LETTER

THE A-TO-Z HISTORY OF OUR ALPHABET

PERFECT

David Sacks

Vintage Canada

VINTAGE CANADA EDITION, 2004

Published in Canada by Vintage Canada, a division of Random House of Canada Limited, and simultaneously in the United States by Broadway Books, a division of Random House, Inc., in 2004. Originally published in hardcover in Canada by Alfred A. Knopf Canada, a division of Random House of Canada Limited, and simultaneously in the United States by Broadway Books, a division of Random House, Inc., in 2003. Distributed by Random House of Canada Limited, Toronto.

Vintage Canada and colophon are registered trademarks of Random House of Canada Limited.

www.randomhouse.ca

National Library of Canada Cataloguing in Publication

Sacks, David
Letter perfect : the A to Z history of our alphabet / David Sacks.

Originally published: Toronto : Knopf Canada, 2003, under title: Language visible.
ISBN 0-676-97488-0

1. Alphabet—History. I. Sacks, David Language visible. II. Title.

P211.S16 2004   411   C2003-905673-2

Book design by Nicola Ferguson

Printed and bound in the United States of America

2   4   6   8   9   7   5   3   1

For my parents, who taught me

PREFACE

This book attempts a voyage of discovery among the letters of the alphabet. Like islands of an archipelago, the 26 letters will be visited and explored, one at a time. Each island's geography and local lore will be examined briefly, also its relationship to other islands in the navigational stream. Some islands may prove more lush or lofty than others. But any one will yield substantial mental nourishment to visitors, along with glorious vistas onto language, literature, and history of the past 4,000 years.

Where do our letters come from? How did they get their shapes, their assigned sounds, their sequence, immortalized in our "Alphabet Song"? Why do we use "Roman" letters for English—also for Spanish, Czech, Turkish, Swahili, Vietnamese, and many others—while some languages (Russian, Greek, Arabic, Hindi, etc.) use different types of letters? What *is* a letter, exactly? What's an alphabet? These are among questions to be answered with authority and zest.

And smaller questions, perhaps more intriguing. Why is X the unknown? What is *The Story of O*? Where did Irish rock band U2 get its name? Why does "mother" start with M? What's Q's source of pride? Which two letters came last to the alphabet? (Answer: J and V.) Why is Z called "zee" in the United States but "zed" in Britain and other Commonwealth countries? Which animal did A originally symbolize? (An ox: the A's legs were horns, pointing upward, 3,000 years ago.)

Every letter has its own chapter here. Typically, the chapter briefly explains the letter's origin in ancient Near Eastern alphabets, including the Phoenician alphabet of 1000 B.C. (In this aspect, the book has benefited from a spectacular archaeological discovery made public in A.D. 1999 that placed the alphabet's invention in Egypt, sometime around 2000 B.C.) Each chapter traces its letter's history through ancient Greece and Rome, medieval England, and subsequent stages, and discusses the letter's noteworthy roles in literature, traditional iconography, modern marketing and pop culture, and other categories. V for Victory. Presidential "Dubya" (W). Xbox, *X-Files*, X-Men.

Each chapter tries, where possible, to find the letter's single chief significance for modern readers—its "personality," as expressed through speech or visual media. For instance, letter A means quality. B is forever second best. C is inconsistent in sound: Its troubles with commitment stem from an unstable childhood. O's shape can be highly inviting. S is the letter of the serpent, whether for evil or for nature. N needs your nose for pronunciation. And H, phonetically, barely qualifies as a letter at all.

Beyond the letters themselves, this book is partly about languages: English first of all, but also Latin, Greek, ancient Semitic tongues (of which Hebrew is the closest modern equivalent), medieval and modern French and other Romance tongues, and German, all relevant to the story of our 26 letters. While I don't speak every one of those languages, I have background in a few and have strived for accuracy in research.

The book uses language topics as the key to explaining the alphabet. Letters are *images* of language: They were invented, around

2000 B.C., to show tiny sounds of speech. Letters, when combined correctly, re-create the sounds of words (whether in English, ancient Greek, Arabic, Russian, etc.). If you take the spoken tongue as your starting point—any language outside of a test tube was spoken long before it began to be written—and you picture an alphabet being fitted to the language, like clothing, amid adjustments, then the history and meaning of the letters become suddenly clearer.

Some books on the alphabet have viewed the letters primarily as items of visual design. Visual, indeed handsome, they surely are. But that approach makes it tough to explain how a letter got its sound(s), especially regarding irregularities. Why does C go soft in pronunciation before E, I, or Y? Why does J mean the sound "j" in English but "h" in Spanish and "y" in German? Such questions are easier to answer if you begin with the language sounds, not the written symbols.

Yet this is no textbook. It does not deal exhaustively with the subject, and I hope it is never boring. Facts are pursued with an eye toward what is enlightening, surprising, fun. The aim is to inform and entertain. I hope to convey how fascinating these 26 little shapes can be, how they contain within themselves thousands of years of culture and history.

The basis for this book was a 26-part weekly series that I wrote about the letters of the alphabet for the *Ottawa Citizen* newspaper (Ottawa, Ontario). The series covered one letter per week, from January to July 2000.

But the first inspiration dates to 1993, when I was at work on my one previous book, the *Encyclopedia of the Ancient Greek World* (Facts On File, 1995). Facing a huge assignment beyond my rudimentary knowledge, I was anxiously researching the ancient Greeks.

One topic was the Greek alphabet, including its origin, sometime around 800 B.C. I had learned in college that the Greeks, with no writing of their own at the time, acquired their alphabet by copying it from the Phoenicians (a Semitic people famed as seafarers, based in what is now Lebanon). I could have written those words on an exam—"the Greeks took their alphabet from the Phoenicians"—without understanding what that meant. I had always imagined some imitation by analogy: that the Greeks, impressed by the Phoenician letters, had gone off and invented two dozen letters of their own, to be Greek letters.

But my studies of 1993 taught me differently. The Greeks had copied more literally than that. (Pardon the pun.) The Greeks didn't copy just the idea of the Phoenician alphabet; *they actually copied the Phoenician letters* and started using them to write Greek.

Does it sound trivial? At the time, the realization stunned me. The ancient languages of Greek and Phoenician were as different as English and Arabic. Greek was (and is) a language of the Indo-European family; its modern relatives include English, German, Spanish, and Russian. The Phoenician tongue, now vanished, belonged to a separate language group, Semitic, whose major modern representative is Arabic, although Phoenician itself was probably closer to Hebrew. Semitic and Indo-European languages do not sound at all alike; their vocabularies are unrelated. And yet . . .

The Phoenician alphabet had 22 letters; the earliest working Greek alphabet, probably 26. The first 22 letters of the Greek list were nearly identical to the Phoenician in sequence, shapes, names, and, usually, sounds (with the exception of five vowel letters, which the Greeks had invented by reassigning certain Phoenician letters to symbolize vowel sounds). In later centuries the Greeks would adjust their alphabet away from the Phoenician model. But around 800 B.C., it seems the Greeks picked up Phoenician letters, made some changes and additions, and began writing.

What if a bunch of illiterate Anglo-Saxons in A.D. 600 had gotten their hands on the Arabic alphabet and started using it to write Old English? Could they have done so? I wondered. Wasn't that basically what the Greeks did?

There must, I thought, back in 1993, be more to these letters than I understood. How could Phoenician letters be so adaptable? Logically, wouldn't most of them be *unusable* for Greek, since the two languages were so different?

Eventually I moved on from the ancient Greece book, got a day job, and turned to a new mental interest: the history of the alphabet. I had never studied it before, but felt compelled to do so now. There seemed something fundamental here that I had missed in my education.

What I found was that alphabets have routinely jumped from language to language, across all sorts of language barriers, down through history, thanks to the adaptability of letters generally. Our Roman alphabet in English is the product of four such leaps: After being copied from Phoenician letters, the Greek letters were copied, in turn, by a different people, the Etruscans of Italy (around 700 B.C.). Etruscan was a tongue as different from Greek as Greek was from Phoenician, yet the letters adapted easily: They now became Etruscan letters, for showing Etruscan speech. Then the Etruscan letters were copied by other Italian peoples, including the Romans, whose language, Latin, was totally unlike Etruscan. Again the letters had made the jump. As Rome conquered Italy and lands beyond, the Roman alphabet became the writing of Roman Europe. Surviving the empire's collapse (around A.D. 500), Roman letters were fitted to newer tongues, including primitive English (around A.D. 600). Today those letters have grown up to become our own.

English is by no means the only example. Roman letters today convey the sounds of other tongues that Cicero never heard of: Polish, Zulu, Azerbaijani, Indonesian, Navajo—and about 100 more, all in daily use. The Cyrillic alphabet works equally well for Bulgarian and Mongolian as for Russian. Arabic letters, devised originally to show the Arabic language, provide writing in Iran, Pakistan, Malaysia, and other places where people don't speak Arabic. Behind such facts lies the letters' ability to leap across languages.

The more I dug into this, the more important it seemed. I was finally getting the idea that the letters have a kind of genius—a genius for showing the sounds of speech. Because they denote the smallest particles of sound ("t," "p," "m," "u"), letters in quantity are beautifully flexible and precise. They can be arranged in endless combinations, as necessary, to capture sounds of words. This allows the letters to be fitted from one language to another: You could easily write English phonetically, in the letters of Hebrew or Cyrillic. (Bored office workers at computers do it idly.)

"People don't understand this concept," I recall thinking. "This isn't being taught at school."

I had learned a new respect for the alphabet, and from this point—for it was just a beginning—I proceeded to dip into other aspects of the story: typography, phonetics, the individual letters' use in brand names and design, the whole psychological message of letters in certain presentations. What I uncovered was a trove of wisdom and lore worth celebrating. And worth sharing.

THE MODERN WORLD'S MAJOR WRITING SYSTEMS

Name of Script	Number of Users Worldwide (Primary Language)	Geographic Range
Roman alphabet	1.9 billion	Americas; Western Europe; parts of Eastern Europe and the former Soviet Union; Turkey; Central and Southern Africa; Oceania; parts of Southeast Asia
Chinese script	0.9 billion	China; Taiwan
Arabic alphabet	291 million	Near East; North Africa; Iran; parts of Central and Southeast Asia
Devanagari script	260 million	Much of India
Cyrillic alphabet	252 million	Russia; other parts of Eastern Europe; parts of Central Asia
Bengali script	125 million	Northeast India; Bangladesh
Japanese script	118 million	Japan

About three-quarters of the world's population live in countries where an alphabet or alphabet-based script is the national writing system. This table takes into account varying levels of literacy around the globe in listing the seven most-used scripts, with approximate numbers of users for whom each script is native and the regions where the scripts are indigenous. Of the seven, only the Chinese and Japanese systems are not alphabetic.

FAMILY TREE OF THE WORLD'S ALPHABETS

Nearly every alphabet, ours included, has been born from a prior alphabet.
The letters have been copied from one language to another

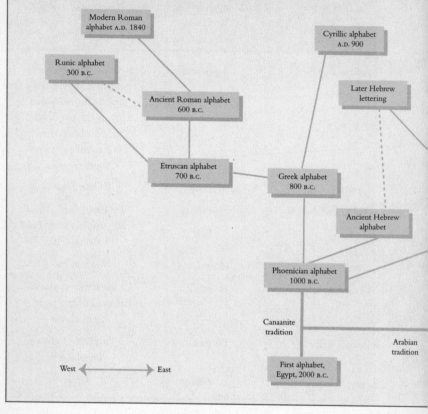

Modern Roman alphabet A.D. 1840

Cyrillic alphabet A.D. 900

Runic alphabet 300 B.C.

Later Hebrew lettering

Ancient Roman alphabet 600 B.C.

Etruscan alphabet 700 B.C.

Greek alphabet 800 B.C.

Ancient Hebrew alphabet

Phoenician alphabet 1000 B.C.

Canaanite tradition

Arabian tradition

West ⟷ East

First alphabet, Egypt, 2000 B.C.

Aside from the nonalphabetic writing systems of China and Japan, almost all major scripts in use today, anywhere in the world, belong to a single "alphabet family," whose principal members are shown here. The family stems entirely from the first Semitic-language alphabet of 2000 B.C. This ancestor produced a prime descendant: the Phoenician alphabet (1000 B.C.), which, from its base in what is now Lebanon, became the launching pad for a global proliferation. By 800 B.C., the convenient Phoenician letters had been copied at least four times into other languages. Two of the resultant alphabets, the Aramaic and the Greek, spawned new alphabets in their own right, and these new alphabets spawned still newer ones, in a steady progress east and west across the ancient world.

As the chart shows, our Roman alphabet comes from one such line of descent. The Phoenician alphabet begat the Greek, which begat the Etruscan, which begat the Roman. Originally created for the writing of ancient Latin, the Roman letters survived the Roman Empire's collapse (A.D. 500) to be adapted to new European tongues, including primitive English. Today aspects of these formative stages live on in our modern letters. Our ABC's are end products of their "prior lives" in the Phoenician, Greek, Etruscan, and ancient Roman alphabets.

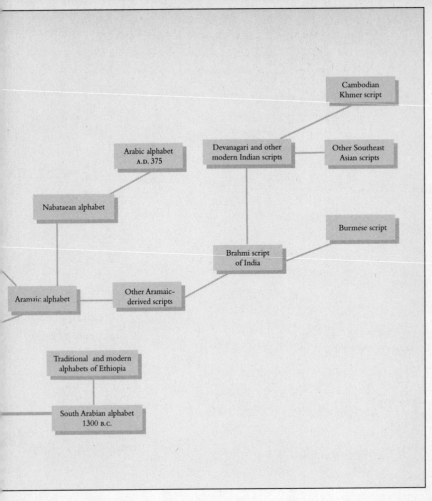

How could one alphabet beget another? Answer: through the magical adaptability of letters. Repeatedly, in the era from about 1000 B.C. to A.D. 1000, the letters of one alphabet were copied and fitted to a new language. The people doing the copying were usually native speakers of the recipient language. (Sometimes, as in the birth of Russia's Cyrillic, the guiding hand of religious missionaries was involved.) The recipients typically had no existing writing system. But they were able to borrow the 22 or 24 or so letters they saw being used for someone else's tongue and to adjust those foreign symbols to fit sounds of their own tongue; individual letter sounds would be modified and whole letters either dropped or invented, as needed. Within a few generations, the copied letters might evolve in shape, growing different from their original models, as influenced by the people's writing materials and visual tastes.

Gradually, the new alphabet would take permanent form, looking different from its mother script yet linked historically to it and perhaps retaining a similar sequence of letter sounds. And if the new alphabet, in turn, was observed by outsiders, speaking their own language and needing a writing system, then the "reproductive process" might begin again.

Only one major modern alphabetic script stands outside this historical family: the 28-symbol Hangul system of Korea, invented from scratch in the mid-1400s A.D.

LETTER
PERFECT

LITTLE LETTERS, BIG IDEA

Ask people to name the most consequential inventions of world history, and you'll hear a list probably including the wheel, the telephone, the atomic bomb, the first computing machine. (Comedian Mel Brooks, in his 1960s audio skit "The Two-Thousand-Year-Old Man," claimed the greatest invention was Saran Wrap.) What might be missing from the answers, overlooked, is the family of little shapes that your eyes are scanning right now: the letters of the alphabet. For the alphabet was an invention, a spectacularly successful one. Judged on longevity and extent of modern daily use, it compares with the wheel.

The alphabet was invented in Egypt around 2000 B.C. as a writing method to show sounds of words. Without doubt, its earliest readers read aloud, their lips forming the words displayed. (Reading aloud continued to be standard practice throughout ancient and medieval times.) The alphabet was not the earliest writing: Egypt, Mesopotamia, and probably China already had nonalphabetic systems. But the alphabet was the most efficient writing system ever found, before or since. Like the wheel, it transformed the ancient world, and, like the wheel, it is still with us and has never been superseded.

Today about 4.8 billion people, over three-quarters of humanity, live in countries that use an alphabet or a writing system modified from an alphabet. About 26 major alphabetic scripts are in place worldwide. The International Three are the Roman, Arabic, and Cyrillic alphabets, each serving multiple nations and languages.

Our own familiar alphabet is the Roman, bequeathed to Western Europe by the Roman Empire and today the most popular script on Earth—weighing in at about 100 principal languages, 120 countries, and nearly 2 billion users worldwide. The Roman alphabet owes its statistical dominance partly to its use by Spanish (330 million native speakers worldwide), by Portuguese (160 million native speakers), and by the languages of Central and Southern Africa (270 million speakers) as well as by English (350 million native speakers). There are variations of the Roman alphabet: For example, English employs 26 letters; Finnish, 21; Croatian, 30. But at the core are the 23 letters of ancient Rome. (The Romans lacked J, V, and W.)

Amazingly, with the sole exception of Korea's Hangul script (invented in isolation in the mid-1400s A.D.), all of today's major alphabetic scripts have a common origin. All can be traced back through history to one source: the first Near Eastern alphabet of 2000 B.C. The family ties are direct and actual. Our Roman alphabet is a third cousin to the Arabic alphabet, a second cousin to the Cyrillic alphabet, and a grandchild of the Greek alphabet. True, different alphabets don't usually look alike (although nearly half of our capital letters strongly resemble their Greek "grandparents"). But alphabets reveal their kinship in general principles and in their sequences of letter sounds. References to "the alphabet," in this chapter particularly, are meant to include any working alphabet, present or past, such as the Phoenician and Aramaic, as well as our own.

Chinese writing symbols typically represent one word each. These translate, from left, as "tea," "hear," and "middle." The "middle" symbol, like other of the oldest Chinese symbols, comes close to being a picture of what it means.

The remaining one-quarter of Earth's population, 1.4 billion people, use nonalphabetic writing. Basically this means China, including Taiwan, and Japan. The Japanese system comes from an adaptation of the Chinese that dates back to the 600s A.D.

What's the big difference? Why doesn't Chinese writing qualify as an alphabet? In Chinese script, each symbol denotes a whole word of the Mandarin Chinese language. We call such symbols "logograms" (from two Greek roots meaning "word letter"). A Chinese symbol is primarily not phonetic; it does not operate by conveying sound. Rather, it conveys the idea behind the word. A few symbols actually *show* their subject as a stylized picture, like the third one in the chart. That sort of symbol qualifies both as a logogram and as a pictograph (meaning "picture writing").

If we English speakers normally wrote the word "dog" as 🐕, that would be a pictograph. If we wrote "dog" with an agreed-on symbol like ∅, that would be a logogram. But we do neither. We write "dog" with three symbols, not one, which together re-create the sound of the word. Each of the symbols (letters) denotes a tiny bit of speech, part of the word's sound. We know the symbol-to-sound code because we had to memorize it in kindergarten or thereabouts, as the doorway to literacy: "A is for 'apple,' B is for 'ball' . . ."

The letter's sound is the smallest amount possible to isolate, what linguists call a phoneme. A phoneme is an "atom" of language, almost always smaller than a syllable. (At most, a phoneme *is* a syllable, as in the long I of "icy" or the English word "a" or certain other vowel uses.) Our word "pencil" has two syllables but six phonemes, each neatly displayed by a different letter.

An alphabet is a writing system based on letters, which by definition symbolize phonemes only. The letters combine to show words of a particular language, shared between writer and reader. The alphabet must adequately represent the language by having enough letters with the right sounds—that is, most of the sounds essential to the spoken language. Yet the number of letters needed is surprisingly small: fewer than 30 for most languages. Russia's Cyrillic alphabet has 33 letters; Iran's Farsi-language version of the Arabic alphabet, 32. While India's Devanagari script hits 48, it and related Indian scripts are not purely alphabetic but also straddle the category of a syllabary (defined below).

Alphabets exploit the fact that human languages tend to use not many phonemes—only around 20 to 40 per language, typically. No matter how many tens of thousands of words there are in a given tongue, the words, once analyzed, yield only a few dozen basic sounds. These are not, of course, the same 40 from language to language: Arabic and English share many sounds, yet Arabic requires certain throat clicks that English speakers cannot make, never having learned them in the cradle. (By the same token, for a mean diversion sometime, ask a Parisian to say the English word "law." He'll struggle to come out with something like "loe.") English has a rather high number of phonemes, between about 44 and 48, depending on regional accent. This abundance is due partly to English's rich heritage, combining Germanic and Franco-Latin influences, from two different language groups. Nearly half our phonemes are shadings of vowel sounds, such as the A in "law" that gives Parisians such trouble.

We don't need 44 letters for 44 phonemes, because letters can do double duty. English spelling assigns several sounds to all vowel letters (go, got, ton, etc.) and finds extra sounds in letter pairings like OI, CH, and TH.

An alphabet enjoys one huge advantage over any other writing system: It needs fewer symbols. No other system can get away with so few. This makes an alphabet easier to learn. Students need memorize only two dozen or so letters to begin building toward literacy, which typically takes about another five years of instruction.

Because the memorization step is simple enough for five- and six-year-olds, the whole process, with an alphabet, can be completed before students reach working age. The learning need not interfere with earning a living. This crucial fact has made the alphabet historically the vehicle of mass literacy. With the alphabet's invention, the farmer, the shopkeeper, the laborer have been able to read and write—unlike the situation in prealphabetic societies. The very first alphabet was invented, scholars today believe, for humble people who were being excluded from the mysteries of Egyptian hieroglyphic writing.

Compare our 26 letters to the Chinese system, which involves at least 2,000 symbols for educated daily reading and writing, out of an inventory of about 60,000 symbols overall. Mass literacy became possible in China only with the communist state of 1949. Today Chinese schoolchildren normally take three years longer than Western children to learn to read and write, with most of that extra time devoted to mastering the symbols.

Despite the symbolization problem, China's writing system serves that nation's needs. China has eight regional languages; its

Simple enough for children to master. Greek letters inked onto a papyrus scroll help provide a literature lesson for a boy in ancient Athens, in the remnant of a painted scene from a ceramic cup, dated between 470 and 450 B.C. The legible words hoi hamera kleei *belong to a phrase meaning something like, "Those whose deeds time makes famous . . . ," perhaps a line of verse.*

logogram system, while keyed to Mandarin vocabulary, is at least partly accessible to non-Mandarin-speakers, more so than alphabetic rendering would be. Also there is the tone factor. Chinese tongues like Mandarin and Cantonese contain many homonyms, distinguished only by being spoken in different tones of voice. The Mandarin word *ma,* for instance, could mean "mother," "horse," "scold," "hemp," or other things, depending on tonal modulation. In Chinese writing, the various *ma*s simply command different-looking symbols, whereas alphabetic writing would have trouble making those words look different from each other. The inadequacy of an alphabet for Chinese is shown in the sometimes-confusing Pinyin system for transliterating Chinese words into Roman letters.

The need to accumulate symbols has hampered most nonalphabetic systems down through history. In the ancient Near East, two major writing forms preceded the alphabet. Both were elaborate, expressive, and confined to specialists. Egyptian hieroglyphics consisted of pictographs, logograms, and phonetic signs: about 700 picture symbols, written usually in combinations. Mesopotamian cuneiform, as typified by the Babylonian version, was mainly a phonetic script of about 600 symbols, half of them used regularly.

Being phonetic, cuneiform reproduced the sounds of words, like an alphabet. However, cuneiform was a syllabary system—a category worth glancing at, so as to better appreciate the flexibility of our letters.

In a syllabary, the symbols denote whole syllables. The word "pencil" would be two symbols, something like ▲⌐, with ▲ meaning the sound "pen" and ⌐ meaning "sil." Simple and reasonable so far—but, depending on the sounds of your particular language, how useful generally would ▲ and ⌐ be? In English, not very. Your ▲ could help spell "pig pen" and ⌐ could go into "silver," but ▲ and ⌐ would spend much of their time out of use. Meanwhile, other symbols would be needed. As you would be continually inventing new ones, the list would grow into the hundreds.

Some modern tongues do fine with scripts that overlap between an alphabet and syllabary: Hindi or Korean, for example. But for English, a syllabary would be chaos. How many lame symbols like ▲ and ⌐ would we need—two hundred? With our letters, two symbols like A and B represent nearly 8 percent of our alphabet. We get much better use from A and B than we would from any two syllabary signs.

Because letters work at the phoneme level and are unencumbered by any extra baggage of sound, they achieve maximum efficiency. Our six letters of "pencil" can easily be broken out and rearranged within countless other words—"lien," "Nile," "stipend," "clip"—that sound nothing like "pencil." Letters are the original snap-on tools: They build on each other as necessary, so you actually need fewer items in your toolkit. With 26, we capture reasonably well the approximately 500,000 words of English. In fact, we could theoretically drop one or two letters—Q, for instance—and spell "queen" as "cween" or "kween."

The genius of the letters is the way they combine simplicity with precision. Although few in number, they are wonderfully flexible and versatile as a group. They can be arranged in endless variations to capture details of sound. Letters fairly cling to the sounds of words, showing the textures: "fill" versus "film," "ascetic" versus "esthetic," "serendipity," "pterodactyl," "Mooselookmeguntic." Organs of speech could hardly be more exact or delicate in their sounds than letters in their showing. At least for most languages.

The letters' precision isn't just a topic for rhapsody. It opens onto the most important fact about the alphabet, the key to understanding the background of our 26 letters and much of world cultural history besides—namely, that letters can jump from language to language. Letters are so clever at showing speech that they need not be confined to any particular tongue but often can be fitted from one right to another.

Even if the two languages are totally unlike, letters often can make the transition. Because their core selection of sounds (inherited from the alphabet's earliest stages) is close to being universal, letters usually can be adapted to a different tongue through only a few changes: three or four letters revalued to new sounds, a letter or two invented, unneeded letters discarded. That is why various modern languages have different numbers of letters for the same general alphabet.

Letters have leapt from language to language throughout history. Originally that was how the alphabet spread across the ancient world, blossoming among people previously illiterate: the Jews, Aramaeans, Greeks, Etruscans, Romans, and others. Each group spoke a different language. Each acquired its alphabet by copying someone else's and then adapting the letters to the new tongue. When Julius Caesar as a Roman general entered Gaul in 59 B.C., he found the inhabitants writing their Celtic language with the Greek alphabet, learned during a prior century from Greek traders at the seaport now called Marseille.

Since the initial spread of literacy, alphabets of the world have kept jumping around, propelled by conquest, missionary religion, or cultural politics. In the early 1990s, three former provinces of the Soviet Union announced they would dump their Cyrillic alphabet (imposed by Stalin in 1940) and switch to the Roman. The newly independent countries of Azerbaijan, Turkmenistan, and Uzbekistan have not altered their spoken languages, which are Turkic tongues, related to Turkish. But the governments have moved to replace Cyrillic street signs, textbooks, tax forms, etc., with new ones printed in a modified, 29-letter Roman alphabet. Elementary schools now teach Roman letters. The massive, disruptive changeover—inspired by westward trade ambitions and hatred of the Soviet memory—was declared officially complete in Azerbaijan, at least, in 2001. The new alphabet is modeled on that of modern Turkey, which switched from Arabic to Roman letters in 1928, under the westernizing regime of Kemal Atatürk.

In centuries before 1940, Azerbaijan, Turkmenistan, and Uzbekistan used the Arabic alphabet, until the early Soviets imposed the Roman one in the 1920s. Thus the three regions have seen all three major alphabets in the last 80 years: Arabic, Cyrillic, and (twice) Roman. Although the three regions' languages are unrelated to Arabic, Russian, or Latin, each alphabet has taken hold in turn.

Other examples abound. In around 1860, Romania switched from Cyrillic to Roman, turning westward from czarist Russia's sphere. Vietnam had Roman letters imposed by French colonialism in 1910; the change displaced a traditional, Chinese-derived script. Today in Ho Chi Minh City, shop signs and newspapers are in Roman letters and Vietnamese language. Meanwhile, in neighboring Cambodia, a kindred language is written in an entirely different way, based on an ancient script of India.

We think of the Arabic alphabet as the written form of the Arabic tongue. Yet Arabic letters have belonged to other languages, too. Carried outward from Arabia by armies and seafarers after the mid-600s A.D., the Arabic alphabet now serves about nine major tongues linguistically unrelated to Arabic: Berber in Morocco, Nubian in Sudan, Farsi and Kurdish in Iran, Urdu and Sindhi in Pakistan, Pashto in Afghanistan, Uighur in China, and Malay in Malaysia. Malay has traditionally been written in either of two alphabets, Arabic or Roman. Roman predominates today, yet in the capital city, Kuala Lumpur, you can still buy a Malay-language newspaper printed in Arabic letters, as well as others in Roman ones.

Malay isn't the only switch-hitter. The African common-tongue Swahili may be written in Arabic letters or the usual Roman. The language known as Serbo-Croatian—shared, with dialectical differences, between Serbia and Croatia—is written in Cyrillic by Serbs, in Roman by Croats. (The split, a legacy of rival medieval missionary churches, has surely contributed to the calamitous distrust between those peoples.) Likewise, India's Hindi and Pakistan's Urdu are fundamentally the same tongue, only using Devanagari script in India, Arabic letters in Pakistan. And Yiddish, while not exactly German, is closely akin to it. Yet Yiddish is written in Hebrew letters, and German in Roman ones.

The "spreadability" of an alphabet means that the future of our Roman letters looks very bright indeed. In Russia's Volga Valley, about 440 miles east of Moscow, the semiautonomous, Turkic-speaking republic of Tatarstan has announced its intent to follow Azerbaijan's example and go Roman. Struggling nations elsewhere, particularly in Central and Southeast Asia, may be expected in coming decades to do likewise, switch to Roman letters for native tongues, as a bid to tie into global trade and communication and to better prepare their people to learn English. Tragically, much that is venerable and spiritually sustaining will be lost. Yet that seems inevitable in the 21st century we are shaping. And it is sobering to reflect that our 26 letters wield such power.

To unlock our letters' mysteries, we begin with the ancient Phoenicians. The Phoenician alphabet of 1000 B.C. would become the great-grandmother of our own. About 19 of our letters can be traced back directly—in their shapes, their alphabetical sequence, and, for most, their sounds—to Phoenician counterparts. Ours is not the only descendant. As shown in the "Family Tree of the

Phoenicia, the Near East, and the Eastern Mediterranean, 1000 B.C.

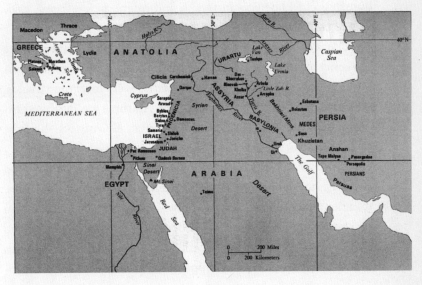

World's Alphabets" (pages xiv–xv), the Phoenician alphabet has been the source for nearly every subsequent alphabet, past and present.

The Phoenicians were a dynamic Iron Age people, based in what is now Lebanon. Today they are remembered as the best seafarers of the ancient world. In the 700s B.C. they spanned the length of the Mediterranean with a seaborne trade network, exchanging luxury goods from the East for raw materials from the West: Babylonian textiles, Egyptian metalwork, and Phoenician carved ivory were traded for elephant tusks from North Africa and bars of silver and tin from Spain. Sustaining the network was a westward string of some 14 major colonies, plus lesser ones—Phoenician seaports on foreign soil, serving as ship stations and local trade depots. Today a handful of these foundations survive inhabited: The southern Spanish Atlantic seaport of Cadiz, for example, began its life as a Phoenician colony named Gaddir ("walled place"). But the most fateful Phoenician colony was Carthage (Kart Hadasht, "new city"), built soon after 800 B.C. on the Tunisian coast. Carthage would grow to a great power of the Mediterranean, eventually dwarfing old Phoenicia in wealth and might, before being challenged and destroyed (146 B.C.) by the Italian city of Rome.

The Phoenician homeland was not a unified nation but a grouping of independent port cities, linked by common language, religion, self-interest. Three cities were foremost: Byblos, Sidon, and the island-fortress of Tyre. All three are inhabited today, as Lebanese cities. Lebanon's capital, Beirut, was likewise once a Phoenician port.

The Phoenicians were Semites, akin in ethnic group and language to the ancient Jews. Phoenician speech would have sounded much like ancient Hebrew. Israel—the Jewish kingdom of David and Solomon—was Phoenicia's southern neighbor and trade partner in the 900s B.C. Unlike the monotheistic Jews, however, the Phoenicians worshipped several gods, chiefly the protective Melkart ("king of the city," sometimes called by the title Baal, "lord") and his consort, the queenly, sexual Astarte.

Sometime before 1000 B.C., the Phoenicians began writing their language in a 22-letter alphabet. They did not invent this alphabet but inherited it from prior Semitic tradition. Created around 2000 B.C. by Semitic speakers, the skill of alphabetic writing had spread gradually through parts of the Near East, learned by one group of Semites from another. Some Semitic peoples may have known of it without using it; non-Semites surely knew nothing about it.

With the Phoenicians, the Semitic alphabet acquired an international platform. As part of a bustling, urban society, the alphabet was taught to Phoenician children, used for government and trade, and carried abroad by merchant fleets. Phoenician writing would have been eyed enviously by foreign trade partners with no writing of their own. Eventually some would copy the Phoenician letters for themselves.

The alphabet was just one of several technologies by which the Phoenicians prospered. They were masters of improved techniques in shipbuilding and navigation (they are credited with the discovery and use of Polaris, the North Star), carpentry, metalworking, and the earliest glass working. Their alphabet surely abetted their technical skills, while their success and travel served to publicize their alphabet, whether they wished so or not.

Although the Phoenicians came along nearly 1,000 years after the alphabet's invention, their version of the alphabet is the earliest that fully rewards modern study. Scholars can analyze and understand the Phoenician letters, thanks to sufficient archaeological remains. The prior millennium has left us with less satisfactory material.

About 500 inscriptions survive from Phoenicia after 1000 B.C., with over another 6,000 from Carthage and its network after

Aboard ships newly beached at a port of Egypt, long-robed Phoenician merchants make gestures of obeisance to Egyptian authorities (not shown) while white-kilted Egyptian harbor pilots come ashore. The Phoenician cargo includes jars, right center, *probably of wine, a drink foreign to Egypt. This modern painting depicts an Egyptian tomb mural from the later second millennium B.C., found near modern Luxor and now sadly ruined by moisture.*

The Phoenicians' trade network brought them into contact with nations of the Mediterranean and Near East: Egypt, Assyria, the Jewish kingdom, the Aramaeans of Damascus, the Etruscans of western Italy, the kingdom of Tartessus in southern Spain, and a marginal but ambitious northeast Mediterranean people, the Greeks. Trade prompted the dissemination of Phoenicia's alphabet. By about 900 B.C. the Jews, Aramaeans, and other Near Eastern peoples had copied Phoenician letters for their own use; by about 800 B.C. the Greeks had done likewise. The Greek adaptation, specifically, was a crucial step toward the formation of our modern letters.

400 B.C. Most are brief: prayers, gravestone epitaphs, statements of ownership on artifacts, and the like. Usually the writing is chiseled or scratched into durable material like stone or ceramic—the material being the reason for the writing's survival. Phoenician letters, conveying the Phoenician language, can gen-

The Phoenicians are described with mixed admiration and distrust in extant Greek and Hebrew literature, such as Homer's epic poem the *Odyssey* and the biblical books of Kings and Ezekiel. Virtues like craftsmanship and intrepid seafaring are counterbalanced with accusations of greed, dishonesty, decadence, and a readiness to kidnap foreign women for the slave trade. Some of this may have been libel, prompted by jealousy.

Our word "Phoenician" comes from ancient Greek. *Phoinikes,* "red people," was what the Greeks called them, probably in reference to their copper skin color. Alternatively, the name may refer to the prized textile dye, ranging in hue from red to dark purple, which was Phoenicia's prime luxury product. Extracted from sea mollusks' dead bodies through a secret process, this uniquely beautiful and expensive purple, exported in woven clothing and furnishings, became an international status symbol in antiquity, its use confined to the very rich, chiefly royalty. Down through the early 20th century A.D., the color purple was associated in Europe with kings and emperors.

What the Phoenicians called themselves we do not know. One possibility is something like *Kananni,* "Canaanites," for the Phoenicians were descendants of people who in the second millennium B.C. had inhabited the biblical land of Canaan (today covered by Israel, the Palestinian Authority, Lebanon, western Jordan, and coastal Syria). Archaeology reveals that some of these Canaanite forebears were using the Semitic alphabet by about 1650 B.C., in a version similar to what the Phoenicians would use.

erally be read with confidence by experts due to the similarity to Hebrew. Among the inscriptions are schoolroom-type exercises, including valuable lists of the letters in alphabetical order.

Such survivals are but a tiny remnant of Phoenician writing that once existed. From Egyptian, Greek, and Roman authors we hear of Phoenician or Carthaginian historical annals, business archives, and volumes of religious lore. Those writings have vanished, as they were normally written in ink on perishable material like animal hide or papyrus (an ancient reed paper), quick to decay. Furthermore, Phoenician literature was not copied and preserved by the Greco-Roman culture that eventually dominated the Mediterranean; in fact, just the opposite: A whole library of Phoenician-language scrolls went up in flames when the Romans sacked Carthage, for example.

Phoenician letters, true to the alphabetic principle, symbolized tiny sounds of speech: "d," "h," "m," "p," etc. The letters were all consonants; there were no vowel letters. Although vowel sounds existed in Phoenician speech, it was not felt necessary to show them in writing. The absence of vowel letters was a feature inherited from the traditional Semitic alphabet. Words were written in abbreviated form, consonant letters only. (Eventually, biblical Hebrew would use the same technique.)

To a modern English speaker, ths sstm wth n vwl lttrs prbbly snds crzy. Vowel letters are essential to identify written English words, especially where a vowel begins the word or *is* the word. Try writing "I am an ass" without vowels. More generally, En-

---

This chart demonstrates how each Phoenician letter's name opened with a consonant sound appropriate to the letter. The names aleph *and* ayin *began with consonants that are unknown to English speech and cannot be clearly shown in our spelling. Thus those two name spellings are misleading.*

Although modern scholars are confident regarding the 22 ancient names themselves (see box, page 23, "How We Know the Phoenician Letters' Names"), the English translation remains uncertain for a few, such as tet *and* tsade. *The third letter's name,* gimel, *used to be translated as "camel"—the crook shape being interpreted as the animal's hump—but today is thought to have meant the boomerang-like "throwing stick" used for hunting small game. Pronunciation tips: The first sound of* gimel *is the hard "g" of "girl." The letter name* he *sounds like "hay." The name* lamed *is* lah-med.

THE PHOENICIAN ALPHABET OF 1000 B.C.

Letter Shape	Sound	Name	Name's Meaning	Descendant(s) in Our Alphabet
𐤀	breathing stop	*aleph*	ox	A
𐤁	"b"	*bayt*	house	B
𐤂	"g"	*gimel*	throwing stick	C
𐤃	"d"	*dalet*	door	D
𐤄	"h"	*he*	shout of surprise	E
𐤅	"w"	*waw*	peg	F, U, and Y
𐤆	"z"	*zayin*	ax	G and Z
𐤇	guttural "kh"	*khet*	fence	H
𐤈	emphatic "t"	*tet*	wheel	—
𐤉	"y"	*yod*	arm and hand	I
𐤊	"k"	*kaph*	palm of hand	K
𐤋	"l"	*lamed*	ox goad	L
𐤌	"m"	*mem*	water	M
𐤍	"n"	*nun*	fish	N
𐤎	"s"	*samek*	pillar	—
𐤏	guttural sound	*ayin*	eye	O
𐤐	"p"	*pe*	mouth	P
𐤑	"ts"	*tsade*	papyrus plants	—
𐤒	"q"	*qoph*	monkey	Q
𐤓	"r"	*resh*	head	R
𐤔	"sh"	*shin*	tooth	S
𐤕	"t"	*taw*	mark	T

glish and other Indo-European tongues assign strong meanings to vowel sounds, for instance in distinguishing "pack," "peck," "peek," "pick," "pike," "pock," and so on.

In Phoenician and other old Semitic languages, not so. Phoenician vocabulary was more uniformly structured. Compounds aside, Phoenician words tended to have two- or three-consonant roots, with one consonant almost always first and another often last. For example, the Phoenicians wrote the word "king" as letters m-l-k, representing a word sounding something like *melik*. Because the vowel sounds were framed between end consonants, the written form m-l-k was pretty clear.

Moreover, although a few other Phoenician words could be written as m-l-k, they all necessarily related to kingship or royalty, for that was the meaning of that root. In writing, context would help to clarify words' meanings.

For ease of learning, the Phoenician alphabet had several built-in memory devices, inherited from Semitic tradition. The letters in abstract were given a strict sequence, so students would not forget any—a feature we retain when we teach preschoolers the "Alphabet Song." The letters had names, as ours do. But *their* names made more sense, as being names of familiar objects: ox, house, throwing stick, hand, water. Every letter's shape formed a stylized sketch of the object named: The "ox" was shaped like two horns; "throwing stick" looked like a boomerang; "water" was a wavy line. And the cleverest touch: Each letter name began with a different sound, the sound appropriate to the letter. The "house" letter, *bayt,* denoted the sound "b." (Indeed, it is ancestor of our B.) The "hand" letter, *kaph,* denoted the "k" sound. (Ditto, it is the K ancestor.) The Phoenician alphabet thus resembled a modern, phonetic, radio-communication alphabet, where words replace the English letter names according to the same principle of the first sound: Alpha, Bravo, Charlie, Delta . . .

The system meant that once a Phoenician child had memorized a list of 22 common nouns, he or she had a handle on each letter's sound (it being the same as the name's opening sound) and on each letter's shape (it being typically a rough sketch of the object named). This is the same sign-for-sound code that we learn, perhaps more laboriously, in kindergarten and first grade.

As mentioned, the Phoenician alphabet contained the seeds of about 19 of our modern Roman letters. Keeping in mind that Phoenician letters were also pictures and tended to project leftward for right-to-left writing (while ours go the other way), you can glimpse some of our letters taking form in the Phoenician list. The sequence of Phoenician letter sounds clearly anticipates our own: "b," "g," "d" . . . "k," "l," "m," "n" . . . "q," "r," "sh," "t." The Phoenician L letter looks like our L and stands at place number 12, exactly where L stands today. Other Phoenician letters clearly anticipate our Q and T in shape and sound and our E, H, and O in shape. Our B, D, K, and others are there, too, in their sounds and general sequence, although with shapes not yet familiar.

Some Phoenician letters sounded far different from ours, as you might expect. The letter *aleph* was a breathing stop and *ayin* a harsh throat sound; most English speakers would be stumped to pronounce either. And Phoenician speech obviously used a lot of sibilance, since its alphabet needed four kinds of S. We retain two today, our S and Z.

But how did it begin? If Phoenician letters belong to a tradition by then 1,000 years old, what preceded? Who invented the alphabet? The answers take us south from Phoenicia, to Egypt of the pharaohs.

During the 1970s, a world-popular TV series was the BBC's *Upstairs, Downstairs*, about the household of a titled family in

THE MODERN HEBREW ALPHABET

Letter Shape	Main Sound	Name
א	[silent]	*alef*
ב	"b"	*bayt*
ג	"ġ"	*ġimel*
ד	"d"	*dalet*
ה	"h"	*he*
ו	"v"	*vav*
ז	"z"	*zayin*
ח	guttural "kh"	*khet*
ט	emphatic "t"	*tet*
י	"y"	*yod*
כ	"k"	*kaf*
ל	"l"	*lamed*
מ	"m"	*mem*
נ	"n"	*nun*
ס	"s"	*samek*
ע	[silent]	*ayin*
פ	"p"	*pe*
צ	"ts"	*tsade*
ק	"q"	*qof*
ר	"r"	*resh*
ש	"sh"	*shin*
ת	"t"	*tav*

THE HEBREW ALPHABET:
ELDEST CHILD OF THE PHOENICIAN

The 22 Hebrew letters were born by being copied from the 22 Phoenician ones, sometime perhaps around 950 B.C. Today the debt to Phoenicia is obvious in the modern Hebrew letters' sounds and sequence, although not their shapes. (As to their names, see box "How We Know the Phoenician Letters' Names," page 23.)

The copying into Hebrew marked the first of several times in history that the Phoenician alphabet would be borrowed by another people. Because the ancient Hebrew and Phoenician languages were so similar, Hebrew speakers would have found the Phoenician letters perfectly usable for their language. The one wrinkle, according to modern analysis: Hebrew could have used three more letters, to show certain sounds existing in Hebrew but not Phoenician. So three Hebrew letters probably did double duty as two sounds each.

Hebrew evidently had no prior writing system; with the adoption of the Phoenician alphabet, there began the permanent recording of Judaism's faith and historical sagas, reaching back into the second millennium B.C. Whatever the antiquity of Jewish tradition, the oldest words of the Bible (written in Hebrew) date only from the 900s B.C.

Of the modern Hebrew letters, only *khet, qof, resh,* and *shin* show any resemblance in shape to their Phoenician models. Yet originally the two alphabets looked identical: Hebrew's alphabet *was* the Phoenician, as revealed by extant inscriptions like the famous Gezer Calendar (page 22). Later, starting in the 200s B.C., Hebrew letter shapes would undergo major changes.

The Hebrew and Arabic practice of writing from right to left derives from the Phoenicians.

Phoenician letters, Hebrew language? The Gezer Calendar is a limestone inscription from the mid- or late 900s B.C., thought to be the earliest survival of written Hebrew. Discovered in A.D. 1908 at the site of the ancient city of Gezer in what is now southern Israel, the "calendar" briefly lists the months of the year by farming duties. It may be a student's exercise: At the bottom left corner, the writer added certain letters that might spell his name, apparently Abijah.

The letters of the inscription are Phoenician. The language could be Phoenician, too, but experts believe it is Hebrew (the two were very similar), partly because of the archaeology: The stone tablet seems to have come from the time and place of the Jewish kingdom ruled by Solomon. If it is Hebrew, then the inscription preserves the newborn Hebrew alphabet, which had been copied recently from the Phoenician alphabet and still looked exactly like it. The text reads: "Two months of harvest. Two months of sowing. Two months of late planting. A month of reaping flax. A month of reaping barley. A month of reaping and measuring. Two months of vine tending. A month of summer fruit."

The 22 Phoenician letter names cited in this book are universally accepted by scholars, given variations in spelling. However, no source from ancient Phoenicia tells us the names. Instead, we rely on reasonable extrapolation.

The 22 Phoenician letter names that we use today are actually the 22 ancient Hebrew names, slightly adjusted. An important written source tells us the ancient Hebrew names, not the Phoenician. The Hebrew versions are assumed to reflect closely the Phoenician ones, from which they came. There would have been no problem of translation, for example: Names like *aleph* and *resh* would have meant "ox" and "head" in both Hebrew and Phoenician.

The Hebrew names are preserved in one of the most important documents from antiquity: the Greek translation of the Hebrew Bible, originating in the Greek-Egyptian city of Alexandria in the 200s B.C. Known as the Septuagint (from the Latin word for "seventy," on the tradition that 70 scholars produced it), this Greek Bible would prove essential to Judaism's survival and the spread of Christianity in the Greco-Roman world. In its book of Lamentations, the Septuagint happens to use Hebrew letter names to order the text's verses. The 22 names appear repeatedly, written out in Greek letters.

Edwardian London. The characters fell into two groups: the well-heeled family and associates, and the socially more humble servants, "belowstairs." Each group had its dramas, sometimes intersecting. The storyline, appealing to democratic tastes, favored the servants, who included the star character.

The alphabet was an invention "belowstairs," in a society far more harshly class-bound than even Edwardian London. Today we believe—from dramatic archaeological evidence, analyzed in 1999—that the alphabet was invented in Egypt sometime around 2000 B.C. (See "The Cradle of the Alphabet," page 29.) The inventors were almost certainly not Egyptians but foreign workers, probably soldiers, employed by Egypt. They spoke a Semitic language, a Bronze Age ancestor of Phoenician, Hebrew, and Aramaic; it was a tongue quite distinct from Egyptian although linguistically related to it.

Extant Egyptian documents from the Middle Kingdom era (roughly 2000 to 1600 B.C.) often mention foreign labor in Egypt: mercenary soldiers, miners, stonecutters, and the like, some of them enslaved war prisoners. Many would have been Semitic speakers from points east: Sinai, Canaan, the Arabian peninsula. The Egyptians knew them by the oft-contemptuous name *Amu* (Asiatics). *Amu*, in Egyptian eyes, were typically desert Bedouin.

As well as being socially marginal, Semites in Egypt were mostly illiterate. Certain individuals of authority—a mining foreman, a military captain—would have mastered a simplified version of Egyptian writing, and a tiny few perhaps knew some Mesopotamian cuneiform, yet as a people they had no writing. They could, however, study their Egyptian masters' ways.

The official Egyptian writing system was hieroglyphics (see box, pages 27–28, "Egyptian Picture Writing"). Hieroglyphic pictures communicated Egyptian words by representing either (1) the idea behind a word or (2) the consonant sounds of the word or (3) often both, using multiple pictures. Almost any picture could be employed in two different ways, although not simultaneously: an image of a tree branch might mean "wood" or it might mean the sounds *k-h-t* (the consonants of the Egyptian word for wood). In its phonetic meaning, *k-h-t*, the branch picture might help represent entirely different Egyptian words, like "after" (which was *k-h-t*, the same consonants) or "strong" (*n-k-h-t*).

Phonetically, most hieroglyphic pictures denoted three consonant sounds each. One group of a few dozen denoted two consonants each. And—most significantly for our present study—there were some 25 pictures denoting one consonant sound each; together, these constituted 25 essential consonants of Egyptian speech. Here was an entire Egyptian "alphabet," embedded in the massive hieroglyphic system.

Evidently someone among the Semites, a lone genius or a group, became inspired by this alphabetic principle in Egyptian writing. A purely alphabetic system was envisioned, to be adjusted to Semitic speech. Like the Egyptian counterpart, the Semitic alphabet would show only consonants: To include vowels would have made the letters too many for easy learning.

Perhaps over a year, perhaps over a generation, the inventors arrived at a list of essential Semitic consonant sounds that would need to be symbolized for writing: possibly around 27 (to guess from later evidence). The list would have differed somewhat from the 25 Egyptian consonants. To their 27 sounds, the inventors married 27 letters, which were pictures.

The choice of pictures was natural, because that's how the Egyptians wrote and because only a picture would possess a name, which was deemed necessary to prompt the reader as to the letter's sound. How could you remember to say the sound "z" unless you were looking at a picture of a zebra? So the Bronze Age reasoning ran.

A letter would be an image permanently agreed on, simple and distinctive in shape, presenting a familiar object whose Semitic name began with the appropriate sound. For visual models, the inventors could look to the beautiful hieroglyphics abounding in public places of Egyptian cities and to the simpler symbols of Egyptian rock-writing practiced in open country. From these they chose pictures to copy as their letters. The new picture letters were known by their Semitic names, with the Egyptian names and values discarded.

For example: To symbolize the sound "r," the Semites borrowed an Egyptian hieroglyph of a man's head in profile. That symbol in Egyptian could mean the word "head"—or "chief" or "promote" or "fetter," in combination with other signs. The two

From Hieroglyphics to E-mail: The Making of Three of Our Letters

Egyptian Hieroglyph	Sinai Alphabet	Phoenician Alphabet	Phoenician Alphabet	Today
2000 B.C.	1750 B.C.	1000 B.C.	800 B.C.	

hand   *kaph,* "hand"

snake   *nun,* "fish" (= eel?)

eye   *ayin,* "eye"

The evolution of three of our letter shapes is traced in this sampling of their ancient forms. The first column shows the Egyptian writing picture from which the letter's shape was copied; the second column shows an early form of the letter itself; subsequent shapes follow. The Semitic letter disregarded whatever meaning the hieroglyph had and instead exploited the name that the image would command in Semitic speech: "hand," kaph, sound "k." The letters began their lives as careful pictorial renderings but steadily morphed toward simplicity and abstraction. Many of our capital letters retain aspects of their ancient forms, sometimes with exactly the same consonant sound as in 1000 and 2000 B.C.

Egyptian spoken words for "head" were something like *tip* and *djedje.* But the inventors didn't care about all that. They saw the hieroglyph of the head and called it *resh,* the Semitic word. Because the name *resh* began with the sound "r," and because the pictorial image was clear and distinctive, they selected that image

Hieroglyphs painted on a tomb wall at Thebes (modern Luxor), in central Egypt, about 1400 B.C. The image resembling a traffic light is meant to be a scribe's wooden palette with two inset paint bowls, attached by a cord to a pouch and brushes.

Writing in Egypt began around 3000 B.C. The official system was hieroglyphics ("sacred carvings"), revered as the gift of the scribe god Toth. Pictures of familiar objects—owl, basket, hand, ox—were used individually or in combination to convey words in a sentence. Any picture could be employed either as (1) a pictograph or logogram or (2) a phonetic symbol. A sailboat image might mean "boat" or "to sail"—or it might simply contribute certain consonant sounds to help spell a different word. In hieroglyphics, an owl and a reed together meant "there," not "an owl and a reed." Read phonetically, the two pictures approximated the sound of the Egyptian word for "there."

Hieroglyphics were works of art, meant for formal presentation. They were always painted, often onto stone-carved reliefs or insets. Normally they ran from right to left. On walls of buildings and monuments, they carried public announcements and expressions of religious faith.

continued

About 700 hieroglyphic symbols were being used in 2000 B.C. In addition to knowing the symbols, there was the exacting job of painting them. Because the system took years to master and constant practice to retain, its use was confined to a literary elite of priests and scribes. Even other high-born types, such as landowners, might not know how to write hieroglyphics.

Less rigorous was the second Egyptian writing system, hieratic. (The name, which is misleading, means "priestly," but other social classes used it.) Hieratic was a simplified hieroglyphic script, designed for ink and brush on papyrus or textile: Pictures were converted to stylized outlines or strokes, with a far reduced vocabulary. Hieratic writing in its most basic form was accessible to most of the Egyptian upper and middle classes: landowners, certain merchants, and military officers.

for the sound. Thus they invented letter R as the sketch of a head in profile. Future generations of Semitic children would look at the *resh* picture and think of sound "r." Today, just erase the second leg of our capital R and you'll see not a P really, but the primordial head and neck in profile.

The earliest alphabetic writing was thus a bunch of pictures. The oldest surviving Semitic inscriptions, from around 1800 and 1700 B.C., show pictures—a head, a section of fence, a human stick figure—arrayed in cumbersome rows or columns like crude hieroglyphics, a whole row spelling out perhaps five words. Yet they were our letters' direct ancestors, as this book will trace.

The alphabet was (and is) a gloriously simple system, invented for the masses. Abruptly, it gave the power to write and read to "little people," foreign laborers in mighty Egypt. Any Semitic

text continues on page 41

How the Search for the World's First Alphabet Has Led to Egypt

Modern experts now believe the alphabet was invented sometime around 2000 B.C. by Semites who dwelled as foreigners in pharaoh's Egypt; the inventors were inspired by Egyptian writing systems. The Egyptian connection has been established through two spectacular archaeological discoveries, one at the beginning and one at the end of the 20th century.

Starting in the mid-1700s A.D., certain European scholars theorized that Egyptian hieroglyphics were the source or inspiration for the ancient Hebrew letters. The decipherment of hieroglyphics in 1823 did not obviously support the theory, for the two writing systems were shown to work on different principles. The question remained alive throughout the 19th century, amid growing awareness of the place in history of the Phoenician alphabet: The emergence of Phoenician and Hebrew writing "next door" to ancient Egypt might not be coincidence, it was argued. But further understanding had to wait for methods of modern archaeology.

The first breakthrough came in 1905 with the discovery and later assessment of about 30 inscriptions in a distinctive script that modern eyes had never seen. It was pre-Phoenician alphabetic writing, although no one knew so at first. The inscriptions were found at a desert locale in central-west Sinai called Serabit el-Khadem, now within modern Egypt. They had been carved into local sandstone and preserved by the site's solitude and absence of destructive vegetation. Their discoverer, British archaeologist William Flinders Petrie, recognized they were novel and important but had no idea how to read them, and decades later he would conclude, wrongly, that they were not alphabetic.

The writing was pictures: carved sketches, arranged in rough rows or columns. The pictures ran continuously (no systematic breaks), and their direction for reading—leftward or rightward, up or down—was unclear. There were about 27 recurring shapes: a fish, a snake, a human stick figure with arms out, a wavy line, the head of an ox or cow, and

continued

others. Certain figures resembled Egyptian hieroglyphic pictures, but the system was not hieroglyphic.

Serabit el-Khadem was foremost an ancient Egyptian site, the scene of intermittent turquoise mining between about 2200 and 1200 B.C. Here agents of the pharaoh, with armies of underlings, had torn out the semiprecious stone from under the desert. The miners probably included non-Egyptians such as Near Easterners, many of whom would have spoken Semitic dialects. As can be guessed, the writing would turn out to be theirs.

The 30 inscriptions had been left amid a mass of more conventional Egyptian relics, similarly carved from local sandstone. These included figurines, panels of hieroglyphics, and remnants of a temple of the Egyptian goddess Hathor, patron deity of the miners. It was Egyptian treasures that had drawn Petrie to the site; he did not come looking for the alphabet.

The writing stood in some relationship to the surrounding Egyptian material. Several of the mysterious inscriptions were scratched onto stone-carved Egyptian figurines, including a small sphinx. Scholars' attempts to date the writing have since relied on (disputed) dating of the sphinx through artistic analysis. British Egyptologist Alan Gardiner believed it to have been carved around 1800 B.C. Later experts put the date at 1500 B.C. But today some believe 1750 B.C. looks like a good guess for the Sinai sphinx and inscriptions.

The symbols remained undeciphered for a decade after Petrie's published report. Then, in 1916, Gardiner published a brilliant article, "The Egyptian Origin of the Semitic Alphabet," which set the stage for all subsequent study. Gardiner argued that the Sinai writing was alphabetic, that the pictures were individual letters, that each of them had been copied from an identifiable Egyptian hieroglyphic picture (with the Egyptian value disregarded), and that when sounded out correctly, the picture letters would yield words of ancient Semitic. As proof, Gardiner offered his decipherment of a single word.

The inscriptions contained about a dozen examples of four symbols together—"box," "eye," "cane," "cross," we might call them—apparently an important word or notion. The four appeared, amid others, on the sphinx figurine. By extreme good luck, the sphinx also carried a hieroglyphic message, scratched into one shoulder, easily translated: "Beloved of Hathor, lady of the turquoise." What if the two texts, hieroglyphic and mystery script, were the same?

From this assumption, Gardiner identified "box," "eye," "cane," "cross" as four letters representing the Semitic word *baalat,* "lady." The respectful term *baalat* was the feminine form of *baal,* "lord," and could be the title or name of a goddess in various Semitic cultures. The sphinx evidently was an offering, dedicated in two writings; "beloved of Hathor" would refer to the worshipper who had donated the figurine to the goddess's temple. The gift was to thank her for help and protection in the mines.

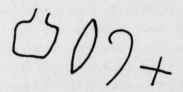

Above, the word baalat, *"lady," as it appears in one of several Serabit el-Khadem inscriptions. Apparently meant to be read from left to right, the letters are* bayt, ayin, lamed, taw—*that is, B, throat sound, L, T. As usual for the early alphabet, the letters show only the word's consonant sounds. The guttural* ayin *has no English-spelling equivalent and is normally left out in transliteration, although linguists might show it with the symbol ' and spell the above word as* ba'alat. *The letters' names mean "house," "eye," "ox goad," "mark." The same four letters in other Serabit inscriptions may have slightly varied shapes, as in the sketch at right. There the word B'LT runs downward, at the bottom right.*

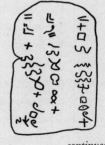

continued

The Semites who wrote the Serabit inscriptions were presumably part of the Egyptian mining operation: laborers, soldiers, concubines, or similar types. They may have been foremen or others of authority, generally skilled and intelligent. Nevertheless, that such people could be literate, in an era before mass education, testifies to the accessibility of alphabetic writing.

Could the Semitic alphabet have been *invented* at the Sinai mining base? That is possible, but experts generally view the 30 inscriptions themselves as being "second generation": The 27 signs, confidently used, seem developed. The Sinai inscriptions (whether dated at 1750 or 1500 B.C.) were probably fruit of a Semitic tradition by then a few centuries old.

Since Gardiner's breakthrough, other scholars have announced decipherments of Sinai inscriptions, yet only Gardiner's *baalat* remains certain. Although we can interpret nearly every individual picture letter, the messages elude us, due to the absence of word breaks and of a fixed writing direction: The Semitic right-to-left writing norm would not take hold until a future century; the earliest alphabet writings could be flowing in any direction, including up or down.

Archaeology of the mid-20th century seemed to lead away from Egypt for the alphabet's origin, toward the Levant—the eastern Mediterranean coast and interior. During the second millennium B.C., this had been the biblical land of Canaan. Canaanites were Semitic speakers whose culture was doomed to wither under invasions by Hebrew tribesmen, seaborne Philistines, and others during the violent birth of the Iron Age, soon after 1200 B.C. Only a northern Canaanite remnant would survive and flourish: the Phoenicians.

In the Levant, archaeologists found two batches of pre-Phoenician alphabetic writing. The unearthing in 1929 of the grand Canaanite city of Ugarit, on the coast of modern Syria, brought to light 1,000 inscriptions in an odd version of the alphabet made up of 30 cuneiform shapes. Dated between about 1350 and 1200 B.C., the relics suggested that Mesopotamian influence on the Levant, earlier on, might have helped prompt the alphabet's invention.

The second batch of discoveries was to the south, at sites now within Israel and Lebanon: some 25 short or broken inscriptions in familiar letters, their shapes recalling both the Sinai and Phoenician writing. The letters had been incised or inked onto household objects: a dagger, arrowheads, pottery (found as fragments). The dagger probably dates from 1650 B.C. or earlier; other items date variously from the 1200s to about 1000 B.C. One incised potsherd may fall within the range of 1750 to 1450 B.C. Another sherd, from around 1200 B.C., carries a list of 22 letters, the same 22 that would later become the Phoenician alphabet. Only some differences in letter shapes distinguish these from the Phoenician versions to come.

The older relics all were found to the south, in southern Israel. This may indicate that the technology of alphabet-writing spread northward up the coast during those centuries. The latest-dated items, arrowheads from Lebanon, in the north, merge into the start of the Phoenician alphabet, both in time and place.

The findings proved the existence of a Canaanite alphabet, in use at some places probably by 1700 B.C., which preceded and became the Phoenician alphabet. The Canaanite version was part of the larger Semitic tradition.

Such facts seemed by the 1960s A.D. to point to the very birth of the alphabet. Of the two earliest groups of Semitic alphabetic remnants, from Canaan and from Sinai, the Canaanite material seemed to many scholars to have begun earlier. Since Canaan could claim the earliest extant letters, and since the early alphabet culminated with Canaanite descendants, the Phoenicians, why not view Canaan as the heart of the tradition and the likely place of origin?

For the rest of the 20th century, at least through the year 1999, books and articles on the early alphabet took their cue from the Canaanite evidence. Your local library has a whole shelf of books

continued

containing the theory that the alphabet was invented in the Levant, around 1700 B.C. Yes, it was inspired partly by Egyptian hieroglyphics (the theory allows), but the inventors were looking at imported Egyptian scrolls and artwork. The inventors belonged to a sophisticated Canaanite society at a crossroads of trade, linked to Egypt by sea and to Mesopotamia by caravan routes east. Impressed with the writing systems of both great cultures, these people culled what they needed.

That reconstruction now goes into the trash can, due to a remarkable recent archaeological find in Egypt.

Like Petrie at Sinai, John Coleman Darnell wasn't looking for the alphabet; he was looking for Egyptian relics. In the early 1990s, the adventurous young Egyptologist of Yale University (today his title there is assistant professor) was absorbed in a field survey of ancient Egypt's road system, which had linked the Nile cities by land and given access to the eastern desert and the Red Sea. The roads had carried Egyptian armies, messengers, caravaners, and other land travelers. To trace the old roads, Darnell and his wife, Deborah, also an Egyptologist, would drive and hike through parts of central and southern Egypt, sometimes camping in the desert, mainly during winter months, when the sun is less ferocious (although night temperatures can plunge into the teens Fahrenheit). Much of their work involved recording thousands of Egyptian inscriptions at hundreds of archaeological sites.

By late 1992, the pair had made an important discovery. In central Egypt, about 30 miles northwest of Luxor (ancient Thebes), amid desert hills seemingly in the middle of nowhere, the Darnells had found a perfectly preserved stretch of ancient road. Part of a desert shortcut connecting the royal city of Thebes with Abydos to the north, the road lay in a valley alongside cliffs of cream-colored limestone. The valley, largely untouched since antiquity, was littered with ancient remnants—many left as litter, including camel droppings, pottery fragments, and bits of rope. Along the base of the cliffs ran hundreds of Egyptian inscriptions, carved into the stone by centuries of travelers along the road.

Here was an open-air archaeological treasure ground, saved, by its remoteness, from the antiquities thieves who are the scourge of Egyptian archaeology. (On the other hand, the Darnells realized they were not the first modern scholars to see the valley. British archaeologists in 1936 had passed through, taken some photographs and notes, and given the forlorn locale a name, based on a nearby place-name: Wadi el-Hol, the Valley of Terror.)

On his first and subsequent visits, John Darnell studied the messages along the cliffs, where "blackboard-like sheets of rock" (his phrase) had invited ancient passersby to carve. The writing looked familiar enough at first. Darnell recognized much of it as a rock-writing style of the ancient Egyptian military: It was a mishmash of hieroglyphic and hieratic symbols, chosen for easy carving, which had reached one typical style during the Middle Kingdom, around 2000 to 1600 B.C.

During much of this era Egypt was a beleaguered state, pressed by invaders from the north and south. Around Thebes, the southern capital, authorities strove to keep roads clear of brigands and desert raiders, for the sake of royal messengers especially. The roads saw frequent, camel-borne, military patrols (amply documented by archaeology). With long stretches of desert and countryside on their routes, senior Egyptian patrol officers had developed a tradition of carving commemorative messages into rocks.

Rock-writing was sober business. Our word "graffiti," with overtones of naughtiness, does not do it justice; it was more like a gravestone epitaph for someone still alive. The writer gave his name and title and ended usually with reference to a deity, a prayer for aid on the desert crossing. The inscription was thought of as permanent and spiritually potent: The writer's name would be seen and spoken by future generations of passersby, a condition good for the soul in the afterlife.

continued

The myriad carvings at Wadi el-Hol seemed to Darnell to belong comfortably to this road-warrior tradition. From specifics in the messages' content and writing shapes, and from analysis of material remains around the valley, Darnell and others would eventually choose an approximate date of 1800 B.C. for peak activity along the road.

It was on his third visit, in 1994, that Darnell noticed two strange inscriptions. They had been carved into the limestone at shoulder level, about 20 feet apart: two short, crooked rows of symbols. Surrounding them were conventional Egyptian inscriptions; all seemed to belong together. Says Darnell, "I saw the method of cutting, the placement on the rock, and I immediately associated them with the Middle Kingdom and Egyptian military rock-writing." Except that the signs themselves were not readable to Darnell. "Some of them seemed to derive from Egyptian signs, but they clearly were being used in a way that was not any Egyptian tradition."

The two inscriptions contained about 16 and 12 signs, including duplicates. Fifteen different signs seemed to be used. Some obviously were pictures. Darnell could discern an ox head, a human stick figure with raised arms, wavy vertical lines, a symmetrical cross. What message they carried, he couldn't guess. He could, however, guess what kind of writing they were. "At a glance, they looked similar to the Sinai inscriptions. So I was certain these, too, would turn out to be alphabetic."

Verification was slow and methodical. By now Egyptian authorities had been informed of Wadi el-Hol, and word was spreading. Amid a new official presence, involving permissions and paperwork—and amid occasional looting raids that saw some of the Egyptian carvings torn wholly from the rock—experts in ancient writing were brought to the valley or shown photographs of the two inscriptions.

The writing indeed proved to be alphabetic. The symbols are letters, closely related to those of Sinai and Canaan. The two inscriptions cannot be deciphered confidently, due to the absence of word breaks and our unfamiliarity with some of the letters. Nobody knows for sure if the writing runs from right to left or left to right. However, assuming the flow is right to left, like that of future Semitic writing, one inscription may begin with the word "chief" and the other one may end with the word "god."

By 1998, Darnell and others had reached a couple of dramatic conclusions. First, the two inscriptions are probably the oldest alphabetic writing yet discovered, certainly the oldest that can be dated confidently: They were carved in about 1800 B.C., give or take a century. More important, the inscriptions can be viewed as signposts that point directly back to the alphabet's invention. On the basis of the Wadi el-Hol evidence, that invention is now assigned to around 2000 B.C. in Egypt—about three centuries earlier (and in a different country) than previously thought. "Finds in Egypt Date Alphabet in Earlier Era," announced the front-page *New York Times* headline of a November 1999 piece reporting on the work.

The evidence is in the letter shapes, Darnell explains. Study has confirmed that every letter of the two inscriptions is copied from some preexisting symbol in Egyptian rock-writing and/or hieroglyphics. That is where the inventors and early users of the alphabet found their letter shapes.

Certain Wadi el-Hol letter shapes suggest a particular moment in time when that copying occurred. We know enough about Egyptian rock-writing to track the evolution of its symbols, and several Wadi el-Hol letters clearly reflect Egyptian symbol forms of the early Middle Kingdom, around 2000 B.C. Yet the Wadi el-Hol date of *carving* looks closer to 1800 B.C. The implication: The Wadi el-Hol writing preserves letter shapes bequeathed from the alphabet's invention, around 2000 B.C.

Most revealing are the M letters. The two inscriptions contain four specimens of a wavy, vertical line. Without doubt, this is the ancestor of the wavy-lined Phoenician M letter, named *mem* (water), and thus is the ancestor of our own M. The Wadi el-Hol M letter strongly resembles a preexisting, vertical, wavy Egyptian rock-writing symbol—obviously the source. But the Egyptian symbol was normally

continued on page 40

Inscription 1

Inscription 1 (augmented)

The world's oldest alphabetical writing yet discovered, the two Wadi el-Hol inscriptions are carved roughly into limestone about 20 feet apart, amid hundreds of other carvings that are Egyptian nonalphabetic writing. In the photograph of Inscription 2, the large "ghost" figure is actually an ankh symbol belonging to a nearby Egyptian inscription.

The inscriptions' letters look like cartoon figures. Yet experts find here the earliest examples of our A, B, E, L, M, R, and other letters. To the untrained eye, the only letter that resembles its future self is T, found twice in Inscription 2: It is the cross or lowercase t shape, at third from the top and again farther down.

Each picture letter denoted a consonant sound. When sounded out correctly, the letters would produce words in ancient Semitic. Only two words have been deciphered, even tentatively. Assuming the writing runs right to left (and that is uncertain), then

Inscription 2

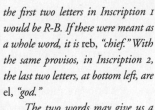

the first two letters in Inscription 1 would be R-B. If these were meant as a whole word, it is reb, "chief." With the same provisos, in Inscription 2, the last two letters, at bottom left, are el, "god."

The two words may give us a guess at both inscriptions' content. The many decipherable ancient Egyptian rock messages at Wadi el-Hol and other road sites follow a standard formula: The writer identifies himself by name and title and invokes a patron deity. The two Wadi el-Hol inscriptions may simply be alphabetic versions of an army-regulation message, "name, rank, and prayer."

Inscription 2 (detail)

The name of God. As read from right to left, the primordial letters aleph and lamed spell el, "god," apparently part of a soldier's prayer for safety in the desert. The ladle-like lamed is the letter L. The ox-head aleph is not an E but rather a breathing-stop like a tiny cough, which began the word's Semitic pronunciation and which does not show up in normal English spelling.

We cannot identify the god, but polytheistic Semitic peoples of later centuries would worship a protective father called Melkart or Baal or sometimes just El. Meanwhile, another Semitic branch, the Jews, would evolve a faith in a single God. In Hebrew, the letters aleph and lamed likewise form the divine name, as contained in the biblical word Elohim ("God") and in familiar names like Elizabeth and Michael. The Arabic word Allah ("God") comes from the same linguistic tradition.

written horizontally. The Egyptian vertical phase was brief, around 2000 B.C. So the vertical shape at Wadi el-Hol betrays the letter's approximate date of birth. Other letter shapes allow similar deductions.

Who were the inventors? Darnell believes they may have been in the Egyptian army: Semitic mercenaries or similar, whom the Egyptians would have called *Amu* (Asiatics). These people were illiterate originally. But the army that they joined happened to have a vigorous writing tradition, which inspired them, it seems, to think of a writing method for themselves.

Perhaps the inventors were junior officers among the *Amu,* individuals who had learned some standard Egyptian rock-writing and were able to work from there. Perhaps, Darnell theorizes, they got help from Egyptian army scribes, who sought to improve the foreigners' organization with the gift of literacy.

As to who might have carved the two Wadi el-Hol inscriptions, same answer as above. Not the inventors themselves, of course, but their great-great-grandnephews, serving in Egypt's camel corps. It was the army that did most of the writing along desert roads.

One last item of information. Quite near to one of the alphabetic inscriptions on the limestone wall is an Egyptian message mentioning someone named Bebi, titled as "expedition leader of the *Amu.*" This can't be coincidence, Darnell maintains: The three inscriptions, alphabetic and Egyptian, were probably carved at the same time. If Bebi was an Egyptian, leading a Semite troop on road patrol, then the "chief" of one alphabetic message could have been one of those Semites, a junior officer or tribal chieftain under Bebi's command. A similar person would have written the other alphabetic message. The two Semitic soldiers were using their "native" writing form, different from Egyptian. Says Darnell, "It certainly looks as though General Bebi wrote his name, and two of Bebi's Semites wrote theirs."

speaker with the opportunity could learn 27 pictures and their names: that, and a few years' practice, brought literacy.

During the second millennium B.C., the new technology spread from Egypt along caravan routes northeast and southeast into the greater Semitic world, to Canaan and the Arabian peninsula. It proved as accessible to the poor as to the rich.

In Canaan and Arabia, the original alphabet apparently evolved into two separate traditions: two different-looking alphabets, adjusted to local speech. In each, the letter shapes morphed away from cumbersome pictures to stylized images, easier to write. The number of Canaanite letters dropped to 22, easier to learn. The Canaanite alphabet passed to the emergent Phoenician culture at the start of the Iron Age (1200 B.C.). The Arabian branch today survives only in the traditional script of Ethiopia.

But the secret power of the alphabet—unknown to its inventors, surely—was that it did not need Semitic speech in order to work. That fact would emerge in centuries to come. With modest adjustments, the miraculous letters would be fitted to diverse tongues of Europe, India, and Southeast Asia, and carry literacy around the globe.

Who today reads hieroglyphics? The upstart notion of the *Amu* has triumphed. Their picture letters were destined for billions of people. Like the wheel or the telephone, the alphabet was an invention to change the world.

An alphabet of (female) personalities is imagined in D. L. May's cartoon "The A-to-Z Line," from the British satirical magazine Punch *(March 23, 1955). Although modern taste might wish for deeper criteria than just clothing and body types, this cartoon still charms, with its 1950s elegance and class consciousness.* Punch *ceased publication in 2002.*

And now for the 26 heroes of our story . . .

The knightly A proclaims "quality assurance," on a red, white, and blue emblem of the United States Department of Agriculture. Among other duties, the USDA inspects and grades food products meant for public consumption, using letter rankings A, B, and C for certain foods, such as poultry, eggs, and dairy. But the A of excellence is also the USDA's own symbol.

A, FIRST AND BEST

Associated with beginnings, fundamentals, and superiority, the letter A has traveled first class down through history. Most modern alphabets start with A or its near equivalent. It was letter number 1 for the ancient Greeks (800 B.C.) and, in an earlier form, for the Phoenicians (1000 B.C.). Almost certainly it came first in the earliest Near Eastern letter lists of 2000 B.C. Being the doorway to literacy, A has enjoyed the richest symbolic value of any letter.

The A can symbolize all other letters by itself. In advertising and other narrative imagery, an A shown chalked onto a school blackboard, or held in the gloved hand of *Sesame Street*'s Big Bird, sends a clear message: "Kids are learning

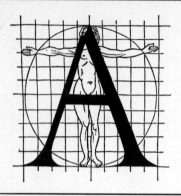 

A human form and a designer's compass and ruler define the ideal proportions of capital A in two ink drawings from the book Champ Fleury *("field of flowers") by visual artist Geofroy Tory, printed in Paris in 1529. A true Renaissance man, Tory was a type designer, painter, engraver, calligrapher, writer, university teacher of French, scholar of Latin and Greek, bookseller, and eventually the official printer to King François I. He wrote his book to demonstrate the "proper and true proportions of the letters" and to correct what he saw as imperfect calligraphy by contemporaries, including German artist Albrecht Dürer. Tory illustrated each letter's design on a grid—reminiscent of recent proportional studies on other subjects done by Leonardo da Vinci—and accompanied his diagrams with a learned, cheerful text on the letters' visual, phonetic, and literary qualities. Tory shared in an idea of the day that letters, as bearers of language and reason, were signs from God. Thus their shapes should reflect a universal harmony and balance.*

the alphabet." No other letter alone could clearly say this; an E or K or Z on the blackboard might blur the signal by seeming to suggest a particular word. "Why E?" the viewer might muse. "For 'e-business,' key to the future? This *must* be an old ad." But A timelessly represents the idea of 26 letters.

It also represents success at school. The use of A, B, C, D, and F to grade students' work is documented in the United States since the late 19th century. The system has survived experimental alternatives and remains nearly universal in American public schools and widespread in the British Commonwealth and Western Europe. Excepting F for "failure," the letters are not initials but ratings by sequence.

Thus the meaning of A as "first rate" is ingrained in us as children, to recur in our adult lives. Like the fair-haired son of a wealthy family, A emanates quality.

For example, in the rating of bonds, stocks, and other credit obligations, both Standard & Poor's and Moody's investors' services use a top grade of AAA, for items carrying very little risk. Investments rated AAA have the right to be called "gilt edged." Next come grades AA and A, then BBB, BB, and B (at Standard & Poor's) or Baa, Ba, and B (at Moody's), and so on to C and, for some categories, D.

Similarly, the United States Department of Agriculture (USDA), which screens food products meant for public consumption, employs letter grades for many. Chicken carcasses are judged as quality A, B, C, or ungraded. To get an A, the carcass must be "normal" in shape, "well fleshed," and "free or protruding feathers and hairs," according to a USDA publication. By the time we reach C, the chicken might look "abnormal" or "misshapen," be "poorly fleshed," and have a "scattering of protruding feathers and hairs." (As if getting slaughtered weren't insult enough.) The point of grading is to provide criteria: Most supermarket suppliers deal only with "A" chickens.

The letter A can signal "top service" in commerce and name branding. Company names like AAA Heating & Cooling have the advantage of coming first in the yellow page listings, as well as being easily remembered and suggesting "no risk" for the customer. The American Automobile Association (AAA) sells itself on a promise of reliability, as does, in its own way, Alcoholics Anonymous (AA).

Our expression "A-1," meaning "first rate," goes back to British nautical language of the early 1800s. The maritime insurer Lloyd's of London, in registering ships, would use notations A or

B to rate the condition of ships' hulls and notations 1 or 2 to rate ship's equipment. Only the most shipshape vessel could advertise as being "A-1 at Lloyd's."

Neat and self-explanatory, "A-1" soon spread to popular use on both sides of the Atlantic. In print, it shows up with no nautical reference in mid-19th-century journalism and in novels like Charles Dickens's *The Pickwick Papers* (1837). The "A-okay" of American speech would seem to be formed by analogy, yet it actually dates from much later, 1961. During the first manned, suborbital NASA spaceflight, a simple "okay" from astronaut Alan Shepard in radio communication was misheard and misreported as "A-okay." The phrase caught on because it captured a niche: The A raised it to the meaning of "excellent," where "okay" might mean just "adequate."

The "A-list," a term favored until recently in snob-appeal journalism and advertising, refers to any select group, the crème de la crème. An A-list tops a B-list and sometimes a C-list. The terminology entered mainstream media in the 1980s, inspired by the "Hollywood A-list"—an unofficial ranking of about 75 movie stars judged to be currently the most "bankable" (able to attract financing for a new film project). Another 100 or so names supply a B-list, with more names on lists C and D. Based on recent box-office returns and film-industry opinion, the lists float around in several versions. *The Hollywood Reporter* newspaper publishes an annual "Star Power Survey," which avoids notations like A and B but is composed of five lists, totaling about 1,000 names. Industry people often refer to these as the A+, A, B, C, and D lists.

Science, unlike Hollywood, mistrusts value judgments. Here the letter A may signify not "best" but "first." Between 1913 and 1916, research chemists mainly at the University of Wisconsin worked to isolate certain organic compounds deemed essential for human health. When one and then a second were discovered, they were called "fat-soluble A" and "water-soluble B," later renamed more spiffily as vitamins A and B. Other vitamin names followed, including subdivisions of B.

A is, of course, a vowel letter. That means it represents certain sounds from the vocal cords—our word "vowel" coming via medieval French from the Latin adjective *vocalis,* "using the voice." Vowels are spoken without much interference or shaping in the mouth. Sounds involving blockage or friction are classed as consonants.

Written English has five proper vowel letters, A, E, I, O, and U. (Y may substitute for I.) Yet spoken English has some 20 shades of vowel sounds. Accordingly, our vowel letters are kept busy, each one symbolizing multiple sounds on any written page. Our letters get some help from rules of spelling, which, for example, can specify the long A of "rate" versus the short A of "rat."

A has about a dozen possible sounds in English. Here are six: "Was Allan's pa all pale?" (Or you may find only five A sounds there, depending on your regional accent.) The first sound in "Allan" is our usual short A. However, the slightly different short A of "pa"—what linguists call the low, back vowel—is A's normal pronunciation in most other European languages and is thought to have been A's pronunciation in the ancient European tongues Greek, Etruscan, and Latin.

This "ah" sound is fundamental to human speech. The mid-20th-century linguist and alphabet scholar David Diringer calls it "the purest and simplest vocalic sound, as uttered by opening the air passage of the throat to its fullest extent. It is regarded as the most primitive vowel sound and is the first sound uttered by a baby." How like our A (first class all the way) to bring home a most essential sound.

Yet it wasn't always so. Three or four thousand years ago, the first letter didn't say "ah." Like every other vowel letter in our alphabet, A began life as a consonant, with a different sound. This isn't a complicated notion: Written letters are mere convention, changeable according to need. Today the familiar letter written as C means sound "j" in Turkish; the letter J means "y" in German and Swedish. The symbol A could mean "z" or "th" or anything else, if everyone so agreed. Early in history, something like that was happening.

The original A is as old as any letter. It makes its entrance in the earliest alphabetic writing yet discovered: two limestone-carved inscriptions at Wadi el-Hol in central Egypt, the work of Semitic speakers, perhaps mercenary soldiers, around 1800 B.C. As all our original letters were pictures, the A was a picture of an ox head, vividly rendered. The picture letter was called "ox"—*aleph* in ancient Semitic tongues.

The earliest letters were consonants, for writing abbreviated words. Vowel sounds, although they occurred in Semitic speech, did not need to be shown in writing. *Aleph* represented a faint con-sonantal sound common in Semitic tongues but rare in modern English, what linguists call a glottal stop. The classic English exam-ple occurs in London's Cockney accent, in the swallowing of the "t" sound of the word "bottle": "bah-owe." A glottal stop is thus a catch in the throat, from which a following vowel sound pushes off.

Insofar as each Semitic letter name began with the very sound that the letter symbolized, the name *aleph* actually began with a glottal stop, a bit of throat before the "a." This fact is hard to ren-der in our own spelling. But some modern scholars print the let-ter name as *'aleph* (alternatively *'alef* or *'alep*), where the mark ' is an international phonetic symbol for the glottal stop.

We know that *aleph* was the first letter of the alphabet in at least 1300 B.C., the approximate date of the oldest Canaanite letter lists uncovered by modern archaeology. Letter lists from Phoenicia, a few centuries later, likewise show *aleph* first. Because letters gen-

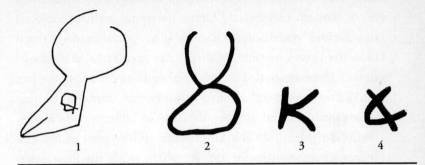

The evolution of the ox. (1) Letter aleph, *the "ox," as it appears in one of the Wadi el-Hol inscriptions, from about 1800 B.C. (Photographs of both inscriptions, including a second carved* aleph, *are shown on pages 38–39.) Unlikely as it seems, this pictorial image was the earliest form of our letter A. Today the horns of the ox remain with us, unnoticed, in the upright legs of our A. (2) Aleph's shape looks simpler in another early Semitic inscription, carved at Serabit el-Khadem in Sinai, perhaps around 1750 B.C. (3) Two horns are still evident in the Phoenician* aleph *of 1000 B.C., but the letter is by now an abstract form, to be written in three quick strokes of an ink brush or pen on papyrus or a stylus on ceramic. (4) By the 800s B.C., Phoenician* aleph *has a new look, rather more like an ox's head, to be written in perhaps two strokes. (Can you guess where the shape would go next?)*

erally stay in the same order over time except for some very good reason, modern scholars consider it a sure bet that *aleph* was the first letter of the original alphabet of about 2000 B.C.

How and why *aleph* was chosen for first place, we will never know. No modern explanation satisfies—especially not references to the sacredness of the bull in ancient Mediterranean and Near Eastern cultures. *Some* letter had to start off the mnemonic string of letter names for the student, and "ox" was a clear concept and image. Because *aleph* came first for the Bronze Age Semites, the letter A comes first for us.

Today a letter called *aleph* or *alef* remains the first letter of the Hebrew alphabet. (Ancient Hebrew letters were originally copied from the Phoenician.) The Hebrew name is still understood to mean "ox," but the glottal stop is gone from the letter's name and sound. Modern Hebrew *alef* carries no sound itself; its job is to show various vowel sounds according to special marks written below the letter's baseline. In shape, a printed Hebrew *alef* looks not very Phoenician: א. The lack of resemblance is due to the fact that Hebrew script underwent a major change during its history. Yet originally, around 950 B.C., the *aleph* of Hebrew and Phoenician looked identical. The kinship can still be seen in modern Hebrew's cursive shape for *alef*, ﬡ, which recalls the Phoenician letter of 1000 B.C.

In Jewish lore, Hebrew *alef* enjoys a philosophical glory greater even than that of our A. According to mystical writings such as the medieval European compilation called the Kabbalah (Hebrew for "tradition"), *alef* symbolizes the divine energy that preceded and initiated Creation. This seeding power existed before any other form could be realized, which is why the opening word of the Hebrew Bible—*bereshith* ("in the beginning")—starts with the Hebrew alphabet's second letter, not the first. Correspondingly, *alef* may represent a person's readiness to act, while the second letter, *beth* or *bayt*, is imagined as the doer of things. Hebrew *alef* could also be used to signify numeral 1 and was a symbol of cosmic unity.

Just as Phoenician *aleph* was the mother of Hebrew *alef*, so was it great-grandmother to our A, by a different line of descent. Ours is the westward branch of the family, linking three ancient European peoples: the Greeks, Etruscans, and Romans.

First, the Greeks. Sometime before 800 B.C., with no existing writing system, they copied and adapted Phoenician letters for writing Greek. The operation was miraculous in light of how different were the two languages, Greek and Phoenician. The Greeks made one major adjustment: They created five vowel letters, by changing the sounds of five Phoenician letters that were otherwise superfluous for Greek. One was *aleph*, representing a subtle, Semitic throat sound unknown to the Greeks. The adapters kept the letter at number 1 but reassigned it to the most basic vowel sound, "ah."

The choice of "ah" was probably prompted by the Phoenician letter's name, whose first syllable contained an "ah" sound: *'a-lef.* Maybe the Greeks couldn't even hear the Phoenician glottal stop in front and thought the Phoenician letter name began with "ah."

To Greek ears, all the Phoenician letter names were just foreign noises, not names of familiar objects. The Greeks altered the names to make them easier to say. *Aleph* became *alpha,* a name also meaningless in Greek (beside denoting the letter) but at least Greek in style.

Today the word *alpha* lives on prestigiously in scientific and technical vocabulary and in name branding, usually signifying something that's first, strongest, or best. The "alpha male," for example, is the strongest in a pack of baboons or wolves. *Alpha* may represent cosmic first principles, for instance in a well-known phrase from the biblical book of Revelation (written in Greek around A.D. 100): "I am Alpha and Omega, the beginning and the ending, saith the Lord." For its effect, the passage brings together the names of the first and last letters of the Greek alphabet. By the way, our very word "alphabet" combines the first two Greek letters' names, *alpha* and *beta.*

Meanwhile, the ancient Greeks were adjusting *alpha*'s shape. The Phoenician letter that they had borrowed had a shape something like this: ⴵ. However, because the name *alpha* did not mean "ox" to Greek speakers, the letter had lost its purpose as a picture, and within about three generations of acquiring it the Greeks decided it looked better standing on two feet: ꓮ.

This mature *alpha* was basically the same as our A. It retained its

1   2   3   4   5

(1) Phoenician aleph *of about 800 B.C., in the era when the Greeks were copying Phoenician letters for themselves. Phoenician writing ran from right to left; thus, the* aleph *led with its point. (2) Greek* alpha, *from one of the earliest extant Greek inscriptions, of about 740 B.C. Like the Phoenician* aleph *that inspired it, this* alpha *lies on its side. However, the Greeks were already experimenting, for this letter is a mirror image of* aleph: *It leads with its feet in a line of Greek writing that runs right to left, whereas an* aleph *would face the other way. (Early Greek writing could run right to left or left to right or, in some longer texts, both ways, using a systematic meander called boustrophedon, "as the plow-ox turns." By about 500 B.C. Greek had settled at left to right.) (3)* Alpha *stands upright in an inscription of about 720 B.C., and thenceforth that is the norm. (4) An Etruscan letter A of about 500 B.C. The Etruscan letters had been copied from the Greek, and they, in turn, would be copied by the early Romans. (5) Roman A of A.D. 113, from a famous inscription at the base of Trajan's Column in Rome. Like most of our capitals, A reached its perfected form in Roman marble-carved inscriptions of the first century B.C. to second century A.D. Roman design refined the letter's shape, widening the right-side leg and adding strokes (which we call serifs) at the feet. Nearly 14 centuries later, early printers in Venice would copy this and other Roman lettering, to create capital letters of the new "roman" typeface.*

shape, sound, and first place when the Greek alphabet was copied by the Etruscans of Italy, around 700 B.C., and when the Etruscan alphabet was copied by Latin-speaking villagers of Rome, around 600 B.C.

Our name for A comes from the Etruscans: Receiving the Greek *alpha,* they simplified the name down to the letter's sound, calling it something like "ah." The Romans did likewise, and "ah" remains the letter's name as pronounced in Latin-derived modern languages like French and Spanish and in some non-Latinate European tongues like German and Croatian.

English gets most of its letter names from Old French, imported to England perforce by the Norman invasion of A.D. 1066. For centuries after the Battle of Hastings, A's name was probably pronounced in England as "ah." But due to fundamental shifts in English vowel sounds during the 1400s and 1500s, the name altered, eventually rhyming with "pay." (Phonetically, A must be Canada's favorite letter—eh?)

During the Roman Empire and early Middle Ages, alternative shapes for A emerged in ink handwriting styles, due to a natural leaning toward greater speed and ease. The Roman penned shape λ led to the late-Roman λ and eventually to a, which was the "Carolingian minuscule," created by churchmen of the French king Charlemagne around A.D. 800 in their reform of handwritten shapes. This particular letter shape had a rosy future. In the 1470s, amid the burgeoning of printing in Western Europe, one school of type designers copied their lowercase letters from the handwriting tradition that perpetuated the old Carolingian shapes, and so a got finalized in print: a. But other print styles used a lowercase shape from a different handwriting tradition: ɑ.

Both forms endure. Today ɑ is our model for handwritten shapes taught in elementary school. In print, it shows up in some fonts that are sans-serif or *italic*. The a dominates, however, as used in ubiquitous roman fonts and in others. Only letters A and G share this odd distinction of owning two modern print-lowercase forms. Every other letter has just one, essentially the same for all typefaces.

Princely as it is, A fails to come first in one category, at least. For frequency of use in printed English, A ranks third, behind the clear front-runner, E, and then T. (Both E and T are helped by the word "the.") Also, A has acquired one actual discredit throughout history. In medieval Europe and Puritan England, A was associated with adultery (Latin: *adulterium*), generally tried as a criminal offense. In addition to punishments like flogging, a convicted spouse might be forced to wear a humiliating badge showing an A or AD. Such facts form the background for Nathaniel Hawthorne's novel *The Scarlet Letter* (1850), set in Puritan Boston in the mid-1600s: Protagonist Hester Prynne is convicted of adultery and must publicly wear an A of red cloth, sewn to her tunic breast.

Hester's tale has touched many hearts, not least that of con man "Professor" Harold Hill in Meredith Willson's 1957 Broadway musical, *The Music Man*. Stuck in local Iowa, Hill sings of his longing to find a worldly, experienced woman, a "sadder but wiser girl":

I flinch, I shy when the lass with the delicate air goes by.
I smile, I grin when the gal with a touch of sin walks in.
I hope, I pray for Hester to win just one more A.
. . . The sadder but wiser girl for me!

The Eastern Mediterranean in 800 B.C.

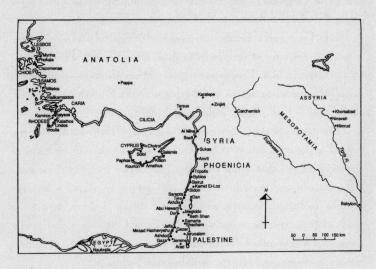

The Greek alphabet may have been born at Cyprus or at nearby Al Mina, on the Syrian coast. In both places, Greeks and Phoenicians lived side by side.

From Phoenicia, the letters of the early alphabet traveled westward to ancient Greece. The Greeks' copying of the Phoenician alphabet, around 800 B.C., was to be one of the most consequential events in history.

The Greeks of that era were an ambitious but relatively humble people, illiterate, disunited, and far junior in wealth and power to Near Eastern nations like Egypt or the Phoenician cities. Greek territory of the day corresponded loosely to the modern nation of Greece—the mainland and the Aegean islands—with the addition of some Greek cities on Cyprus and the west coast of Asia Minor.

Unlike Egyptians or Phoenicians, the Greeks spoke a language of the Indo-European family, to which ancient Latin also belonged. Today some 60 major Indo-European languages exist worldwide, including French and Spanish (descended from Latin), also English, German, Hindi, Farsi, Russian, Irish, and other tongues of Europe, Central Asia,

continued

and India. Linguists classify modern Indo-European tongues into eight subfamilies; English belongs to the Germanic subfamily.

Indo-European languages are capable of wonderful precision, for example, in variations of verb form to show many possible differences in tense. As a rule, Indo-European tongues rely heavily on vowel sounds to establish word meanings, as in distinguishing the English words "hall," "hail," "heel," "Hell," "hill," "hole," and "hull."

The destiny of the Greeks was to be shapers of the West. During the heyday of the 400s and 300s B.C., Greek minds would pioneer many of the civilizing arts that define us today. The Greeks invented democracy, stage tragedy and comedy, Western philosophy, investigative history-writing, biological research, and political theory. They perfected the study of geometry, the sculpting (in bronze and marble) of the human form, and a monumental architecture that we imitate for our courthouses, museums, and other venerable public buildings.

Obviously, their alphabet and literacy were essential to such achievements, and their alphabet is part of their legacy. The Greeks bequeathed to the West an alphabet that had been adapted to an Indo-European language (Greek) and was therefore accessible to other European tongues. Specifically, the Greeks had introduced vowel letters—the equivalents of our A, E, I, O, and U—where earlier, Semitic versions of the alphabet had contained none. Vowel letters brought the alphabet forward to a point where it could be fitted to most other languages. The Greek letters were the necessary background to the creation of the ancient Roman letters, which later became our own.

All of that lay in the future in 800 B.C. Greek genius meanwhile showed itself elsewhere: in religious awe; in a wealth of myths and legends, handed down through oral-poetic tradition; in an enthusiasm for trade and seafaring; and in a talent for copycatting (and often improving on) other peoples' skills. As the Greek philosopher Plato would later claim, "Whenever Greeks take anything from foreigners, they eventually bring it to a greater perfection."

The early Greeks had opportunity to study the Phoenicians. The two peoples were trade partners at locales mainly on the Greek side: Phoenician merchant ships brought Near Eastern luxury goods to exchange for Greek raw materials like silver, iron, and slaves (these being mostly Greeks, enslaved by other Greeks in the internal wars that blighted their society). Phoenicians sailed to and from ports of mainland Greece and of islands like Crete and Rhodes. More significantly, Greek and Phoenician communities coexisted on the south coast of Cyprus and at an important trading station in the north Levant, now called Al Mina.

Modern study reveals several Greek borrowings from the Phoenicians. Among them: (1) improved ship designs, for merchant and war vessels; (2) techniques of long-range navigation; (3) certain visual motifs in artwork, including the Near Eastern tree-of-life design and an imaginary, dragonlike beast, the griffin; (4) the religious cult of a protective, sexual goddess whom the Phoenicians called Astarte and whom the Greeks renamed Aphrodite, along with a belief in her doomed human consort, known in Greek as Adonis (from the Phoenician Semitic word *adonai,* "lord"); and (5) the Phoenician alphabet.

The oldest surviving Greek alphabetic inscriptions are scratches in ceramic or stone, dated from about 775 to 700 B.C. The earliest of these seem to come from the second or third human generation of Greek alphabetic literacy. In the inscriptions, the Greek letters display their origins: They closely resemble Phoenician letter shapes, with many (not all) of their sounds being the same as for the Phoenician versions, except that the letters are now being used to convey the speech sounds of Greek.

Despite the fact that Phoenician and Greek were languages as different as Arabic and English, the Greeks evidently had picked up the 22 Phoenician letters, made some changes, and started writing. The adaption was possible partly through the Greek genius for tinkering and partly through the magical flexibility and aptness of the letters themselves.

Only one major change the Greeks made, as mentioned: Out of a Phoenician alphabet of all consonants, they invented five vowel letters,

continued

the equivalents of our A, E, I, O, U. In a future century, the mature Greek alphabet would contain seven vowel letters, with long E and long O distinguished from short E and O. But in the meantime, five was the number of vowels that would reach Italy and be copied into Italian alphabets like the Roman. That's why our alphabet has only five vowel letters today.

Regarding the details of the transmission from Phoenicians to Greeks, we know nothing: not who, where, or when exactly. Probably the Phoenicians were merchants, on good terms with Greek counterparts. A later Greek legend acknowledged the debt to Phoenicia, although distortedly: Once upon a time (the tale ran), a Phoenician prince named Cadmus had immigrated to an illiterate Greece and had taught local people to use *Phoinikeia grammata,* "Phoenician letters."

Wherever it was born, the invention spread very quickly through the small Greek world, along sea routes. Probably by 600 B.C., every Greek city had a literate upper and middle class. The swift transition to literacy, in a Greece still imbued with an oral tradition of myths, meant that these could be written down, fresh in memory. Two masterpieces of Western literature are among the results: the epic poems *Iliad* and *Odyssey,* written down around 750 B.C. and ascribed to the blind poet Homer. But many other tales went into writing then, which is why today we have record of a rich Greek mythology. Those legends were captured, as in a photograph, by alphabetic literacy.

THE PHOENICIAN ALPHABET OF 800 B.C.			THE GREEK ALPHABET AFTER 800 B.C.		
Letter Shape	Sound	Name	Letter Shape	Sound	Name
⪤	breathing stop	aleph	A	"a"	alpha
⅁	"b"	bayt	8	"b"	beta
⅂	"g"	gimel	⅂ or 〉	"g"	gamma
◿	"d"	dalet	◁ or △	"d"	delta
⅂	"h"	he	⅂	"e"	e psilon ("naked E")
Y	"w"	waw	⅂	"w"	wau
I	"z"	zayin	I	"zd"	zeta
目	guttural "kh"	khet	目	"h"	eta
⊕	emphatic "t"	tet	⊕	"th"	theta
⅃	"y"	yod	l	"i"	iota
⅄	"k"	kaph	Ж	"k" (1)	kappa
⅃	"l"	lamed	⅃	"l"	lambda
⅂	"m"	mem	⋎	"m"	mu
⅃	"n"	nun	⋏	"n"	nu
⪥	"s"	samek	⊞	"ks"	ksi
O	guttural sound	ayin	O	"o"	o mikron ("little O")
⅂	"p"	pe	⅂	"p"	pi
Ⱶ	"ts"	tsade	⋀	modified "s"	san
φ	"q"	qoph	⅋	"k" (2)	qoppa
⅂	"r"	resh	⅂	"r"	rho
W	"sh"	shin	〉 or 〈	"s"	sigma
†	"t"	taw	⊤	"t"	tau

Four Greek letters added by about 750 B.C.

	Y	"u"	u psilon ("naked U")		
	φ	"ph"	phi	OR	×	"ks"	ksi
	×	"kh"	khi	OR	φ	"ph"	phi
	Ψ	"ps"	psi	OR	Y	"kh"	khi

Last letter added by about 660 B.C.　　Ω　　long "o"　　o mega ("big O")

The early Greek alphabet followed the Phoenician in its letters' shapes, sequence, names, and (for the most part) sounds. The very earliest Greek list perhaps had 22 letters, ending with the T letter, like the Phoenician. Within the 22, the Greeks reassigned a few letters to new sounds, discarding certain Phoenician sounds unneeded for Greek.

continued

In this way, the Greeks invented four vowel letters, the A, E, I, and O equivalents. The first of them was the first letter of the Greek alphabet, alpha.

The 22 letters proving not adequate, the Greeks soon created four more, including vowel U, adding them to the end of the letter row. Finally they added a 27th letter, o mega or omega ("big O"), to denote the long-O sound. The earlier O letter, thenceforth confined to short O, was renamed o mikron ("little O"), or omicron, as we usually spell it. Eventually the underused wau, san, and qoppa dropped out, leaving the number of letters at 24.

The early Greek alphabet had three slightly differing forms, used in different regions. The East Greek variant, adopted by the influential city of Athens around 400 B.C., would grow into the modern Greek alphabet. The West Greek variant would travel to Italy to become the "grandmother" of the Roman alphabet.

The three alphabets varied at the end of the letter row, just before omega. The chart (page 61) shows the more familiar East Greek ending at center, with the West Greek alternative at right—containing our future letter X, with its relevant sound, "ks."

The Greek names of the first 22 letters mainly echoed the Phoenician names, in a Greek form. But where the Phoenician letter names were also Semitic common nouns ("ox," "house," "throwing stick," etc.), the Greek names had no prior meanings in Greek: They just denoted letters. Today Greek letter names live on in our scientific and technical vocabulary, our fraternity and sorority names, and our business and brand names. The favorites are alpha, beta, gamma, delta, and omega.

One quirk of the Greek alphabet has fascinated scholars. The original Greek adapters apparently made minor mistakes in transcribing the Phoenician sibilants (letters involving S-type sounds). For their letter zeta, the Greeks took the sound and name of Phoenician tsade but the shape and sequence position of Phoenician zayin. For their letter sigma, the Greeks took the sound and name of Phoenician samek but the shape and position of Phoenician shin. Other substitutions tied up the loose ends. Sibilants, with their often-subtle shadings of sound, are notorious tripping points between languages generally: To Greek ears, Phoenician tsade and zayin probably sounded similar—but still that doesn't explain why the Greeks combined elements of both for zeta. It seems even the Greeks were only human.

Power to the people. The alphabet, in delivering mass literacy, has for ages been a cornerstone of democracy—a relationship embodied in these ceramic potsherds, incised with Greek letters, from ancient Athens, the world's first democracy. Falling in date between about 485 and 440 B.C., each sherd carries the name of a prominent Athenian politician of the era. Clockwise from top left: Aristeides, son of Lysimachos; Themistokles, son of Neokles, of the Phrearros city ward; Perikles, son of Xanthippos; and Kimon, son of Miltiades. About half the letters look just like ours.

These items are votes to have the men banished. Ceramic sherds (ostraka in Greek) being the ancient world's version of scrap paper, the four scraps have been used as ballots in a practice called ostrakismos (ostracism), unique to Athenian democracy, whereby the Athenians had the chance annually to vote to banish any citizen. Ostracism was not a punishment for crimes committed. Rather, it was the people's safeguard against the rich—specifically, against politicians who might scheme for supreme power and an end to democracy. An ostracism vote had no announced candidates; people simply voted, secretly, in writing (most Athenian citizens being literate). Ballots were collected in a controlled procedure. If a quorum of 6,000 votes was reached, the man with the most votes had to leave the city for 10 years. Of the four powerful men named here, only Perikles avoided a "winning" vote; the other three were exiled.

Imitating medieval manuscript illumination, a decorative print B dominates the opening page of the famous 1457 Latin Psalter, a collection of psalms for church use, printed by Johann Fust and Peter Schöffer at the German city of Mainz. The text presents the start of Psalm 1: "Blessed is the man (Beatus vir) that walketh not in the counsel of the ungodly. . . ." The letter shapes are based on a traditional German handwriting style. This was among the first books printed from metal type, following Johann Gutenberg's Bible of about 1455. Fust had been Gutenberg's investor and had sued and bankrupted him, evidently seizing Gutenberg's letterpress and tools—and probably Gutenberg's design for this fine Psalter.

elow the best, or second in sequence: That's the message we get from letter B. Think of Plan B, the B-list, B-rated bonds, grade-B eggs. More so than other letters, B has lived centuries in the shadow of its exemplary sibling, A. The whole point of B, in many uses, is that there exists an "A" version, which is better.

The eloquent term "B-movie" refers to a Hollywood-type film that's inferior, with shallow plot or characterization and maybe a cheap production look. B-movies often come from B-scripts. The B doesn't stand for a word (these movies aren't bombs, necessarily); it just announces a shortfall. We don't even have an expression like "A-movie." The B creates the whole comparison.

The B-girl appeared in print in the early 1930s, not long after the repeal of Prohibition, and remained familiar until at least the 1960s. Here B *did* stand for a word, "bar." The girls were young women, hired by nightclubs and such to sit at the bar and pretend to be customers. Their job was to enhance the atmosphere and induce male customers to buy them drinks; the women might be served glasses of lukewarm tea, disguised as liquor. Again, B comes off as a bit tacky.

Despite such imperfect impressions, the letter B has done yeoman service in the alphabet for 4,000 years. It symbolizes a sound that is basic to human speech, categorized by linguists as the voiced bilabial stop—in other words, the sound engages the vocal cords, is formed by two lips, and involves stoppage of air through the nose. With no tricky use of tongue or teeth, "b" is relatively easy to say. Babies say it all the time (the thirsty 16-month-old wants her "bah-bah"), and many of the world's languages, past and present, have included it. Our B represents probably the same sound carried by the analogous letter in Near Eastern alphabets of 30 or 40 centuries ago.

It is a consonant sound. Therefore, B is a consonant letter, the first in alphabetical sequence of our 21. If asked at a dinner party to define the word "consonant," someone might venture, "Well, I know it's not a vowel . . ." and that actually is the best starting point. Whereas vowels are pronounced from the vocal cords with minimal shaping of expelled breath, consonant sounds are created through obstruction or channeling of the breath by the lips, teeth, tongue, throat, or nasal passage, variously combined. Some consonants, like B, involve the vocal cords; others don't. Some, like R or W, flow the breath in a way that steers them relatively close to being vowels.

We get the term "consonant" via medieval French from an ancient Latin word, *consonans,* "sounding along with." The idea is that while vowel sounds can be pronounced on their own ("Eee! I owe!"), a consonant normally can be pronounced only with a vowel before or after. Try saying the "b" sound alone and you'll probably wind up cheating, tacking on a vowel sound: "bih."

This rule isn't bulletproof. A few consonants *can* more or less be pronounced alone, particularly those with a continuous sound, like F or Z. Still, you'll need effort not to relax into "fih" or "zuh" at the end.

The oldest version of B appears in the earliest-known alphabetic inscriptions, discovered at Wadi el-Hol in central Egypt and dated to 1800 B.C. The letter is a prominent presence in other Near Eastern alphabetic inscriptions of about 1750 to 1200 B.C. But the early letter is most familiar to us from its systematic use in ancient Phoenician writing, after about 1000 B.C.

The Phoenician letter had two traits we recognize easily: It represented sound "b" and came second in the alphabet. Like every Phoenician letter, it was named for a familiar object, the object's

1   2   3   4

(1) The Egyptian "reed shelter" hieroglyph represented sound "h" in Egyptian picture writing, around 2000 B.C. This symbol is believed to have inspired certain non-Egyptian Semites, living in Egypt, to invent a letter that they called "house," bayt, carrying sound "b." (2) The hieroglyphic shape is strongly recalled in a bayt from a Canaanite inscription (ink on ceramic) of about 1200 B.C. The Canaanites were a Semitic people of the Levant, ancestors of the Phoenicians. Bayt came second in their alphabet, which is why B comes second in ours. (3) The Phoenician bayt of 1000 B.C. was derived from the Canaanite letter shape but allowed for simpler strokes of the ink brush or pen. It faced left, consistent with the right-to-left direction of Phoenician writing. (4) Early Greek beta, about 680 B.C., facing left in a right-to-left line of writing. The Greek letter at that stage still slightly resembled Phoenician bayt, from which it had been copied perhaps 120 years before.

name starting with the appropriate sound (an aid to memorization). The letter's name was *bayt* or *beth*, "house" in Phoenician and other Semitic tongues. In shape, it resembled our figure 9.

Between about 1000 and 800 B.C., the Phoenician letters were copied by other eastern Mediterranean peoples, including the Jews (whose language was very similar to Phoenician) and the Greeks (whose was not). Today, in the Hebrew alphabet, the second letter is still called *bayt* or *bet* or, more traditionally, *beth*. The Hebrew name means "house" and the letter carries the "b" sound, although its shape no longer resembles its ancient Phoenician model.

Apart from the letter name, the Hebrew common noun *beth* has had a lively history of its own. It contributes to such familiar place-names as Bethlehem (house of bread), Bethel (house of God), Bethesda (merciful house), and Bethpage (*bet faj,* "house of unripe figs").

When the ancient Greeks adopted the Phoenician alphabet, they kept *bayt* much the same as it had been. The letter remained at the number-2 place for the Greek alphabet, with the useful sound "b." However, to the letter's foreign name the Greeks added a Greek-style ending, turning the name into *beta,* pronounced "bay-ta." Unlike the "house" of Phoenician and Hebrew usage, the name *beta* had no meaning in Greek beyond denoting the letter.

Greek *beta* departed in shape from Phoenician *bayt,* eventually looking just like our B; indeed, it is a source of our B. Among several alternatives, the shape ꓭ or Ɓ shows up in Greek inscriptions by the 600s B.C. (Mirror imaging occurred because early Greek writing could run from right to left *or* left to right, before settling on the latter, around 500 B.C.) The Greeks had given *beta* a second loop, at the bottom, probably to distinguish it from the very similar-looking R letter, written as ꓘ in Phoenician and in early Greek. Today capital B and R still resemble each other in our own alphabet.

Above: *The* beta *can easily be picked out in an early Greek inscription on a ceramic bowl sherd found near Athens, from around 680 B.C. (This* beta *shape also appears in the letter chart on page 67.) Crudely scratched into the fired clay, the letters run right to left, presenting the start of the Greek alphabet:* alpha, beta, gamma, delta, epsilon. *Probably the whole alphabet ran clockwise around the bowl's exterior, for beauty and magic, in an era when writing was thought spiritually powerful.* Below: *Letters more expertly carved grace a marble inscription of 334 B.C., from the Greek city of Priene on the central west coast of Asia Minor. Starting with a handsome* beta, *the words honor the Macedonian conqueror Alexander the Great, who had freed Priene from Persian rule and rebuilt its patron goddess's temple: "King Alexander dedicated the temple to Athena of the City." The letters of "King Alexander" fill the top line:* BASILEUS ALEXANDROS.

The word *beta* as a common noun turns up in ancient Greek literature, meaning an item second in sequence or value. For example, Eratosthenes of Cyrene, director of the famous Library at the Egyptian-Greek city of Alexandria in the latter 200s B.C., was a scientist, mathematician, geographer, historian, philosopher, poet, and literary critic, best recalled today for accurately calculating the polar circumference of Earth from systematic measurements of shadow angles. He was fondly nicknamed "Beta" by colleagues, for while he excelled at many studies, he specialized in none and generally came second in knowledge, behind the resident expert of each field.

Today the word "beta" lives on, sometimes pronounced "bee-ta," in scientific and technical vocabulary. It still means "second place," usually in context with its brother alpha. The beta version may be weaker, later, or more refined.

For astronomers, the beta in any constellation is the second-brightest star there, behind the alpha star. Zoologists say that wolves, baboons, and other grouping mammals tend to produce two types of males: leaders and loyal followers. Leader types are called alpha males; followers are—you guessed it. In autumn 1999 the term "beta male" blazed to notoriety in the United States when the press learned that a campaign adviser to Democratic vice president and presidential candidate Al Gore was using those words to refer to Gore's perceived subservience to President Bill Clinton. The adviser, an author aptly named Naomi Wolf, urged Gore to challenge the president on issues and thus appear more like an alpha male. Gore lost the 2000 election to George W. Bush (on whom see Chapter W, page 330).

The beta version of a software program is the second prerelease stage, from which the worst bugs of the cruder "alpha" have been ironed out. The manufacturer distributes the beta to cooperating companies so they may "beta test" it in time to generate helpful criticisms for the sales version.

Back in 1931, European chemical research into the body's creation of vitamin A from certain foods had focused on the role of carotene, a hydrocarbon pigment in carrots and other vegetables. Carotene was found to have at least two components, which scientists named alpha-carotene and beta-carotene. Today beta-carotene, available in vitamin pills, is prized and even overrated as a health booster.

But onward from beta. When ancient Greek traders brought their alphabet to Italy in the 700s B.C., the Etruscan people there copied the Greek letters for themselves. *Beta* was adopted into the Etruscan alphabet and from there into the alphabet of the early Romans, whose letters would eventually become our own. The Romans and Etruscans, abridging the Greek name *beta,* called the letter something like "bah" or "bay."

Like most of our letters' names, our name for B entered English from Old French after the Norman invasion of England in A.D. 1066. The French evidently called it "bay" (they still do today), a name derived from French's parent tongue, the Latin of ancient Rome.

If you could ask a medieval Parisian to spell the letter's name, pronounced "bay," she would probably reply "B-E"—that is, the

1   2   3

(1) The Roman B of the 200s B.C. looked just like its Greek and Etruscan forebears. (2) Later Roman B attained more balance and elegance, as in this example from the inscription on Trajan's Column, A.D. 113. This letter has an amply enlarged lower loop to "support" the upper one, along with finishing strokes (called serifs) at the stem. The shape survives today in our "roman" typeface and other serif typefaces. (3) Our lowercase b shape emerged around 500, in the Latin ink handwriting style known as semi-uncial. Scribes began omitting B's upper loop for the sake of speed. Just under 1,000 years later, early European type designers would adapt this traditional penned shape to be their print lowercase b.

Phonetically, B has attachments to several other letters. If you try to say the sound "b" without using your vocal cords, you more or less say "p." Thus P is the "unvoiced" counterpart of B. The relationship comes out in a word like "spin," rather different-sounding from "pin."

That B and P should look similar as well as sound similar may not be coincidence. Within our alphabet are several informal pairings: letters alike in both sound and shape. Examples include C and G, M and N, S and Z, and B and P. Although the stories behind the pairings differ in detail, they typically begin with two letters that have related sounds, followed by a gradual change in shape of at least one of the letters, so that it grows to resemble the other. Usually this happens during an early stage of Greek or Roman writing, in the centuries before Christ.

Such convergence was probably deliberate on the part of the people doing the writing: Ancient Greeks and Romans may have found that moderate pairings made the letters easier to learn. In the case of B and P, the P letter changed its appearance completely, from about 800 to 500 B.C., in order to reach its present resemblance to B.

B also has a relationship with M—and not just through the old, polite initials for "bowel movement." While the two letters sound different, they use much the same speech mechanism, both being voiced bilabials. To discover the connection, pinch your nostrils and say, "My mommy meets me." It comes out a bit like, "By bobby beets be." (This shows also that sound "m" relies on airflow through the nose, while sound "b" relies on blocking it, which you do

letter itself plus a long E. Likewise, a Londoner of Geoffrey Chaucer's day (1380) would have said "bay," spelling it "B-E." So would a modern Frenchwoman, Spaniard, Italian, German, or Pole. To the ears of all of them, the "ay" sound would mean long E. We modern English speakers accept the spelling "B plus long E," yet of course we pronounce it "bee."

Modern English is the oddball here, due to tidal shifts in our without thinking.) Similarly, if you'll please let go of your nose now, you'll have no trouble saying "mmba." The sound of B launches naturally from M.

The "mb" combination shows up in English in words like "combination" and "dumbbell." It occurs frequently in some of the Bantu languages of Central and Southern Africa, contributing, for instance, to place-names like Zimbabwe, Mombassa, and Mbandaka.

Lastly, V. Among languages of the Indo-European group, the sound "b" has a tendency over centuries to decay, slurring to "v" or some other sound. This has happened strikingly in Greek. Since about A.D. 400, Greek words and names that once contained "b" now have "v" in the same place, with the result that modern *beta* represents purely sound "v." The northern Greek town name written as Bolos is pronounced "Volos," where Socrates would have read it as "Bolos." The ancient word for "king," *basileus* (featured in the Priene inscription shown on page 69), survives in modern Greek, only now pronounced as "vassil-effs." From this pronunciation, used by the medieval Byzantines, came the Russian first name Vassily and similar Eastern European names.

When Old French emerged from Latin in the early Middle Ages, many words contained a slurring of what had been Latin sound "b"—with consequences for English after the Norman invasion of England in A.D. 1066. Here changes can be traced in spellings. The old Roman *taberna* became a French *taverne* and English "tavern." The Roman military slang word for "horse," *caballus,* became medieval French *caval* and *ceval,* which have produced English "cavalry," "cavalier," "cavalcade," and modern French *cheval* (horse) and *chevalier* (knight, gentleman). Meanwhile, Spanish, generally less changed from Latin than French is, holds on to Latin "b" in *caballo* and *caballero.*

vowel pronunciations, during the 1400s and 1500s. Amid countless changes in sounds of English words at that time, B's name went from "bay" to "bee." For a sense of the old pronunciation, ask an Irishman to say "B," and you may hear something like "bay." It's a name reaching back to the *bayt* of the Bronze Age Near East.

From Ancient Greece, the Alphabet
Traveled Swiftly West to Italy

Looking largely familiar, letters of the Etruscan alphabet adorn a rooster-shaped ceramic jug, possibly a child's possession, from an Etruscan tomb at Viterbo, 30 miles north of Rome, from about 550 B.C. The letters, 26 in all, continue around the circumference; they were scratched in after the clay was fired. Copied originally from the West Greek alphabet, the Etruscan letters would provide the model and inspiration for the Roman alphabet.

Just as the Phoenician letters could not be confined to the land and language of Phoenicia, so did the newly created Greek letters soon take hold in a foreign land: Italy. During the same era when the Greeks were copying the Phoenician alphabet—and in the same aspiring spirit of acquisition—certain Greek maritime cities were exploring long-distance trade contacts with peoples of Italy, non-Greeks, chief of whom were the Etruscans. The Greeks' goal was the mineral wealth of Italy and farther West Europe: silver, iron, and the two components of bronze, copper and tin. The Etruscans, as owners or middlemen, could help provide these.

Because the Etruscans were based along parts of Italy's west coast, the Greek shipping route first had to reach there, by rounding Sicily and the foot of Italy. The exploration of the route, around 800 B.C., is probably re-

Italy in 600 B.C.

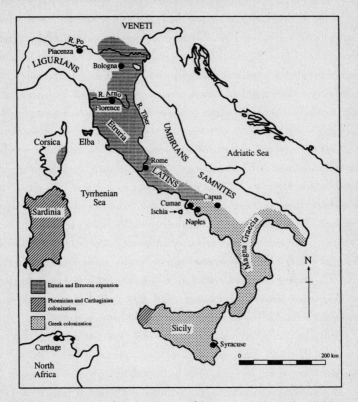

Although based in cities of Etruria, the powerful Etruscans had a southern holding at Capua, from where they traded with Greek settlers around Cumae, on the Bay of Naples, from about 775 to 475 B.C. In the same era, many non-Etruscan cities of Italy were ruled by Etruscan overlords, including one city with a special destiny: Rome. This map helps explain how the letters of the alphabet passed from the Greeks to the Etruscans to the Romans all within about a century, 700 to 600 B.C.

called distortedly in the Greek hero Odysseus' legendary voyage among monsters and witches of the western seas, in books 9 to 12 of the *Odyssey* (written down around 750 B.C.).

Modern archaeology reveals that Greeks arrived in Italy in about 775

B.C., setting up a trade depot at the Bay of Naples, on an offshore island now called Ischia. Undoubtedly they did so with Etruscan permission. Later the depot would move ashore and become the Italian-Greek city of Cumae, whose remnants still stand. Later still, Greeks from Cumae would establish a nearby "New City" (Greek: *Neapolis*), today the Italian seaport of Naples. In exchange for raw metals, the Greeks probably offered luxury goods: wine, perfumes, and metalwork including utensils, jewelry, and weaponry. Greek settlers and imports would have profound effects, good and bad, on native Italian peoples. Regarding writing, Italy had none at the time, neither alphabetic nor another form.

Significantly, one of our earliest known Greek inscriptions from anywhere comes from Ischia. Archaeology has turned up a Greek ceramic cup, dated to around 725 B.C., with a jovial message scratched into its outer surface. Probably relevant to businessmen's drinking parties where female slaves entertained, the words read: "I am the cup of Nestor, a joy to drink from. Whoever drinks from this cup, immediately will desire of lovely-garlanded Aphrodite seize him." The phrase "cup of Nestor" involves a sophisticated joke: The Nestor of legend was a Greek king, one of the heroes of the Trojan War, who is described in Homer's *Iliad* as owning a huge goblet of beautifully worked gold. The clay cup of Ischia could hardly compare.

Still, the cup is very valuable to *us*, for its inscription proves that the Greeks of Italy were using the Greek alphabet in the decades before 700 B.C. No doubt they were observed in this by their illiterate trade partners.

Enthusiasm for Greek goods and culture was to be a defining trait of the Etruscans. Over time, many Etruscan religious beliefs, social customs, military practices, and styles of art and architecture would be inspired by Greek examples. Modern scholars often reserve the very term "Etruscan" for the Greek-influenced civilization that took shape during the 600s B.C. and peaked just prior to 500 B.C. The earlier, formative stage of the same people is distinguished as the Villanovan Culture (named for an archaeological site near Bologna). A rough cutoff between the two is 700 B.C.

The Etruscans were a federation of city-states, joined by language and culture, each city typically governed by a king. Their home region lay between the rivers Tiber and Arno—from north of Rome to Florence and Arezzo on a modern map—and their name survives in the modern regional names Tuscany and Tuscia. Yet Etruscan power ranged far beyond: By 800

B.C. they held Capua (they may have founded it), far to the south. Capua became their conduit to Greek trade on the Bay of Naples. By 550 B.C. they had reached northward, also, to the Po Valley and the foothills of the Alps.

Among many non-Etruscan cities in their domain was a humble Tiber settlement called Roma (Rome). The Romans spoke Latin, a language of the Indo-European family, related to Greek and modern English (among other tongues) but not to Etruscan. The Romans were not partners in Etruscan power, although they were deeply influenced by Etruscan civilization. According to later Roman legend, Etruscan kings ruled Rome from about 616 to 509 B.C., before being ejected by the people. The Romans had a grand destiny in store. Eventually, during the 300s B.C., they would challenge and destroy Etruscan power, subsuming Etruscan culture into their own. By 250 B.C. the Romans would rule Italy, a prelude to greater conquests.

But back to the Etruscans and Greeks. Around 700 B.C., the Etruscans began writing their language in letters of the Greek alphabet. The fact is shown in archaeology: At a certain point, tombs of wealthy Etruscans begin to yield samples of Greek lettering, yet conveying a language not Greek. The writing typically appears incised on objects of ceramic or (more often) metal—a silver cup, an iron sword blade—that were entombed with their owners.

The letter shapes belong to the West Greek style of the Greek alphabet, the style in use among Greeks at the Bay of Naples. Beyond doubt, those Greeks were the source: Probably they cooperated gladly in the transmission to the Etruscans. Just as the Greeks of 800 B.C. had adapted Phoenician letters to the writing of Greek, so now did the Etruscans copy Greek letters and begin using them themselves.

One artifact from an Etruscan tomb near Florence, dated to about 660 B.C., tells practically the whole tale. It is a carved-ivory miniature writing tablet, perhaps designed to be worn around the neck, on whose frame are incised 26 letters of the alphabet, running right to left. They are West Greek letters but probably are meant to represent the Etruscan alphabet; the two at that moment in history looked identical.

The 26 letters omit what would be the 27th Greek letter, *omega*. This tells us the Etruscans copied the Greek alphabet before Greek *omega* was invented. (Back in Greece, *omega* starts showing up in inscriptions around 660

B.C., which squares with archaeological dating of the Etruscan writing tablet.) *Omega* never would make it into the Etruscan alphabet; in fact, five of the original 26 Greek-derived letters would later drop out, as representing sounds unused in Etruscan speech. The Etruscan alphabet would be finalized (about 400 B.C.) at 22 letters, including a final, invented letter.

Today we have some 13,000 Etruscan inscriptions, dating down to the end of the 1st century B.C., when Etruscan culture finally died out. Preserved mainly on durable material (stone, ceramic, metal), the messages include epitaphs, legal documents, prayers and other devotions, and ownership declarations.

Despite the abundant material—a tribute to Etruscan society's vigor and affluence—we can decipher only the shorter, formulaic messages. Why? Because the language behind the writing remains largely a mystery to us. The Etruscan language was related to perhaps no other tongue on Earth, then or since. Unlike Latin and most other Italian languages of the day, Etruscan did not belong to the Indo-European family nor to any other known family. It has left no modern descendant for us to compare it with. In the inscriptions, we can read every word's sound yet often don't know what the words mean. Only 500 have been deduced, mostly kinship terms, office titles, personal names, and words for material objects: "I am the pitcher (*qutun*) of Lemausna."

According to modern analysis, spoken Etruscan sounded nothing like Greek, the language whose alphabet it had borrowed. Among other differences, Etruscan had no voiced stops: no sounds "b," "d," or "g." Etruscan speech had only their *unvoiced* counterparts, "p," "t," and "k." Even odder-seeming from our viewpoint, Etruscan had no vowel sound "o" and no need for the Greek O letter, although the Etruscans kept it in their alphabet for a couple of centuries. At the same time, Etruscan employed three shades of sound "k," about four shades of "s," and a particular "f" sound, which were inadequately represented in the Greek alphabet. Still, the Etruscans were able to fit the Greek letters to their language by reassigning a few letters' sounds. Here again, credit must be given to the adaptability of the letters.

Arriving in 700 B.C., at the threshold of two centuries of Etruscan greatness, the alphabet surely boosted Etruscan achievements, abetting communication, organization, artistic expression, and so on. Like the Greeks before

ECOYPᴚATITAYFNDIAZMᴬⱯᴬP ᴚᴅ ꓕꓕ

The beginning of our Roman alphabet can be seen in these crude letters scratched onto a ceramic wine container, from the vicinity of Rome, around 620 B.C. "I am the urn of Tita Vendia. Mamarcos made me" runs the apparent message, although obliterated toward the end. From left to right, without word breaks, the Latin words of the top line can be read clearly: eco urna tita uendias mamar—. (The two letters resembling Y are really U; the two resembling P are R.) The word eco would come to be spelled ego in classical Latin, while urna speaks for itself.

them, the Etruscans quickly became a literate society, in which the merchant class (among others) could write. Merchants, specifically, traveling and needing friends, might teach the trick to foreigners. What happened next: At least *seven* different non-Etruscan peoples of Italy began writing with Etruscan letters.

In the archaeology of Rome and vicinity, the oldest inscriptions are pure Etruscan: Greek-derived Etruscan letters, with the Etruscan language behind them. But at archaeological levels around 620 B.C., something remarkable happens. In two inscriptions from separate sites, the Etruscan letters now form words of Latin, the language of Rome. (See illustration above.) The Romans had copied, or were in the process of copying, Etruscan letters for themselves.

Roman writing for the next 350 years, to about 250 B.C., is represented by 650 surviving inscriptions. Unfortunately for us, they include no letter lists to show the whole alphabet. Still, scholars can trace through these years the emergence of a truly Roman alphabet of 21 letters.

For writing the sounds of Latin (much different from Etruscan), the Romans gradually made changes to the Etruscan letters. They dropped three received letters as unneeded; they resuscitated the old Greek letters for the "o," "b," and "d" sounds; and they reassigned a couple of letters to new sounds, creating our F and G. Also, between 600 and 250 B.C., about a third of the Roman letters altered shape, leaving behind their original West Greek forms for a different look, more familiar to us today.

In the 21 Roman letters of 250 B.C., the five letters absent (per our 26) were J, V, W, Y, and Z. Their sounds were either unknown to ancient Latin or already covered by existing Roman letters.

Equipped with its alphabet and other resources, the Roman Republic of 250 B.C. stood as a new world power. Rome had by then subdued Etruscans, Greeks, and other peoples of Italy, unifying the peninsula under Roman rule. Now the Romans looked abroad. In coming centuries they would conquer and annex nations around the Mediterranean—Carthage, Macedon, and others—and the rugged tribes of Western Europe. To these places, in the wake of Roman legions, the Roman alphabet would go.

Our Roman alphabet takes shape in these three columns of letter shapes. The early Etruscan alphabet retained all 26 received Greek letters, including four that the Etruscan language never used. One Greek letter had its sound changed: Letter number 3, symbolizing Greek sound "g," now became sound "k"—thus supplying the third "k" letter in the Etruscan alphabet. (The Etruscans had no sound "g" and seem to have distinguished three "k" sounds in speech.) This Etruscan quirk lives on in our redundant C-K-Q combination today. Etruscan also recognized about four shades of "s" sound, including "z" and "ks," distributed among four letters. Etruscan writing could run either left to right or right to left, but the latter direction was favored and is reflected in the chart. (Letter shapes would face the opposite way for left to right.)

The early Roman alphabet copied the Greek-Etruscan letter shapes while dropping five Etruscan letters unneeded for Latin. Over time Roman writing settled at left to right (the early stages could run either way), and many of the letter shapes morphed to forms more familiar today. Around 250 B.C. the Romans re-created the "g"-sound letter that the Etruscans had removed but that Romans felt was necessary for showing Latin speech. Instead of going to the end of the letter row, Roman G was inserted at number 7 to replace an "s" letter that had proved superfluous for Latin.

ETRUSCAN ALPHABET OF 650 B.C.		ROMAN ALPHABET OF 550 B.C.		ROMAN ALPHABET OF 250 B.C.	
Letter Shape	Letter Sound	Letter Shape	Letter Sound	Letter Shape	Letter Sound
A	"a"	A	"a"	A	
8	[unused]	8	"b"	B	
>	specialized "k" (1)	>	"k" (1)	<	
◁	[unused]	◁	"d"	D	
ꓱ	"e"	ꓱ	"e"	E	
ꓺ	"w"	ꓺ	"f"	F	
I	"z"	I	"s" (1)	G	"g"
目	"h"	目	"h"	H	
⊕	"th"	—	—	—	—
I	"i"	I	"i"	I	
ꓘ	specialized "k"	ꓘ	"k" (2)	K	
ꓳ	"l"	ꓳ	"l"	L	
ꟺ	"m"	ꟺ	"m"	M	
ꓴ	"n"	ꓴ	"n"	N	
⊞	[unused]	—	—	—	—
O	[unused]	O	"o"	O	
ꓶ	"p"	ꓶ	"p"	P	
ꟽ	"s"	—	—	—	—
ꝗ	specialized "k" (3)	ꝗ	"k" (3)	Q	
ꝗ	"r"	ꝗ	"r"	R	
ᛣ or ᛋ	modified "s"	ᛋ	"s" (2)	S	
ꓔ	"t"	ꓔ	"t"	T	
Y or V	"u"	V	"u"	V	
X	"ks"	X	"ks"	X	
Φ	"ph"	—	—	—	—
Ψ	"kh"	—	—	—	—

Letter C's intriguing shape—an incomplete circle, suggesting attraction or advancement—has for many decades been employed in advertising and marketing. The Coca-Cola logo of 1886 (shown here, slightly different from the modern design) imitates a person's elegant signature, thus conveying quality and trustworthiness. To some, the two sinuous capital C's suggest images of an outstretched arm and a smile (although there is no evidence that was the founders' intent).

C OF TROUBLES

Critics have chafed at C's inconstancy. As used in English, the letter has sounds that are too diverse. Not always pronounced as "k," it turns into the sound "s" before E, I, or Y, according to a fundamental rule of our spelling. Thus we have hard C and soft C. The discrepancy appears all over the printed page and in many individual words, like "discrepancy."

Elsewhere, C joins with H to signify a new sound (say "cheese") or not (say "chorus"). C also has a fondness for the sound "sh," which it occasionally takes in partnership with E or I (ocean, glacier) or with H in postmedieval word borrowings from French, such as "champagne," "chic," and "machine" (a word originating in ancient

Greek, bequeathed to French via Latin, but appearing in English not until the 1500s). As a fifth possibility, C may be silent: muscle, indict.

To have more than one sound is in itself no sin for a letter in English. Our vowels run long and short, with extra shades of pronunciation besides. Our consonant letters, more confined in interpretation, include a few that carry two or so main sounds, for instance, G (green giant) or X (Xerox). The letter S pushes the envelope with three frequent sounds (hiss, his, sure), however, as a mitigating factor, all three are sibilants, phonetically akin.

C's problem is that its three main sounds are so unlike each other—the stop "k," the sibilant "s," and the affricate "ch," formed with letter H—as to seem arbitrary: What exactly is this letter about? Making matters worse for C is the notorious turf war, with letters K and Q laying claim to what is supposedly C's principal sound. K has contested C in dictionary spellings like "disk" versus "disc" and British "kerb" versus American "curb," also in deliberate, name-brand misspellings like "Kool-Aid." Sometimes K even has to rescue C, as in the change from "traffic" to "trafficking," where C would otherwise go soft before "-ing." Q proves itself as good a worker as C, for instance in the homonyms "queue" and "cue" or in the English-language title of Islam's holy book, which since the 1700s has evolved from "Coran" to "Koran" to the now-favored "Qu'ran." The wasteful overlap of C, K, and Q dates back to the ancient Greco-Roman world, as explained below.

In an alphabet that is otherwise understaffed, needing a few more letters, C's position looks embarrassing. You get the impression of a difficult personality, left over from prior management, occupying a big-title job of patchy duties, jealously on guard against her colleagues. Sure, she still looks great, especially when she wears serifs, and in some of her work you glimpse glories of ancient Rome, in words like "capitol," "fiscal," and "concord."

But does that justify her salary? Letter C ranks around 13th in frequency of use in English-language print, appearing more often than half the other letters, including K and Q, yet only in the soft "ch" sound does C contribute anything unique to spoken English. In all its other sounds, C is redundant with other letters.

No wonder that purists have taken aim at C. Spelling reformers through the ages have wished to reduce C's role in English or even erase it from the alphabet. Comparison has been made with spellings in German, Swedish, and other northern European tongues, which greatly favor plain K over C. In German, C is reserved for letter combinations—CH, pronounced gutturally in *Nacht* (night) or as "k" in *Wachs* (wax), and SCH, pronounced as "sh" in words like *schwartz* (black)—and for non-German terms like "CD-ROM" or "Enrico Caruso." For most "k" sounds, German uses spellings like *Kontakt, Korn, Reaktion,* and, of course, *Kapital,* all of which could be English words, too.

As early as 1551, changes of this kind were being urged in England by scholar John Hart in an earnest treatise, *The Opening of the Unreasonable Writing of Our Inglish Toung.* During an era when English vowel pronunciations were actually shifting and when spelling was not yet strictly uniform, Hart sought to make spellings more reliable phonetically. Although his specific suggestions would wind up mostly in history's wastebasket, his general criticisms, such as that spellings of his day often used too many letters for the sounds, did influence subsequent generations of dictionary writers.

To clean up the mess of C, K, and Q, Hart said, elevate K: Keep symbol C only to mean sound "ch" (thus spelling "latch" as "latc") but elsewhere replace C with K or S and replace Q with K. "So should we need no *q* or *c* in the sound of *k*."

Other thinkers have simply complained. John Baret (or Barrett) was a pioneering English lexicographer whose 1580 masterpiece, a revision of a prior work, bore the memorable title *An Alvearie, or Quadruple Dictionarie Containing Foure Sundrie Tungues:*

Namelie, English, Latine, Greeke, and French, Newlie Enriched with Varietie of Wordes, Phrases, Proverbs, and Divers Lightsome Observations of Grammar. (An alvearie is a beehive or any partitioned container.) Of all his verbal enthusiasm, Baret could spare little for C: "This letter troubleth me worst of all, and maketh me wonder how it got this third place of honour. . . . If C were a proper letter, then art and reason would it should have his proper sound, and ever to keep the same uniformally in speaking, not wavering like *Proteus* or *Chamaelion.*" Since it functions only by trespassing on the sounds of K and S (Baret concludes), the C is "no letter at all."

Ditto from Ben Jonson. The English playwright-poet-scholar, best recalled for his stage comedy *Volpone* (1606), wrote a handbook titled *The English Grammar,* published posthumously in 1640. In an otherwise innocent section that introduces the individual "letters and their powers," Jonson indulges himself against C: "A letter which our fore-fathers might very well have spar'd in our tongue. But since it hath obtained place, both in our writing and language, we are not now to quarrell orthographie or custome, but to note the powers." Mee-ow!

Another in the fray was Benjamin Franklin, whose boundless imagination embraced science, mechanical invention, journalism, and nation building. In 1768 the 62-year-old Franklin wrote a proposal for spelling reform. The essence was to discard letters C, J, W, and Y and reassign their values to other letters and to new symbols (including similar-looking symbols for sounds "ch" and "j," insofar as those two sounds are related); also, vowels would be shown more phonetically. Living in London at the time, Franklin sent his proposal to a young female friend there, Polly Stevenson. She replied in a letter, written in experimental Franklinese and incidentally revealing her high-toned accent, that she could "si meni inkanviiniensis" in the scheme.

The letter C's struggle with identity and commitment stems from an unstable childhood. We turn, for insight on these formative years, to C's favorite sibling, G. No two letters of the alphabet are closer than C and G, fraternal twins in shape and sound. Settle your tongue and make the sound "k," which shoves air along the rear roof of your mouth (the velum, or soft palate). Leave your tongue in place but this time start from your vocal cords: "g." Thus C (or K) is the unvoiced velar stop; G is the voiced velar stop. The kinship can be heard in the word "scorn," which would be pronounced much the same if spelled "sgorn." (Another example: On your next memo to your boss, try writing across the top "As we disgust.")

G is our key to understanding C's psychology. The two letters grew up inseparable, in tumultuous households. Today G shares some of C's symptoms, turning soft itself before E, I, or Y.

Back in 1000 B.C., the third letter of the Phoenician alphabet was the G letter. It came after B and before D. It was called *gimel* (with a hard "g" sound, as in "girl"). The opening sound of the name was the letter's sound, too, as always in the Phoenician alphabet. The *gimel* had been inherited from a Near Eastern alphabetic tradition stretching back to 2000 B.C. No letter like C yet existed. For sound "k," the Phoenicians had two letters, differing slightly in pronunciation, the ancestors of our K and Q. For "s" sounds, they had several forms of S.

When the Greeks copied and adapted the Phoenician letters, around 800 B.C., they kept *gimel* at number 3, with sound "g," but altered the name to make it more Greek: *gamma*. Today *gamma* lives on as the third letter of the modern Greek alphabet. Similarly, in modern Hebrew, the third letter is the G, called *gimel*.

The ancient Greek alphabet began with letters equivalent to A, B, G, D, E. Farther down the row came letters equivalent to K, Q, and S. Still no letter C.

Complications arose after Greek merchants brought their writing to the western shores of central Italy during the 700s B.C. There the Greeks' trade partners were the powerful Etruscans, who would eventually copy the Greek alphabet for their own writing.

The Etruscans spoke a language very unlike Greek—indeed, unlike most European tongues then or since. Among other peculiarities, Etruscan evidently had no sound "g." The Etruscan speech sound nearest to "g" was the unvoiced counterpart, "k." Therefore, *gamma,* the third letter of the Greek alphabet, would be a letter the Etruscans didn't particularly need.

Extant Etruscan letter lists from the 600s B.C. show that the Etruscans had dutifully copied *gamma* in place, to be their letter number 3. Other inscriptions clearly show the letter being used to mean the sound "k." What the Etruscans had done was to change the letter's agreed-on sound, from "g" to "k." Fair enough. However, letters K and Q also appear regularly in Etruscan inscriptions to mean "k."

Why did the Etruscans need three separate letters to show the "k" sound? Apparently there were small differences of pronunciation. Etruscan writing used the *gamma* letter frequently. It was always sounded as "k," never "s."

Meanwhile, the letter acquired a standardized shape. Three or four different shapes show up in early Etruscan writing, reflecting various styles of early Greek *gamma.* The form that soon predominated was a stubby crescent, copied from the crescent *gamma* favored at certain Greek cities of Italy and Sicily. This Etruscan crescent, meaning the sound "k," marks the beginning of our C.

The Etruscans dropped the irrelevant name *gamma,* instead calling the letter something like "kay." (Their K they called something like "ka.") If asked to spell out the letter name pronounced as "kay," an ancient Etruscan would probably have replied "C-E," that is, the letter itself, plus long E. Today, over 25 centuries later, that spelling, but not the pronunciation, supplies our own name for the letter: "ce" or "cee."

Around 600 B.C. Etruscan letters started being written by Latin speakers in the region of the village of Rome. Latin being a language totally unlike Etruscan, the Romans must have had a low opinion of the Etruscan arrangement for velar stops: three letters for "k" and none for "g." The Romans eventually concocted their own G letter (which is our G today), and they sim-

(1) Phoenician gimel *from an inscription of the 800s B.C. The letter's name, which scholars previously translated as "camel," is now thought to have meant a hunter's "throwing stick," and indeed the shape resembles a boomerang. The letter took the hard "g" sound, signaled by the name. (2) Early Greek* gamma, *from an inscription of around 685 B.C. The letter imitated Phoenician* gimel *in shape, sound, and number-3 alphabetic place. This particular letter faces left in right-to-left writing. Early Greek writing could run in either direction. (3) A different-shape* gamma, *from a left-to-right inscription from the Greek city of Corinth, around 675 B.C. The crescent* gamma *was used also by Greek settlers on Italy's Bay of Naples who traded with the Etruscans and would help to inspire the Etruscan alphabet. The Greek letter still meant the hard "g" sound. (4) Etruscan C of the 500s B.C. Although copied in shape from the Greek crescent* gamma, *the Etruscan letter took the sound "k." (5) Classical Roman C from a marble-carved inscription of the late 1st century B.C. This appealing shape with its serifs (finishing strokes) became the model for our familiar "roman" print C today. (6) A penned C in the late-Roman and early-medieval handwriting style known as uncial clearly imitates the inscriptional shape. This example comes from a Christian Latin prayer book of the 400s A.D. (7) The semi-uncial pen style, emerging in Italy and France by A.D. 500, gave many of the letters a new look, much later finalized in lowercase print shapes. This letter is from a Latin manuscript written probably in France in the 500s.*

plified the Etruscan "k" letters by heavily favoring C in their spelling. Q became restricted to one particular use. K was virtually ignored, although kept in the Roman alphabet.

The Roman Empire, from the mid–1st century B.C. onward, saw letter C's heyday. This was the ubiquitous C of classical Latin, enshrined in names like Cicero, Caesar, Seneca, the Colosseum, the god Cupid. Latin writing, like Etruscan, used only hard C. Sounds of "s" were written with S. Thus the Latin word for storeroom, *cella,* was pronounced "kella." The name Cicero was really "Kick-ero." Caesar was "Kye-sar"—incidentally the origin of the German imperial title, kaiser.

The emergence of a soft C was a linguistic sea change (pardon the pun) of the later Roman Empire. Modern scholars have traced how the Latin C gradually became slurred in certain uses, as spoken by everyday people of Roman Europe: Before an E, I, or Y—which are "front vowels," pushing the tongue forward— the C began to be pronounced "ch." The Latin word *processio* (advance, procession) was pronounced as "pro-*kess*-io" in 100 B.C. but by A.D. 400 had turned to "pro-*chess*-io." After Rome's fall in around A.D. 500, the slurred C became part of the Romance languages (Italian, French, Spanish, Portuguese, Romanian, to name the main ones) which arose from dying Latin. In that era, pronunciations were changing faster than old Latin spellings, bound by tradition. Therefore, the letter C entered the Middle Ages with two normal pronunciations: "k" and "ch." In modern Italian, soft C is still "ch." In other Romance tongues, the sound gradually decayed to "s."

Soft C entered medieval English from French. The Norman invasion of England in A.D. 1066 forcibly imported Norman French vocabulary and spelling rules, which mixed with Old English to create the rich compound known as Middle English, starting around 1150. Among many other effects, Middle English spellings became riddled with soft C's. A medieval French word like *procession*, pronounced as "pro-*sess*-i-un," would become the source of a modern word in English as well as in French.

The pattern is still apparent. Today the vast majority of our soft C words—like "cellar," "citizen," "reconcile," "grace"—entered the English language from Norman French, having come previously from Latin. Words that were formed more recently, like "bicycle" or "cybernetics," usually follow the older rules.

Our variable C can require fancy footwork in spelling. Reference has been made here already to formations like "picnicking," where K is added to keep the second C hard. Conversely, soft C must hold on to its E, as in the change from "trace" to "traceable," where modern spelling rules would otherwise want the E out. Which is why we have a movable feast but a peaceable kingdom.

The solid and steadfast nature of letter D is captured in this illustration from a children's book, published in Paris in 1844. The book's title translates as Wonderful Stories—Tales from every land, collected and arranged by P. Christian.

DEPENDABLE D

own 40 centuries or so, across many languages, this letter has stood loyally at place number 4 in the alphabet, carrying sound "d." Constancy and plainness are its virtues. Long before the birth of English, the D already stood for "door."

Like B and G, D represents a voiced stop. To say "d," you place your tongue tip at the roof of your mouth, just behind the teeth, and push off, sounding from your vocal cords. Try it again with *no* vocal cords, and you'll say "t." Thus T is the "unvoiced" counterpart of D.

The "stop" of a voiced or unvoiced stop refers to your nasal airway. You close your nose from the inside each time you say "d" (or "t," "b," "p," "g," or "k"). Yet not one person in 10,000 could be aware of doing this, unless they happen to have read about it.

That we pronounce such sounds automatically, blind to the mechanics, is part of the miracle of how our brains learn language while we are babies. In the company of family and caregivers who systematically produce certain speech sounds—often exaggeratedly when speaking to a baby—the child by about five months is learning to recognize these and is preparing to imitate them; the process involves a subconscious level of brain-mouth coordination, so the child won't forever have to think about each sound each time. The child learns to imitate perfectly the sounds she hears (certain pronunciations, like "shoe" versus "soo," may take till age four or five), but she is restricted in this certainty to those language sounds around the cradle. The sounds of Japanese, for example, are not those of Hindi, despite an overlap.

Your first year or two of life represent your golden chance to become bilingual, while your brain is malleable that way. Given the environment, you could grow up learning Hindi and Japanese, no problem—to say nothing of Spanish and English, relatively similar to each other, which is the most usual North American bilingual pairing. After about age two, if you learn a new language, you will probably fail to imitate perfectly those sounds you are not used to: Your brain is by then shutting down that department. You will speak the new tongue probably in a foreign accent, however slight. While it is true that certain German or Dutch speakers can learn perfect English in high school, this is because the sounds *they* heard in the cradle are close enough to English to narrow the gap. (Yet still, some German speakers have thick accents in English, including trouble with "w" and "th.")

The sounds of D, B, and G are learned early in English. Among the most usual talk sounds from a seven-month-old in an

English-language environment are "ba," "da," "ga," "ka," "ma," and "pa," of which the first three begin with a voiced stop. So it may be hard for us to imagine a language that's missing voiced stops. Yet such tongues exist—for instance, Mandarin Chinese. The English sounds of B, D, and G do not strictly occur in Mandarin, despite those letters' conventional use in transliterating words like "Beijing." The consonantal difference can be heard, for example, when a Mandarin speaker mispronounces English "sad" as "sat," thwarted by the voiced stop. (Yet bilingually raised Chinese Americans have no trouble: Their brains mastered both languages' sounds in babyhood.)

Modern scholars believe that the ancient Etruscans of Italy, bearers of the alphabet after about 700 B.C., had no voiced stops. Etruscan babies didn't say "ba," "da," "ga"—or, if they did once, they quickly forgot how, because no nearby adults were using those sounds. Instead, the babies said "pa," "ta," "ka." The Etruscan substitution of "k" for "g," specifically, has relevance for the birth of our letter C.

But back to D. In the Phoenician alphabet of 1000 B.C., the second, third, and fourth letters were the three voiced stops: sounds "b," "g," and "d" in that order, sensibly grouped together. The D letter, at place number 4, was named *dalet* or *daleth* (door); as always in the Phoenician system, the sound of the letter was also the opening sound of the letter's name. Today the Hebrew D letter, at number 4, is still called *dalet,* understood as meaning "door."

The Phoenician letter looked like a blunt triangle lying on one side: △, a shape not particularly suggesting a door. In fact, of all Phoenician letter shapes, *dalet* is the most disappointing as a picture. Those accomplished people couldn't draw a better door?

A halfway explanation may exist. A few of the earliest alphabetical inscriptions, from Serabit el-Khadem in Sinai (perhaps 1750 B.C.), include a striking-looking letter that is a picture of a

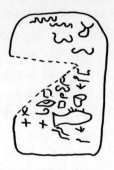

A fish shape, possibly a primitive form of letter D, stands out among picture letters carved into a rock face at Serabit el-Khadem in Sinai, dating perhaps from 1750 B.C. The message in this early alphabetic writing eludes us. But see, next to the fish's tail, four letters running downward that spell the word baalat, *"lady" (as explained back on page 31).*

fish. Some experts interpret the fish as a primitive D letter, in which case it could have been named *dag* (Semitic for "fish"), thus fitting the ancient requirement of first sound of name equals sound of letter. Seven hundred years later, that the fish picture should be by then reduced and stylized to the Phoenician sideways triangle seems reasonable, even likely. So the Phoenician *dalet* shape could theoretically be the remnant of the earlier fish letter. Yet the Phoenician letter's documented name was "door," not "fish." How the substitution might have occurred, in the Near East around 1600 B.C., is a question tentatively answered in Chapter N, pages 241–42.

When the Greeks adapted the Phoenician letters sometime prior to 800 B.C., they ushered *dalet* right into their alphabet, at spot number 4, to mean sound "d." The Greeks made only two small changes. They adjusted the letter's foreign name to be more

Two ancient Greek styles of delta.

Greek in form: *delta* (a name that at that moment meant nothing in Greek aside from denoting the new letter). And they straightened up the letter's shape somewhat. Extant Greek inscriptions show two alternative shapes for early *delta*. One was a half-moon outline that would be the source for our modern D. The other was an isosceles triangle, which would later become the prevalent Greek *delta* shape, in the writing style of the influential ancient city of Athens. Modern Greek's capital *delta* is an isosceles triangle.

In time, the ancient Greek word *delta* took on a second meaning: a triangle or something triangle shaped, whether in geometry, carpentry, land survey, or other pursuits. By the mid-400s B.C. the Greeks were using this word to describe northern Egypt's region of fertile alluvium, formed by the Nile River's outlets diverging toward the Mediterranean Sea. On a modern map, the Nile Delta appears as a solid triangle, tip pointing southward. The ancient Greeks, with no aerial photography, must have named it from the ground: Passing what is now Cairo on their way up the Nile, Greek mercenary soldiers and other visitors could look back from some vantage point (the top of a pyramid?) and see a vast triangle tip of green farmland, fanning north to the horizon, contrasted with the desert alongside. They called it the *delta*. Today the word lives in our Mississippi Delta and similar uses.

D IS FOR DUTY

The useful, inoffensive D bears at least one unhappy association. During the American Civil War (1861 to 1865), the Union Army customarily punished an attempted deserter by branding a letter D on the man's cheek, hip, or buttock. Regulations specified the letter be one and a half inches tall. This grim punishment supplies a pivotal episode in Simon Winchester's biography *The Professor and the Madman* (1997), about lexicographer William Minor.

Like other Greek letter names, "delta" has gone into modern technical vocabulary. In math, "delta" represents the increment of change in a series. In science, more true to its Greek etymology, "delta" means something triangular (deltoid muscles) or something fourth in sequence.

To astronomers, the delta is the fourth star of any constellation, in decreasing order of power, after the alpha, beta, and gamma stars. There is delta of Orion, delta of Cepheus, etc. *Delta of Venus,* a 1950s pornographic fiction collection by French-American author Anaïs Nin, cleverly combines in its title the astronomical phrasing with the meaning of delta as a triangle.

Delta is a surprisingly popular brand name among many kinds of products: Delta Faucets, Delta Machinery, Delta Dental Plans. Delta Airlines refers to the Gulf of Mexico region, but in Maine or Nevada you might find Delta Landscapiµng or Delta Taxi Service, with no geographical reference. The Greek name sounds like quality (if you overlook the potential meaning of "fourth best in town"), and it offers a visual opportunity to business owners— namely, to signpost a triangle, with its message of expert workmanship and fair dealing. The Washington State–based Delta Society, which promotes the use of pets and therapy animals for

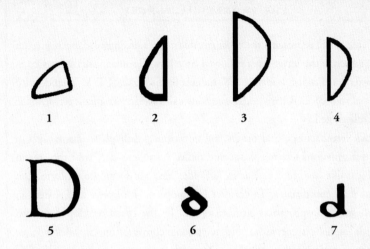

1   2   3   4

5   6   7

(1) Phoenician dalet, *the "door," 800s B.C. The letter stood at place number 4 and took sound "d," as our own D still does. (2) Early Greek* delta *from a right-to-left inscription from a Greek trading base at the Bay of Naples in Italy, around 725 B.C. Soon peoples of Italy would copy Greek letters for themselves. (3) Greek* delta *in the left-to-right writing of certain Greek cities of southern Italy, about 525 B.C. This half-moon shape had by now been copied into the alphabet of the Etruscans and, from there, of the Romans. (4) Early Roman D, from an inscription of perhaps 500 B.C. (5) Roman D from the Trajan Inscription, A.D. 113 (shown on page 104). Here the old half-moon shape has been elegantly modified. This design supplies our print capital D today. (6) Our modern print lowercase d shape starts to emerge in the inked capital D of the uncial handwriting style, this one from a Latin manuscript of Italy, mid-400s A.D. Uncials were thought of as old Roman capitals reduced to a single pen motion. (7) A semi-uncial inked letter from a Latin manuscript of the 500s A.D., also from Italy, shows a further step in stylization. Nearly 1,000 years later, such handwriting traditions would inspire the designs of early European printers' lowercase type.*

human health, chose its name *for the sake of* a triangle logo, to symbolize the linking of pets, pet owners, and μmedical people.

Delta may owe some of its current popularity to the Delta Force, a U.S. Army antiterrorist commando unit, formed in 1977 and glamorized in computer games and movies. Delta Force's

Our name for D represents the most common form of English-language letter name, which is the letter itself followed by a long-E sound, usually spelled as -ee. American English has nine "ee" names: B, C, D, G, P, T, V, Z, and (with no initial sound) E. British and Commonwealth usage recognizes eight, the Z being called "zed."

Such letter names, and others, are notoriously difficult to distinguish in vocal transmissions like telephone and radio. A spoken "dee" over the air can sound just like "tee" or "vee," or an "eff" like "ess," thus jumbling information such as map coordinates. To counter the problem, European and American military and transportation authorities had by the 1940s developed various phonetic alphabets for radio and telephone conversation, in which letter names were replaced by words that began with the letter in question: "Charlie" meant C, "Dog" meant D, and so on. Significantly, this modern expedient re-creates an aspect of the earliest Bronze Age alphabet: the use of familiar words to help represent the letters, by virtue of the words' opening sounds. (See pages 18, 25–26.)

Here are the two official phonetic alphabets that have been used in American military and civil-aviation radio talk. The second version replaced the first as being easier for foreign-language speakers.

The current version, containing our old friends *alpha* and *delta,* saw use during the Vietnam War (1964 to 1975) and has become associated with that monstrous tragedy through TV news clips, written memoirs, and Hollywood

official title is First Special Forces Operational Detachment, Delta— which means just that it was designated originally as unit number 4 in a larger Special Forces structure. But today the name "Delta," by association, takes on possible meanings of "toughest" or "elite."

When the Etruscans copied the Greek alphabet for their own use, around 700 B.C., they preserved (at first) all the Greek letters in order, even those unneeded for Etruscan speech, like *beta* and *delta.*

During World War II and Aftermath		From 1956 to Today	
Abel	November	Alpha	November
Baker	Oscar	Bravo	Oscar
Charlie	Papa	Charlie	Papa
Dog	Queen	Delta	Quebec
Easy	Roger	Echo	Romeo
Fox	Sugar	Foxtrot	Sierra
George	Tare	Golf	Tango
Howe	Uncle	Hotel	Uniform
Item	Victor	India	Victor
Jig	William	Juliet	Whiskey
King	X-ray	Kilo	X-ray
Love	Yoke	Lima	Yankee
Mike	Zebra	Mike	Zulu

films. The communist-partisan Vietcong, the main adversaries of American troops, were known by the initials VC and the call words "Victor Charlie," thus prompting their loveless American nickname, "Charlie." And in radio communication regarding combat casualties, U.S. soldiers wounded in action (WIA) were reported through the inappropriately beautiful and evocative words "Whiskey India Alpha."

Greeks in Italy were using a half-moon–shape *delta,* which now became the Etruscan alphabet's letter number 4. Soon the Etruscan alphabet had been copied by a neighboring Italian people, the Romans (600 B.C.). The Romans spoke Latin, a language that used voiced stops and needed letters for them. The half-moon D, at place number 4, became a Roman letter, later passing into alphabets of Western Europe after the Roman Empire's fall (A.D. 500).

Our letter name "dee" comes from ancient Rome. Unlike the Greeks, the Romans used mainly one-syllable letter names that simply demonstrated the sounds: D was called *da* or *de* (pronounced "day"). Bequeathed from Latin to the Romance languages, the letter's name in medieval French was "day"—it remains so in modern French—and as "day" was imported to England with the Norman invasion of A.D. 1066. The great English vowel shift of the 1400s and 1500s, affecting many English word pronunciations, turned the name into "dee." Still, from *dalet* to "dee," with a small shift in shape, down 4,000 years, across six or seven languages, is change modest enough. Steady at the tiller, that's our faithful D.

ROMAN EMPIRE, ROMAN LETTERS

The Empire in A.D. 113

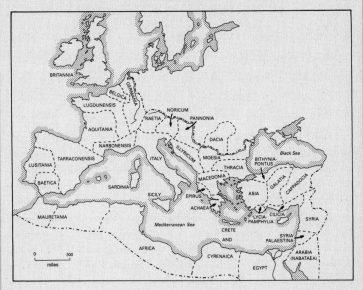

Under the emperor Trajan, the Roman Empire reached its greatest extent. From southern Scotland to the first cataract of the Nile, it covered about 2.5 million square miles, including the Mediterranean Sea. Across the empire, the Roman alphabet was used primarily for writing the Latin language, spoken by Roman authorities every-where and by the populace in Romanized regions like Spain, Gaul (modern France), and eventually Dacia (southern Romania), as well as in Italy. Today people in those countries speak Romance languages, derived from Latin.

The Roman alphabet blossomed to maturity in the heyday of the Roman Empire. Under efficient, benevolent emperors like Trajan (ruled A.D. 98 to 117) and Hadrian (A.D. 117 to 138), Rome securely held a vast domain and thrived on the taxes of subject peoples; the alphabet, meanwhile, had progressed to a stage where we today can easily recognize it as our own. Empire and alphabet are embodied together in the remarkable monument of Trajan's Column, com-

SENATVSPOPVLVSQVEROMANVS
IMP·CAESARI·DIVI·NERVAE·F·NERVAE
TRAIANO·AVG·GERM··DACICOPONTIF
MAXIMOTRIB·POT·XVII·IMP·VI·COS·VI·P·P
ADDECLARANDVMQVANTAEALTITVDINIS
MONSETLOCVSTAN····IBVSSITEGESTVS

The most beautiful lettering in the world is often said to be found in this marble-carved inscription of A.D. 113, which survives, although damaged, on the large pedestal of Trajan's Column in Rome. The column also survives, marble plated and 115 feet tall; in ancient times, it formed the centerpiece of Trajan's Forum (marketplace), a building group that the emperor added to Rome's business center. The column's height specifically demonstrated the height of a previously existing corner of the Quirinal Hill that Trajan's engineers had to dig away to create his forum. The inscription records the finished column being "dedicated" to the emperor. Across the top line runs the famous, official phrase of Roman legislation, Senatus Populusque Romanus *(easily translated once you know that the suffix* -que *just means "and"): "The Senate and People of Rome dedicated [this column] to the emperor Trajan"—his various titles follow—"to make known how high was the hill terrain removed for these great public works," that is, the forum buildings. Notice the V shape of the U letters and the I for J in the name* TRAIANO *(line 3). The ancient Romans had no letter J; its modern use in ancient Roman words is a later convention.*

pleted in A.D. 113 and still standing in the middle of the city of Rome: The column displays marble-carved scenes of Roman military conquest along with, on a plaque at its base, the perfected expression of Roman carved capitals. (See the two photographs here.)

Aside from Latin, for which it had been created, the Roman alphabet of the empire was sometimes used to write certain Celtic and Germanic tongues on the western frontier. But most of the European languages destined for Roman letters had not yet been born. Romance languages like French and Portuguese were as yet nothing

On a pontoon bridge of boats, standard-bearers of Roman legions lead the army north across the Danube River into territory of the warlike Dacians, in a marble-carved scene from Trajan's Column. The column, completed in A.D. 113 and dedicated with its famous inscription, features a spiral band of about 155 scenes, narrating the emperor's conquest of Dacia (the Translyvania plateau of southern Romania) in A.D. 101 to 106. Afterward repopulated with Roman settlers, Dacia would remain a Romanized enclave of Eastern Europe, as maintained today in the country's name, Romania, and its Romance language, written with Roman letters. Romania's neighbors Serbia, Bulgaria, and Ukraine, meanwhile, use Cyrillic.

more than regional dialects of spoken Latin. Old English was centuries in the future, prefigured only in a Germanic dialect of certain
wild tribes living at that time in north Germany.

From 21 letters, the Roman alphabet had by A.D. 100 grown to
23: Two new letters were welcomed officially, after perhaps 200
years of being used informally in Roman writing. Like most newcomer letters anywhere, the two were placed at the end of the letter
row: our Y and Z.

They were borrowed from the Athenian Greek alphabet of the
day, where they were, respectively, the 20th and 6th letters in order:
the vowel *upsilon* and consonant *zeta*. *Upsilon*, written in Greek as
Y, represented a narrowed "u" sound: "ew" or "ih." *Zeta*, written as
Z, took sound "z" (having slurred from the "zd" of Iron Age Greek).
The Romans wanted the two letters for help specifically in transliterating Greek words into Roman writing.

Why did the Romans care? Because for centuries, even while
Greece had been subdued by Roman armies, Greek culture and
technology had been potent forces in Roman life. Greek loan words
had been moving into Latin as the necessary vocabulary for whole
fields of knowledge—medicine, architecture, theater, astronomy,
and others—that the Greeks were masters of and the Romans as yet
were not. Greek terms like *symphonia* (symphony) or *zoidiakos* (zodiac) involved language sounds that Latin lacked, and lacked letters
for. To avoid the tedious expedient of switching to Greek to write
problem words, Latin needed those two Greek letters at least. Latin
had its own letter U, but Greek *upsilon*'s sound fell somewhere between Latin's U and I, and apparently the Latin U was felt inadequate for showing the Greek sound.

The new Roman Y and Z were never written for native Latin
words, apparently, only for Greek and other foreign noises. The Roman Y was always a vowel. Our English use of Y as a consonant
(yes), as well as a vowel (fly), is unusual. Although French and Span-

ish occasionally use Y as a consonant, too, most modern languages see Y foremost as a vowel.

The sounds of Roman letters generally were similar, not identical, to our own; specifics are detailed in chapters on the relevant letters. As for the letters' shapes, they speak to us, down 2,000 years: They could simply be our own letters.

The reason for this is that Roman letters were preserved in stone. A thousand years after Rome's fall, early European printers would copy the beautiful, revered shapes in designing capital letters for the first "roman" typefaces ("roman" for being first designed in Renaissance Rome, and "roman" as opposed to type shapes by Gutenberg and others that imitated German medieval handwriting). Two printers associated with early roman type were Nicolas Jenson, around 1470, and Aldus Manutius, around 1495, both based in Italy. Their work, in turn, would serve as models for typefaces like Garamond, Bodoni, and Times New Roman, which have come to define newspaper and book print.

The classic look of ancient Roman lettering emerged in carved inscriptions of the late 1st century B.C. and reached finest form in the era of the Trajan Inscription. The designs involved two abiding techniques by Roman stonemasons. First, certain parts of each letter were subtly widened—one leg of the A, two opposite sections of the O—in contrast to others. This gave the shape a sense of perspective and graceful solidity. The second technique was to add small finishing strokes (we call them serifs) at the letters' end points: Clear examples include letters E, G, H, S, and T. Serifs first appear in Greek letter carvings; the earliest known example may be the "King Alexander" inscription of 334 B.C., shown here on page 69. The Romans copied the idea and enlarged it, to good effect.

Of course, most Roman letters of A.D. 100 would have been written in ink, not stone. But as in any study of the ancient world, we are frustrated by the near-total disappearance of Roman ink writing, normally penned onto perishable material: papyrus or animal skin (of which the most refined versions were vellum and parchment). Only the sands of Egypt and a few other protective

Ink letters from a Latin manuscript in the "rustic" handwriting style, probably from the 500s A.D. (a late example). Done with much rotation of a broad-nib pen, the careful shapes resemble carved letters, with serifs and widened sections.

environments have yielded Roman ink samples on papyrus, parchment, or wood—or (at the Roman city of Pompeii, buried in volcanic ash in August A.D. 79) Roman messages painted onto building walls: see page 315.

Two distinctive handwriting styles of the empire are known today as old Roman cursive and rustic capitals. The first was a script for minor documents and everyday use, evidently penned quickly (cursive means "running") and often nearly illegible as compared with Trajan's Inscription. More formal and painstaking was the misleadingly named rustic, used for important documents and literary manuscripts.

Sometime around A.D. 300, there emerged a distinctive new Latin handwriting style, which we today call uncial. (The name is explained on pages 142–43, in a section on medieval writing.) Arriving in the late afternoon of the Roman Empire, uncial writing would survive Rome's fall and disintegration (A.D. 500), to be the first important pen style of the Middle Ages. Less imitative of carved letters and more adapted to swift but legible penmanship, uncial would point the way to subsequent ink styles of the Middle Ages—styles appropriate to a new order, including new languages of Europe.

The crooked E. Days before the beleaguered Enron Corporation filed for bankruptcy and laid off 4,500 workers in December 2001, a man carried belongings from the energy giant's Houston headquarters, behind the five-foot-tall, stainless-steel Enron logo. The trademarked, tilted E was meant to symbolize ascent and power (particularly electricity, Enron's main product). But when the biggest-ever American bankruptcy was followed by accusations of stupendous fraud, the unlucky logo became a media symbol for corporate greed and dishonesty, and acquired the nickname "the crooked E." This headquarters sculpture has since been removed for auction; a similar E, from another Enron building, fetched $44,000 at auction in September 2002.

A handsome E in the medieval ink style known as late unical looks right at home amid modern typeface (opposite page).

CAN'T SPELL ENGLISH WITHOUT E

Easily the most-often-used letter in English-language print, E out-distances runners-up T, A, and I by ratios of 10 to 7.7, to 7.28, and to 7.04, respectively, according to one analysis. That's quite a long lead. E's fairly pepper our printed pages—just look *here* and *there*—and one reason is in the many shades of vowel sounds that E can represent: about 15 sounds in all. For example, E takes a different sound in each of the following words: be, mere, red, alert, sadden, new, sew, latte, and (with a partner vowel) great, heart, and height. In an alphabet that is under-staffed with vowel letters, E does the job of two, at least. As our most visible worker, it enjoys a certain symbolic value: Where letter A might embody the whole alphabet, E could be said to represent our English vowels or even English itself.

Add to this dominance a more recent coup by E, or rather e, in symbolizing the digital communication revolution. In 1982, little e, for "electronic," went into the new word "e-mail"—and today we can't live without it. Well beyond company and product names like eBay (online auctions), eToys (toy sales), eDecor (home furnishings), eTravel (travel information), and e Café, we think nothing of seeing coinages like e-commerce, e-solutions, eStuff, e-tailing, and (following the dot-com bust) e-bankruptcy. English will never be the same.

Also au courant is "E" meaning "ecstasy," as in methylenedioxymethamphetamine, the euphoria-and-hallucination-inducing drug of choice for misguided young people at raves.

E is Everywhere. Unfortunately, amid its honors, E could be said to cheat a bit. Unlike other letters in our spelling, E regularly gets to show up and say nothing: It has an important silent role, which adds greatly to its number of appearances. By a uniquely English spelling rule (carefully taught to us in grade school), an E at the end of a word, following a consonant preceded by a vowel, is always a mute E; its job is to signal that the other vowel is long. Thus: "fate" versus "fat," "wine" versus "win." Only in foreign word borrowings (café) is the rule ignored.

How did English acquire a silent E? Some words from Old English, like "name," carry an E that was always there and was at one time pronounced. However, more often a silent final E has been *added* to the word in the last three hundred years. It is a convention, a device, that English lexicographers and teachers agreed on by the late 1600s, to help relieve what was then the chaos of English spelling. People began writing and teaching according to the new rule. Thus the traditional English word *wif,* with a long-I sound, received an added E to become "wife," with no change in pronunciation. The choice of E for silent duty, versus another letter, was prompted probably by the example of "name" and similar words.

The final-E rule is a clever way by which we compensate for our Roman alphabet's shortcoming in vowel letters. Many languages that use a Roman alphabet (English certainly) would have been grateful for a couple more letters, to help distinguish long vowels from short. The ancient Greek alphabet, for example, included two letters to mean O, one long and one short, and two to mean E, long and short. In English, we have had to get there partly by developing a coded E.

One early prophet of final-E spelling was the Elizabethan grammarian and teacher Richard Mulcaster. Although reputed to have been the model for the farcical pedant Holofernes in Shakespeare's comedy *Love's Labour's Lost* (circa 1590), Mulcaster himself seems to cast a warmer glow. An advocate of liberal education and a true fan of the English language, he was headmaster of London's Merchant Taylors' School, where his students included the future poet Edmund Spenser and playwright Thomas Kyd. In an era when some thinkers wanted to solve English spelling inconsistencies through complete overhaul, Mulcaster argued to keep traditional spellings but tinker to make them work. Accordingly, in 1582, he published a combination grammar book, teacher's manual, and 8,000-word spelling dictionary, titled *The First Part of the Elementarie which entreateth chefelie of the right writing of our English tung.* (An "elementary" was a primer.) In the book, discussing the letters individually, Mulcaster praises E for its many sounds, qualifying it for multitasking in an improved English spelling: "a letter of marvelous use in the writing of our tung. And therefore it seemeth to be recommended unto us speciallie above any other letter." One hundred years after his time, many of Mulcaster's spelling suggestions would be adopted, including the use of a final E.

Linguists classify vowels by the tongue position involved in their pronunciation. E's main sounds in English, the long E of "beet" and the short E of "bet," belong to the category of "front vowels," so named because they push the tongue forward. Other front vowels include our long-A sound, as in "day"—a sound we might also find sometimes in E, typically in words borrowed from continental languages, for example, "café" or "ballet" (from French) or "latte" (from Italian).

This "café" E is the normal long E of continental Europe. When a Spaniard, Dutchman, or any other continental European thinks of long E, he hears the sound "ay" (as in "café"). Our English long E—"ee"—would to continental European ears be the sound of long I. Insofar as the names of Roman alphabet vowels are generally the naked sound of the long letter, the name "ee" belongs to the letter I, by the continental standard. E's name in modern French, German, and others is "ay." (Short E, meanwhile, has no such identity problems but is pronounced much the same in English and continental tongues.)

The continental practice here is the proper and traditional one, reaching back to the ancient European languages of Greek, Etruscan, and Latin. English is the odd man out, due to the Great Vowel Shift, a vast and mysterious change in the English pronunciation of long A, E, I, O, and U, and OW, culminating in the 1500s. Prior to the Shift, Middle English was pronouncing long E as "ay."

Like all of our vowel letters, E began its life as a letter showing a consonant sound, in the Near Eastern alphabets of the second millennium B.C. This original or ancestral E was called *he* (pronounced "hey"), and it carried the "h" sound exemplified in the opening of its name.

As mentioned in prior chapters, every letter name of the early alphabet was a common noun in the users' Semitic language: house, hand, water, and so on. Every letter's shape was a rough picture of the object named. What the *he* meant—and this is no kidding—was "Hey!" The letter's name indicated a shout of surprise. And the letter's shape illustrated it strikingly.

The earliest surviving example of a written *he* appears in the oldest known alphabetic writing, carved into limestone in central Egypt in about 1800 B.C. The letter shape is a human stick figure, half crouching, perhaps leaping upward, arms raised at the elbows. The person is probably meant to be shouting, in an ancient Semitic expression that by coincidence resembles our "Hey!"

The vivid stick person *he* also shows up in the next-oldest extant batch of alphabetic writing, in rock carvings at west-central

The letter he, *carved into a limestone rock face at Wadi el-Hol in central Egypt, part of a (yet undeciphered) message left by a Semitic-language speaker, around 1800 B.C. The stick figure's posture is probably one of surprise. Denoting an "h" sound, the* he *is one of two stick figures among the early letter shapes.*

Sinai, from perhaps 1750 B.C. In the plaque sketched on page 31 a *he* can be seen among the letter shapes, fifth from the bottom in the far right-hand column.

But evidently the stick figure proved too exacting for convenient writing as a letter, and the shape became reduced to an abstract form by the next era of the alphabet: namely, the Phoenician alphabet of 1000 B.C. The Phoenician *he* shows up as the fifth letter in alphabetical order, the future place of our E. The Phoenician *he*'s shape, no longer human, looks like, well, a backward E, with a short tail: ⅎ The letter still took the consonant sound "h."

The biggest change came when the Greeks copied and adjusted the Phoenician letters for the writing of Greek, around 800 B.C. Choosing a handful of Phoenician letters whose consonantal sounds were unneeded for Greek, the Greeks reassigned these to be vowels. One letter affected was *he,* which now became the Greek E vowel. No doubt the choice of *he* for E was prompted by the Phoenician letter name, pronounced "hey" or "hay." The vowel sound in "hey" was the sound the Greeks wanted for their long E.

At first, the Greek letter stood for both long and short E. Later the letter would be specialized as short E only, and another Greek letter, named *eta,* would be developed for long E. At some point in the process, the former *he* letter received the Greek name *e psilon* (or *epsilon*), "naked E."

During the time while there was still only one Greek E letter, the Greek alphabet reached the shores of western Italy, where it was copied by the Etruscans (around 700 B.C.). The Greek E letter now became an Etruscan letter: The Etruscans kept it as letter number 5, gave it the name *ay,* and recognized it as meaning the sounds "ay" (long) and "eh" (short). These aspects of E remain absolutely the same today among continental European languages.

E passed to the Romans in about 600 B.C., when Etruscan letters were copied for writing Latin. Here the letter shape gradually reached a form exactly like our capital E. This E, called by the name *ay,* was bequeathed to newer European languages after the fall of Rome (A.D. 500). Meanwhile, in the ink handwriting of late antiquity and the early Middle Ages, there emerged a second shape for E, condensed for easy penmanship: e. This shape would much later, around 1470, inspire early European printers in designing their lowercase e.

Like X and a couple of other letters, E serves an important role as a symbol in math and science. The E of Albert Einstein's famous equation $E = mc^2$ is an abbreviation for "energy," while *m* is the "mass" of the object in question and *c* (for Latin *celeritas,* "speed") means the speed of light in a vacuum. In mathematics, lowercase e denotes a numerical constant, equal to about 2.71828, vital to the study of logarithms; the e commemorates the great Swiss mathematician Leonhard Euler, who first derived the number, in 1748.

The "ee" of English long E is one of three vowel sounds identified by researchers as typically the earliest sounds of infant speech the world over. The other two are "ah" and "oo." As the three are universal to human speech, any infant will hear them in the cradle, and because they are easy to articulate—vowels in general requiring no tricky use of the tongue or throat—a baby might here find her first success in imitating adult speech. Basically, the child just pushes the simple sound through her open throat, perhaps as early as age two months. From that stage, she typically will advance to floating a consonant in front of the vowel, forming "coo" or "yee" or something similar.

This phenomenon of the first sounds did not escape the notice of people in prescientific eras. In Elizabethan England, there existed a belief that female babies, particularly, were apt to begin speaking with the sound "ee"—in deference to their first forerunner, Eve.

Here is the order of the 26 letters in their frequency of use in printed English, according to three different surveys:

Dictionary of Phrase and Fable by Ebenezer C. Brewer, 1870	Codes and Ciphers by Frank Higenbottam, 1973	World Book Encyclopedia, 2002
E	E	E
T	T	T
A	A	A
I	O	O
S	N	N
O	I	R
N	S	I
H	R	S
R	H	H
D	L	D
L	D	L
U	C	U
C	U	C
M	P	M
F	F	F
W	M	G
Y	W	Y
P	Y	P
G	B	W
B	G	B
V	V	V
K	K	K
J	Q	X
Q	X	J
X	J	Q
Z	Z	Z

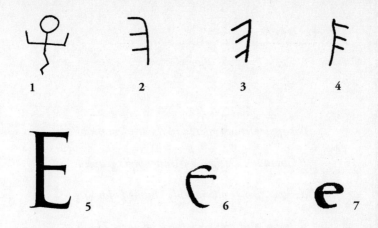

1   2   3   4

5   6   7

(1) *The Semitic letter* he, *from the Wadi el-Hol inscriptions, about 1800* B.C. *At this date, perhaps 200 years after the alphabet's invention, the letters were still being treated as pictures, similar to the Egyptian hieroglyphics from which they had been copied. The* he *took the "h" sound, the opening sound of its name.* (2) *By 1000* B.C., *in the Phoenician alphabet, the letter shape had settled to an abstract shape, facing leftward for right-to-left writing. The letter still meant "h."* (3) *The Greek version, from an early inscription, around 725* B.C. *The Greeks had copied the Phoenician* he *in shape and number-5 alphabetical place, but reassigned it to be a vowel: the letter E.* (4) *Early Roman E, about 600* B.C., *from an inscription that runs left to right. As Roman writing gradually settled on this direction permanently, E would be finalized as rightward facing.* (5) *Classical Roman E from the carved Trajan Inscription at Rome,* A.D. *113. The serifs of Roman design have here a most satisfying effect.* (6) *This inked E in the uncial handwriting style, from a Latin manuscript of about 450, seems to hover between an old Roman E and the beginning of our lowercase e shape.* (7) *A letter in the semi-uncial pen style, from a Latin manuscript of the 500s, clearly anticipates our lowercase print form.*

No apologies are offered in the trademark of F Company Design, a Minneapolis graphic design firm, memorably named for its founder and owner, John R. Falker. The F, in austere Futura typeface, seems to mean business, while the background dot could embody the whole science of graphic design.

F IS FOR—FORGET IT

Forever saddled with an obscenity, the letter F can seem vulgar or comical just by itself. Adding to F's tacky aura is our second f-word, "failure," which in the late 19th century suggested F, not E, as a pupil's flunking grade, below D. Of the alphabet's other letters, only P can even approach the stigma of being F.

At one time, F was handled carefully in the media—a loaded symbol, a walking punch line. The title of the comedy-western TV series *F-Troop* seemed positively daring in 1965, which was the same year that Neil Simon's stage comedy *The Odd Couple* opened on Broadway. *The Odd Couple* juxtaposes the fastidious Felix Ungar with the tougher, slobbier Oscar Madison as reluctant Manhattan apartment mates; the playwright's choice of Felix's name is rewarded in a scene where Oscar complains angrily about an innocent housekeeping note that Felix has left him. "I told you a hundred times," Oscar snarls, "I can't stand little notes on my pillow. 'We're all out of corn flakes. F.U.' . . . It took me three hours to figure out that F.U. was Felix Ungar."

Such coy treatment seems quaint nowadays, when clothing companies named Fuct and f.c.u.k. (French Connection, U.K.) push the envelope for the youth market's attention in ways that many of us find demoralizing.

The F-word's ugliness and impact benefit from its sizzling, opening sound. The F belongs to a category of consonants called fricatives, which involve breath expelled through some constriction of the mouth. Fricatives in English include the letter V, the sound "th," and, by some reckonings, a subcategory known as sibilants—the hissing sounds of S, Z, and "sh."

Exemplified in the very name "fricative" (from Latin *fricare,* "to rub," related to the word "friction"), the F sound results from air pushed through the barrier of the front teeth and lower lip. If you start saying a continuous F, then switch to a vibration of your lip and vocal cords, you'll be saying V. Thus F, with no vocal cords, is the unvoiced labio-dental fricative ("labio-dental" referring to the lip and teeth), while V is its voiced counterpart.

In running air over the lower lip, F and V resemble another letter, not a fricative: W. The kinship can be heard, for example, in the imperfect English of certain native speakers of German or Slavic tongues, who may substitute the sound "f" or "v" for the (to them) more difficult "w," saying "fich" for "which" or "faht" for "what."

F's crude sound attracted comment long before English was born. The ancient Roman statesman Cicero called it the "unsweetest" (*insuavissima*) sound in Latin, in a book on oratory written in 55 B.C. The Roman grammarian Quintilian, in *his* book on oratory, around A.D. 90, demeaned F as "harsh and unpleasant . . . a sound scarcely human or even vocal." The letter's hiss seemed to him to belong outside the organs of speech.

Ironically, this sound that has been F's ball and chain isn't even the sound that F started out with, historically. Back in about 700 B.C., the symbol F denoted not "f" but the kindred sound "w." Only later was F reassigned to become the unlucky fricative. Here is how it happened:

F is our alphabet's sixth letter. In the Phoenician alphabet of 1000 B.C., the sixth letter was called *waw*. The name meant "peg" in the Phoenicians' Semitic tongue, and the written letter looked like a Y-shaped peg or bracket: Y. (Through a different line of descent, the *waw* would also supply our letter Y.) *Waw* took the "w" sound, demonstrated in the name's opening sound. As for the sound "f," the Phoenicians didn't use it in their language and so had no letter for it.

When the Greeks copied and adapted the Phoenician alphabet in about 800 B.C., they kept the letter at place number 6 and sound "w," but for a new look they slapped the pronged head down to the side, as ⅂ or ⅂ or Ϝ. (Like other early Greek letter shapes, this one could project leftward for right-to-left writing or rightward for left-to-right writing.)

Why change the shape? The Greeks seem to have been influenced partly by the shape of their alphabet's preceding letter, *epsilon*: ⅂. They wanted the two to look similar, apparently. Since *epislon* was the ancestor of our E, the resemblance in shape between E and F continues to this day.

The Greek F-shape letter eventually had two names. At first called *wau* (pronounced "wow," slightly different from the Phoenician name), it was by about 500 B.C. also known as *digamma*, "double gamma." *Gamma* being the Greek G letter with a shape like ⌐, the name *digamma* referred to the shape of two *gamma*s, piggybacked. By any name, the letter still denoted the sound "w." Although Greek speech did have a sound somewhat similar to "f," that was covered by another letter, called *phi*.

After the Greek alphabet reached the shores of Italy in the 700s B.C., the *wau* or *digamma* was copied into the Etruscan alphabet to be letter number 6, symbolizing "w." Here it enjoyed a long and happy life, serving as the Etruscan W for seven centuries, until Etruscan culture and language finally evaporated amid the dominance of Rome.

Greek *wau-digamma,* meanwhile, fared less well at home. Eventually it dropped out of the Greek alphabet as being inessential for writing that language. Ancient Greek simply didn't need a "w" letter the way that Etruscan did or English would, and this fact gradually came out in the wash. Along with *san* and *qoppa,* two other superfluous Phoenician-derived Greek letters, *digamma* would not be included in the classical Athenian alphabet of 400 B.C. nor in the modern Greek alphabet, descendant of the Athenian.

Thus far historically, we've seen the F-shape letter to mean the sound "w." The switch from "w" to "f" came with the Romans, who copied the Etruscan alphabet shortly before 600 B.C. The Romans made adjustments on letter number 6: They assigned the "w" sound to their letter U as a secondary job, and, thus enabled, they gave the F-shape letter a brand-new sound— the strong Latin fricative not adequately represented among the Etruscan letters, the sound "f."

So finally, F for "f." Roman F thrived in its new job, symbolizing a Latin sound that was *frequent* and *fundamental* (the disdain of intellectuals like Cicero and Quintilian notwithstanding). F occurred often at the start of Latin words; most of the respectable F-words in a modern English dictionary derive from Latin: family, faun, feast, fracture, future, and so on.

With its dash of harshness, Roman F even served the poets.

Easily read from right to left, these Etruscan letters—incised on a silver cup from a tomb at Praeneste, 20 miles west of Rome, from about 650 B.C.—spell out the word Wetusia, *pronounced perhaps as "Weh-tuhs-ia." The initial F shape denotes the sound "w," not "f," and the Y shape is a U. Modern scholars recognize the root word as an Etruscan male name and the "-ia" as a possessive ending; thus the meaning is: "I belong to Wetus." Intriguingly, the name Wetus seems to correspond to a later-known Roman name, spelled* Vetus *and meaning "old."*

One phrase of the Roman poet Ennius (about 200 B.C.), describing woodsmen chopping trees, is recalled for its zesty onomatopoeia: *fraxinus frangitur* (meaning: the ash tree is felled and sectioned). And Vergil, in his epic poem, the *Aeneid* (about 20 B.C.), imagining a mythic embodiment of violence or evil, calls it *Furor impius,* "godless Frenzy"—the F sound contributing to a sense of menace.

After Rome's fall (around A.D. 500), its alphabet lived on; the letters were fitted to the writing of other European tongues, including Old English (about 600). There being as yet no letter V in the European Roman alphabet, the Old English F did double duty, representing the "f" of "fallow" and the "v" of "love"—a word originally written as *lufu* and pronounced probably as "luv-uh."

Meanwhile, the Romance languages were writing the sound "v" with the letter U, a practice that would eventually give rise to a variant U, the letter V. Starting in the late Middle Ages, V would oust F from many English word spellings where the sound was "v." Still, the Old English F-for-"v" survives in a few of our words today, notably "of."

Like Latin, Old English was fond of "f" as a word's opening sound (example: fond). This English quality mirrors an ancient development of the Germanic branch of the Indo-European language family, in which an initial "p" sound in prehistoric Indo-European became an "f" in primitive English. The development can be glimpsed by comparing certain native English words with corresponding words in other old Indo-European tongues, distantly related to English. Our word "father," for example, connects back to ancient words including Greek *pater,* Latin *pater* (with its descendants, such as Spanish *padre* and French *père*), and the Sanskrit root *pitar-*. Our "fire" corresponds to Greek *pur* and Czech *pýř*. And our "foot" represents the Indo-European root *pod-* or *ped-*, which steps out in the vocabularies of Greek (root *pod-*), Latin (root *ped-*), Sanskrit (*padas,* "foot"), Lithuanian (*pèdà,* "footstep"), and other Indo-European languages.

With F we reach our first example, in alphabetical order, of a minority letter name. As mentioned in the D chapter, the most common formula for English names of consonants is: The letter's sound plus long E equals the name. Eight consonants (or seven, if you call Z "zed") have "-ee" names of this kind, the others being B, C, D, G, P, T, and V. The F is the earliest sign of the alphabet's Opposition Party, wherein consonants are named with a *prefixed* vowel sound, usually short E. The others here are L, M, N, R, S, and X.

Why an Opposition Party? Why don't F, L, M, and the rest stick to the main pattern, with names like *fee, lee,* and *mee?* The first thing to say is that all these letter names entered medieval English from Old French after the Norman Conquest of England in A.D. 1066. Old French, in its turn, had received its letter names mostly from late Latin. So our focus shifts back to the Roman Empire, around A.D. 300. What was up then with the names of F, L, M, N, R, S, and X?

Significantly, the X aside, these letters all represent continuous sounds. You can make one long noise of F, L, M, N, R, or S until your breath runs out. Two other ancient Roman consonants were continuous, H and Z, and H we can add to the above-mentioned letters. But Z stands apart because Roman Z had a special, imported Greek name, *zeta*. (As for our modern alphabet's other continuous consonants, namely J, V, W, and Y, the first three were unknown to the ancient Romans and their Y was purely a vowel, not a consonant.)

From scant references in writings of ancient grammarians, it looks as if F, H, L, M, N, R, and S all underwent a name change during the Roman Empire, at least in common parlance. Each received in its name an initial vowel sound, where none had existed before. The purpose, apparently, was to create a buffer that would demonstrate more clearly the letter's sound in its name. For instance, Roman F probably started out, around 600 B.C., being called something like *fe* ("fay"). But by the early centuries A.D. the name had changed, through a vowel prefix, to something like *effe* ("ef-fay")—retained today as the modern Spanish name for F. The new Latin name better exemplified the "f" sound, for clarity among the letter names.

Ditto for other letters of the group. The benefit can be heard in L's change from "lay" to "ellay," in R's change from "ray" to "erray," and in the clearer contrast between "emmay" and "ennay" (M and N). Such names, delivered from late Latin to early French, passed to medieval English, with slight modifications through the centuries.

X, the maverick here, apparently never changed it name: It was called *eks* from the start, as inherited by the Romans from the Etruscans, around 600 B.C. Perhaps its name served as a model for the eventual renaming of F and its fellows.

For obvious reasons, F has never been a favorite of English-language product marketing. Today its use belongs mainly to a spirit of youth or rules-breaking, as in F-Group (software) and F Club (University of Florida sports fans). One place where F *has* found steady work is in science and technology: F can be Fahrenheit, fluorine, farad or faraday (measurement units of electricity, named for 19th century British physicist Michael Faraday), or frequency (as in FM, "frequency modulation," a method of radio broadcasting).

The lurid-sounding "f-number" of photography simply involves the ratio between a camera's focal point and its lens diameter (f for "focus"). Hence the "f stops" of a camera's iris adjustment. Hence, too, the reassuring name of Nikon's popular series-F camera, introduced in 1959.

But probably F's most familiar job has been in designating "fighter" aircraft—as opposed to "B" bombers or "C" cargo planes—of English-speaking armed forces, a usage that goes back to World War I and to Britain's Bristol F.2 Fighter and Sopwith F.1 Camel, biplanes mounted with machine guns. Today the F's proliferate overhead, in the names of such daunting American supersonic war birds as the F-16 Fighting Falcon, the F-18 Hornet, the F-22 Raptor, and the F-117 "Stealth" Nighthawk. Is it embarrassing to fly around in an "F"? Most fighter pilots would probably say they don't give a darn.

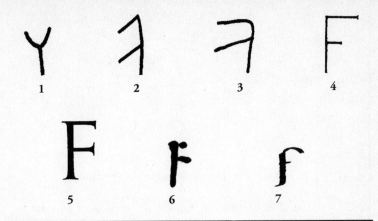

1   2   3   4

5   6   7

(1) Ancient Phoenician waw, the "peg," of 1000 B.C. Number 6 in the Phoenician alphabet, this letter took the "w" sound, exemplified in the start of its name. (2) A Greek wau, later also known as digamma, from a leftward-running inscription of about 700 B.C. The Greeks had altered the letter's shape but had kept it at alphabetic place number 6, with the sound "w." (3) The Etruscan letter—this one from the Wetus inscription of about 650 B.C., shown on page 125—imitated the Greek version in shape, alphabetic placement, and "w" sound. Like the Greek, the Etruscan letter could face either left or right, depending on the direction of the text. (4) This Roman F from a carved inscription of the 200s B.C. shows several changes. The shape, now more even, faces rightward, for normalized Latin left-to-right writing, and the tips of the horizontal bars have small serifs (finishing strokes), hallmarks of mature Roman lettering. But the most important change: Roman F took the sound "f," not "w." (5) Roman F from the marble-carved Trajan Inscription, A.D. 113. This handsome shape would become the model for our modern capital F, particularly in "roman" typefaces. Aspects of the letter's design, such as its serifs and its setting of the crossbar slightly above the midpoint, remain essential to roman print F's today. (6) An inked F in the late-Roman uncial pen style, from a Latin manuscript of Italy, mid-400s A.D. The shape recalls the old carved capital, yet, with its reduced top bar, it also starts to anticipate a modern print lowercase f. (7) The look of our lowercase f emerges in the semi-uncial pen style, this specimen from a Latin manuscript of the 500s A.D., from southern Italy. Reducing the letter to two quick pen strokes, the semi-uncial shape became part of a medieval handwriting tradition that would later (about 1470) inspire the lowercase type designs of early European printers.

Capital G in the medieval ink style known as black letter or Gothic. Flourishing in Northern Europe during the 1200s through 1400s A.D., this handwriting reflected the look of spires, pointed arches, and vertical struts in certain church architecture of the day—an architecture likewise known as Gothic. The adjective Gothic originally meant "German" but today has come to include, internationally, a dark kind of teen music, computer fantasy, and personal grooming.

GORGE-OUS G

lory. Grandeur. Glamour. Ghoul. Slag. The visceral G sound seems to reach for extremes. How fitting that it gongs twice in "gargantuan" but stays silent in "gnat." Equally at home with the good and the ugly, G thinks big, has gusto.

With G, we revisit the honest category of voiced stops. B and D are the two other English voiced stops, and the trio's general phonetics have been mentioned in the chapters on B and D. The hard "g" sound of G is the voiced velar stop—"voiced" designating the vocal cords and "velar" the roof of the mouth. Hard "g" belongs also to the loose category called "gutturals," or throat sounds.

Our English adjective "guttural" comes via medieval French from an ancient Latin noun *guttur,* "throat." Two related roots in Latin and Greek, *gurg-* and *garg-,* have bequeathed to us words like "gorge," "regurgitate," "gargle," and "gargoyle" (a sculpture that typically spouts drainage water from its throat). That such roots should showcase the throaty "g" sound—along with another throaty letter, R—seems beyond coincidence: Thousands of years before the alphabet came along, prehistoric Indo-European tongues were forming "throat" words partly around the appropriate sound "g."

Or compare with this primordial layer the modern appeal of Kellogg's-cereal character Tony the Tiger and his full-throated description of Frosted Flakes as "G-r-r-eat!" The G and R go together as naturally as, well, sugar and cornflakes.

G is a more complex letter than its straightforward fellows B and D. Its hearty "g" sound may cloak a frail and inconsistent nature. G actually has five possible pronunciations, including a silent one, all demonstrated in the Prohibition-esque phrase "mighty rough garage gin."

The soft G of "gin," with the same sound as our J, is G's alternative personality. By a rule of English spelling, G takes this pronunciation on most (not all) occasions when it falls before the vowels E, I, or Y. In flipping between hard and soft sounds, G of course resembles one other English letter: C. The C turns to "s" before E, I, or Y.

This odd mannerism, unique to G and C, is a legacy of their teenage years spent in medieval France. Soft G and soft C came to English from Old French, brought with French vocabulary and spelling rules after the Norman Conquest of England in A.D. 1066.

Relevant to this historical background, the soft G of modern English occurs mainly in words derived from medieval French: gentry, pageant, giant, and engine, among hundreds of examples. It is also found in Latin or Greek borrowings as traditionally anglicized: genius, gymnasium. But G may stay hard where the English word comes from a different language, including Old English, whence our "get," "give," "girl," and "gelding." Other hard-G source languages include biblical Hebrew (Gideon, Gethsemane), Japanese (ginkgo tree), and Malay (gecko lizard).

In a few French words borrowed by English since the Middle Ages, the soft G retains a distinctly French pronunciation, sounding more like "shj" than "j." Thus: corsage, garage, rouge, and luge.

Letters G and C share more than just a tendency to go soft. In an alphabet where certain letters are informally paired—including B and P, M and N, and S and Z—the closest two are G and C. They look similar; they sound similar (the kinship may be heard, for example, in the word "scold," closer to "gold" than "cold"); and their histories are deeply entwined . . . although not in the healthiest way.

Oversimplifying somewhat, we can say that C stole G's identity. G was the alphabet's original letter number 3, centuries before C existed. Then, a change: G disappeared and C became letter number 3—similar to G yet lacking its voice. Where had the real G gone? Not dead, but banished from the developing alphabet, G wandered four and a half centuries in limbo, until, its services being at last missed and appreciated, it was recalled to the letter row, to spot number 7 (ousting another letter). There G abides today, staring with who-knows-what emotions at the back of C, four places ahead.

G goes back to the earliest Semitic alphabets, as exemplified by the Phoenician alphabet of 1000 B.C. The Phoenician letters 2, 3, and 4 were the three voiced stops, the equivalents of our B, G, and D. The G letter was called *gimel,* the "throwing stick," the hard "g" of *gimel* being also the letter's sound. Today *gimel* remains the third letter of the Hebrew alphabet.

In the Greek alphabet, copied from the Phoenician in about

800 B.C., *gimel* became the Greek *gamma,* still a hard "g," still at place number 3. Today *gamma* remains the modern Greek third letter.

The misfortunes of this early G began around 700 B.C., when the Etruscans of Italy borrowed the Greek letters for their own use. As detailed in the letter C chapter, the Etruscans, with no voiced stops in their language (and thus with no need of a G letter), reassigned the third letter from the sound "g" to "k," terminating *gamma* and creating C in its place.

It was this G-less Etruscan alphabet that the Romans inherited for the writing of Latin in around 600 B.C. Unlike Etruscan, Latin was a tongue of the Indo-European family. Related to Greek and (distantly) to modern English, Latin included the familiar Indo-European sound "g." But Latin spoken "g" had no letter to represent it in the received alphabet.

Without doubt, the early Romans had contact with Greek traders and Greek writing in Italy, and they must have known that such a thing as a G letter existed, at place number 3 in the Greek alphabet. For several centuries the Romans used their letter C to mean either the sound "k" or the sound "g," according to context. This expedient would survive in one corner of later Latin writing: in the use of C to abbreviate the Roman male given name Gaius (not "Caius") and the use of Cn to abbreviate the name Gnaeus. Still, the double use of C was evidently felt to be inadequate, and a change was coming.

Among the letters bequeathed from the Greeks to the Etruscans to the Romans, the letter at place number 7 was proving superfluous for writing Latin. With the shape I, this letter denoted the sound "z," a sound employed by Greek and Etruscan yet not, as it happened, by Latin. The Greek letter was called *zeta* (pronounced "zayta") and the Etruscan one probably *ze* ("zay"). Through a dramatic detour encompassing several centuries, *zeta* would crop up eventually as our letter Z—though not, obviously, as our letter number 7.

Landing in the Roman alphabet of 600 B.C., Etruscan *ze* denoted a sound that the Romans couldn't even articulate. If the Romans used it at all, it was as a second letter for the sound "s" (their principal "s" letter being S). Thus the Roman seventh letter languished, a mere duplicate S.

Sometime around 250 B.C., Roman minds got the idea to connect this dud letter with the needed sound that was missing from the Roman alphabet, the sound "g." Roman tradition would ascribe the breakthrough to one Spurius Carvilius Ruga, a freed slave who supposedly opened Rome's first school of grammar. Letter number 7 was reassigned to mean the sound "g" and was renamed as something like *ge* ("gay"). The name *ge* would be the direct ancestor of our modern English name for G.

The Romans quickly gave *ge* a new look. The inconvenient shape (too similar to the I of the letter I) was changed, through stages, to a modified C shape: *G*. So G was born.

Presumably the new letter shape's resemblance to C was deliberate on the Romans' part. Some kind of attraction was at work: Since C was close in sound to G and had doubled as the G letter in

1   2   3

(1) Derived from the Greek letter zeta, the Etruscan letter number 7 denoted the sound "z." Around 600 B.C., it went into the newborn Roman alphabet as a letter not actually needed for writing Latin. (2) Around 250 B.C., the Romans reassigned the letter to a sound they did need represented, "g," and they began to give the letter a more distinctive shape. (3) By about 200 B.C., Roman G had reached its mature shape: a C with a small crossbar. The resemblance between G and C was presumably deliberate, an aid to memorizing the new letter.

the old days, the Romans evidently felt that their newly created G would be easier to learn and remember if it resembled C in shape.

For centuries Roman G remained a simple letter. The classical Latin of Cicero or Seneca knew only a hard G, regardless of what letter followed. In the Latin word *gemma* (jewel), G was pronounced as in our word "gum." Ditto for the poet whose family name was Vergilius (Wer-gill-ius) but whom we call Vergil or Virgil (Vur-jil). Ditto, too, for such recognizable Latin words as *religio, generosus, generalis,* and *vestigium:* All had hard G. Classical Latin carried no sound "j" and no letter for it; our letter J is postmedieval. Today the existence of soft G in countless English words derived from Latin—religion, generous, general, vestige—is due mainly to the intervention of medieval French.

Soft G arose in the spoken Latin of the later Roman Empire. Starting around A.D. 150, G began to be slurred when it fell before E, I, or Y (which are "front vowels," sharing certain aspects of pronunciation). Modern scholars trace this slurring partly through analysis of variant manuscript spellings: A Latin word like *gemma* apparently passed through a stage of being spoken as "dyemma" before reaching "jemma" by the time of the empire's collapse (around A.D. 500).

Thereafter, soft G was borne along as regional Latin dialects evolved into early versions of the medieval Romance languages. Today soft G is a prominent Romance feature: It is still pronounced as "j" in modern Italian, while in French and Portuguese it has slurred further, to something like "shj," and in Spanish to a guttural "h."

Our English soft G is a medieval French import, a legacy of the Norman invasion of England in 1066, as mentioned. It so happens that our "j" pronunciation, similar to Italian's, preserves the sound of medieval French soft G more faithfully than does the modern French pronunciation (as in "rouge"). The medieval

French "j" settled down permanently in Middle English, around 1300, whereas in France it continued slurring, to "shj."

By bad luck, the vicissitudes of soft G have affected the letter's very name. Our name for G goes back to the Latin name pronounced as "gay" and spelled as *ge*: that is, the letter itself plus a long E, with the ancient Latin values for the G and E. This name "gay" would have slurred to "jay" by the era of early French, and so "jay," arriving in England with the Norman Conquest, became the name in Middle English, as well as in French.

"Jay" would have offered no confusion with the letter J, for two reasons: (1) The J did not begin to appear systematically in English writing until the 1600s, and (2) J's early name in English was "jye."

From medieval "jay," the path forks toward both the modern English and French names for G. In France, the "j" sound softened to "shj," producing the modern French name, "shjay," still spelled as *ge*. In England, conversely, the "j" sound stayed put but the attached *vowel* sound changed: Amid the great English vowel shift of the 1400s to 1500s, long E went from "ay" to "ee," bringing us to G's modern English name, "jee." The one item of continuity has been the name's spelling: G plus long E, through differing pronunciations, in ancient Latin, medieval French, and modern English (albeit for clarity we might prefer two E's: "gee").

While the modern French name for G is "shjay," the name for J is pronounced "shjee." Thus, in French, "J" for G's name and "G" for J's, a detail that has irked students on both sides who are learning the other tongue.

The irregular GH spelling of "sigh," "night," "tight," "enough," "slough," and others commemorates medieval pronunciations of certain English words. Medieval "night," for example, was probably pronounced as something like "neehkt," comparable with modern German *nicht* or Scots-dialect *nicht*— as in the classic Lowland phrase, "'Tis a bra' [brave], bricht, moon-licht nicht, ta-nicht." While the GH spelling was fairly accurate for that breathy, guttural sound, such English pronunciations would change by the Middle Ages' end, leaving the GH spelling behind. Today, in words like "tough" versus "light," GH is both inaccurate and inconsistent.

This GH has distressed purists, including the Irish playwright, philosopher, and 1925 Nobel laureate, George Bernard Shaw. Among his many studies, Shaw—probably best remembered today for his 1913 play *Pygmalion* (basis for the 1956 musical *My Fair Lady*), featuring the brilliant phonetics expert Henry Higgins—was a lifelong advocate of English spelling reform. On his death in 1950, Shaw left a bequest of prize money for a contest to create an improved alphabet for English spelling: The competition, held in 1958, produced a winning alphabet of 48 new "letters," each symbolizing one sound exactly. During his lifetime, Shaw was fond of demonstrating English spelling inconsistencies by observing that the word "fish" could logically be spelled as *ghoti*—that is, the "gh" of "rough," the "o" of "women," and the "ti" of "nation."

G enjoys a modest 21st-century prominence in brand names and international relations, often as an abbreviation for "global" or "group." The title "G-7," for "group of seven," denotes those nations with the biggest industrialized economies: Canada, France, Germany, Italy, Japan, the United Kingdom, and the United States. For "G-8"—as in the 2001 Genoa G-8 conference disrupted by mass protests—add Russia.

As used in lowercase, g represents a unit of gravity, a factor in high speeds of spacecraft and supersonic aircraft. A G-suit may be worn by pilots and astronauts to help them withstand multiple g's.

In "G-man," a term reminiscent of 1930s gangster movies, G stands for "government" and refers to the FBI and similar federal law enforcement agencies. The expression is said to have been coined by real-life Public Enemy Number 1 "Machine Gun" Kelly at his arrest in 1933: "G-men, don't shoot!" Some criminals may be carrying 100 G's (100 grand, $100,000) when the G-men pick them up.

The G spot—a small region of female sexual sensitivity, distinct from the clitoris and located somewhere along the vagina's front wall—is named for German gynecologist Ernst Grafenberg, who announced its existence in writings of 1950. Since then, generations of husbands and boyfriends have failed to find it.

The G-string of the vaudeville stage was a cunningly skimpy and sometimes spangled loincloth worn by strippers or dancers, typically female. While G-strings themselves live on in modern performance and photography, the name's origin has been forgotten. The G perhaps stood for "genital," but even more tantalizing than that line of thought are the earliest journalistic references to a "gee-string" or "G-string," which all come from the American West, starting in the 1870s, and concern the attire of various male American Indian groups. "Some of the boys wore only 'G-strings' (as, for some reason, the breech-clout is commonly called on the prairie)," runs a December 1891 *Harper's Magazine* passage. So maybe the G commemorates some relevant word, sounding like "jee," of a Plains Indian language.

Johann Sebastian Bach presumably had other things in mind when, in about 1723, he wrote his "Air on a G String" (actually so named by a later arranger). Part of a larger piece for string quartet, the "Air" includes a violin solo that fits entirely on the G string, the lowest of the violin's four strings.

Since the 19th century, a few thinkers have held the letters' shapes to be subconscious expressions of a collective human mind. According to this (unconvincing) line of thought, the shapes evolved over centuries due to guiding human principles rather than to mere convenience in scribbling. In a far-out 1961

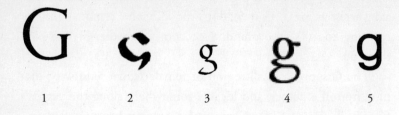

1   2   3   4   5

(1) Carved Roman capital G from the Trajan Inscription, A.D. 113. This perfected Roman shape would become the model for all print capital G's. (2) An inked G in the uncial handwriting style, from a Latin manuscript of the mid-400s B.C. Uncials were basically capital shapes adapted to pen strokes. Like the capital, the uncial letter sat atop the text's baseline. (3) The beautiful Carolingian minuscule ink letter, from a Latin document written in England in A.D. 1018. The Carolingian version clearly anticipates the modern lowercase print letter, both in shape and in venturing below the baseline. (4) Lowercase g in Garamond typeface, a traditional French design originating in the 1500s. Like all "roman" typefaces, Garamond employs lowercase shapes based on Carolingian minuscules of centuries earlier. (5) The lowercase g in Futura typeface—the trend-setting sans-serif design from 1928 Germany—looks different from the g of roman typefaces like Garamond. The g form shows up in many (not all) sans-serif and italic typefaces. Only our G and A have this quirk of possessing two different lowercase print shapes, derived from separate medieval-handwriting traditions.

book titled *Sign and Design: The Psychogenetic Source of the Alphabet,* mystical British scholar Alfred Kallir explained the alphabet as a sexual picture code, a "magic chain of procreative symbols destined to safeguard the survival of the race" of humankind. The shape of A, for example, sticking into the air and associated historically with the ox's horns, is a cinch to symbolize the erect male member. The curve of D is the full womb of a pregnant lady. And G turns out to be a most explicit letter, showing the act itself, with a female circle and male crossbar. Watch for it on *Sesame Street!*

After the Roman Empire's Collapse, Roman Letters Survived and Evolved, Fitted to New European Languages, Including English

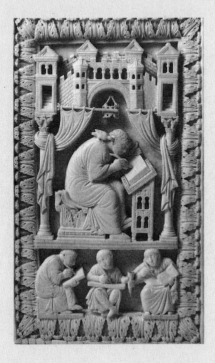

Pen and ink. St. Gregory the Great, pope from A.D. 590 to 604 and a shaper of the medieval church, receives dictation from the Holy Spirit as a dove in this beautiful French carved-ivory plaque from the late 800s. Gregory was remembered for reforming the Roman Catholic mass—whence our term "Gregorian chant"—and the scene shows him composing the mass's new Latin text (a section of which appears on Gregory's ivory book page, readable with a magnifying glass). The three scribes symbolize the church organization that would copy and distribute the master's words throughout Christian Western Europe. Among the scene's details, note the writing materials: the scribe's ink horn, the pens that are not quills but hollow tools of carved bone or horn, and the book format of parchment sheets bound along one edge, versus a scroll of papyrus or leather, as in earlier times. (Parchment was process-smoothed animal skin, typically sheep or goat, finer than standard leather.) During the often brutal and tempestuous Middle Ages, the church kept alive the legacy of classical Roman learning—copying and preserving works of pagan authors like Vergil and Cicero as well as of church fathers—and helped to marry Roman letters to newer, Northern European tongues, such as German and English.

continued

Shapes of things to come. This Latin manuscript page of about A.D. 450, in the uncial handwriting style, shows the early stages of certain letter shapes that would inspire European printers' lowercase forms in the late 1400s, a thousand years in the future. Among the emerging shapes to be found here are: a, d, h, m, p, q, and u. Penned in Italy, the manuscript is a translation and continuation of a Greek work of about 325, the World History by the bishop and scholar Eusebius of Caesarea. The page's text concerns the reign of the famous ancient Persian king Darius (the "DARII" of the second full line and elsewhere).

In the Roman alphabet's long history, uncial handwriting represents the next important stage after the carved capitals of imperial Rome. Derived from a Greek handwriting style, Latin uncial arose around A.D. 300, during the late Roman Empire. It was a quick but legible pen style for the yielding surface of parchment, particularly parchment sheaved in the new-fashioned format of the book. (Books of the era often were bound before the writing went in, as shown in the "St. Gregory and the Scribes" scene, page 141.) Uncial letters as a group looked different from, and required different pen positions than, the two older styles of Roman formal handwriting: the "square" and "rustic" capitals. These took careful, slow pen strokes, traditionally applied to sheets or scrolls of papyrus or leather, laid flat on a hard surface. Uncial was an adaption to more modern book materials and more productive work standards.

Uncial became the premier Latin book hand of late antiquity ("book" as opposed to the daily "business" hand). It survived the empire's collapse, around A.D. 500, being among the Roman cultural elements preserved by the Roman Catholic Church, and it remained the foremost Latin book hand in the early Middle Ages, virtually monopolizing the production of Bibles and Christian religious texts. Even today, uncial-style letters can be found on our product labels, announcing "medieval tradition." Uncials are favorites for the signposting of Irish-themed taverns in the United States.

The name "uncial" is a scholarly invention of the 1700s, extrapolating from a Latin reference by St. Jerome to litterae unciales, "inch-high letters" (about 400). Compared with the Trajan Inscription capitals of A.D. 113, shown on page 104, some uncial letters show little change, such as N, O, S, or T, while others look quite developed, such as the A, D, E, or H. Regardless, all uncial letters were considered to be the capitals, adapted to easier penmanship. A letter shape like ❧ was thought of as D, not as a minuscule or lowercase d. Letters in those days had mainly one shape in any text. Not until the 800s would texts begin to combine writing styles so as to include various shapes for any letter.

Older Roman lettering, such as rustic capitals, had employed letter shapes of uniform height. Uncial was the first book hand to regularly break uniformity, with about nine letter shapes that extended either above or below the others: D, H, K, and L were the "ascenders" and F, G, P, Q, and Y, the "descenders." Nowadays those letters, plus a few more, supply the ascenders and descenders of normal lowercase print. Similarly, the uncial practice of opening a chapter or section with a letter writ larger (see the big E and Q on the manuscript page, opposite) was the first step toward our modern, two-tiered system of using an uppercase letter to begin a sentence.

Uncial reigned for nearly 600 years, until the late 800s. It spawned at least two derivative Latin handwriting styles: the widespread business hand today known as semi-uncial, used for minor documents and workaday writing through the 800s, and the decorative "artificial uncial" (now called), which proved too exacting to be practical but found a certain use in manuscript headings and ornate opening letters. Uncial and semi-uncial were both displaced by the highly legible and easily penned Carolingian minuscule, sponsored by the French king Charlemagne.

continued

The millennium from A.D. 500 to 1500—the "middle" ages, bridging the end of antiquity and the birth of modern Europe—saw our Roman alphabet through most of its final growth. At the era's outset, the alphabet comprised 23 letters for writing Latin. By 1500, the same alphabet had been fitted to about 30 different Western and Central European languages; its letters could now number 24 or more, according to the tongue being represented; and the whole category of European "writing" had been revolutionized by a practical printing method invented by Johann Gutenberg in Germany in around 1452.

One language that began being penned in Roman letters during the early Middle Ages was Old English. By the year 1500, English had been enriched and developed through mixture with medieval French, and it stood within a few generations of its finest expression, in the stage plays of William Shakespeare (around 1600) and the King James translation of the Bible (1611).

Such vast developments can be but sketched here. The milestones of the Middle Ages in regard to the alphabet are:

• *The collapse of the Roman Empire.* By the 400s, the authority of the Roman emperor and government was crumbling amid invasions of Germanic tribes, not only in the provinces but in Italy itself. The empire's end is traditionally dated to A.D. 476, the year in which Rome's last emperor was deposed by a mutineer. Yet in ways the empire lingered: The city of Rome was not destroyed; the title "emperor" continued to be used by rulers at the eastern capital, Constantinople; and aspects of Roman society lived on, particularly in the villa organization of the countryside. Latin in various dialects remained Europe's major spoken tongue west of the Rhine River, and Latin supplied the religious and administrative language of the Roman Catholic Church. Latin writing, in the 23-letter Roman alphabet, was preserved by church-organized education, primarily the monastic schools (particularly of the Benedictine order) and the episcopal schools, often urban, which were associated with a bishop (Latin: *episcopus*) and his cathedral and which might admit well-heeled lay students as well as intending clergymen.

• *A new map of Europe.* The western Empire broke into multiple kingdoms, ruled typically by Germanic newcomers. After 450, most of Roman Britain fell to seaborne invaders from northern Germany: Angles, Saxons, and Jutes, who would create on the island a new "Angleland." Much of Italy was held in the 500s by a Germanic people called Lombards (whence the modern name Lombardy, the region of Milan). And a swathe of territory from the Elbe River to the Pyrenees was won by an aggressive, resourceful tribe called the Franks—whose name lives on in the modern name of France, in the western German city's name Frankfurt ("the Franks' ford" on the river Main), in our noun "franchise" (originally denoting Frankish citizenship rights), in our adjective "frank" (citizens may speak freely), in our verb "to frank" (to rubber-stamp, usually with postage value), and in the Italian word for postage stamp, *francobollo*. The postal references commemorate an era when a Frankish nobleman's wax seal or outer signature could ensure an envelope's delivery along the roads. The greatest Frankish king would be Charlemagne, or Charles the Great, reigning from 768 to 814.

• *The birth of the Romance languages.* Modern Europe has five major languages that derive directly from Latin; they are, from west to east, Portuguese, Spanish, French, Italian, and Romanian. (The adjective "Romance," coming to English from Old French, refers in this case, of course, to the ancient Romans.) By the middle years of the Roman Empire, around A.D. 150, certain changes were under way in the common people's spoken Latin. After the empire's collapse, the changes accelerated along local lines: Western Europe became a patchwork of Latin dialects, many more than five. Of these, a certain few, belonging to important cities like Paris or Castile, were able to spread at the expense of others, through

continued

centuries of nation building. Today a few minor Roman languages survive alongside the five major ones, such as Catalan in the Barcelona region or Rhaeto-Romance in the southeastern Swiss Alps.

Regarding the mechanics of the Latin-to-Romance transformation, suffice it to say that the changes encompassed language structure, pronunciation, and vocabulary, with differences from one Romance tongue to another. Latin's expressive but complex system of noun, adjective, or verb endings (whereby the endings would change according to the words' use in a sentence) became vastly simplified; the new languages confined word-end changes mainly to verbs and relied more on word order and dedicated prepositions. Thus, in the Latin phrase "mother of God," *mater Dei,* the preposition "of" is indicated by the specific form *Dei* (versus *Deus, Deo,* etc.), while modern Italian or Spanish shows the preposition as a word: *madre di Dio, madre de Dios.*

Much of modern Romance vocabulary has shifted in pronunciation from Latin yet remains recognizably Latin at core. Thus the Latin word *rota* (wheel) has yielded Romanian *roata,* Italian *ruota,* Portuguese *roda,* Spanish *rueda,* and French *roue* (from Old French *ruede*) as well as English borrowings like "rotate." The Latin verb "to sleep," *dormire,* has become Italian *dormire,* Romanian *dormi,* and Portuguese, Spanish, and French *dormir.*

The modern Romance language closest to classical Latin in grammar is probably Romanian, while Italian tends to be the closest in written vocabulary. The tongue that has evolved furthest from Latin is French, its development due partly to an early introduction of Germanic phonetics from Frankish invaders and partly to medieval France's dynamic role as a center of commerce and learning, open to outside influences. French is of particular interest as being the single other language most relevant to the history of English.

The earliest stage of French, to about A.D. 1300, is known as Old French. The emergence of Old French as a tongue distinct from Latin is traditionally dated to 842. This misleadingly late and precise date reflects the earliest written document we possess in a language that can be called French, not Latin—in fact, it is our earliest document for *any* Romance tongue; early Italian and Spanish are not documented until the 900s. The French item records an alliance treaty between two kings of separate Frankish territories (they were brothers, Charles the Bald and Louis the German). Known as the Oath of Strasbourg, after the eastern French city where it was ratified, the treaty is preserved within the Latin writings of a contemporary Frankish historian. The treaty was a public declaration to be understood by both rulers' armies, and so it is bilingual, in French and German (being of great value, too, for German studies). The French portion offers a fascinating glimpse at a language in transition between ancient Latin and modern French. The opening words are: *Pro Deo amur et pro christian poblo et nostro commun salvament, d'ist di in avant* (For the love of God and for the safety of the Christian people and our community, from this day forth).

Although written in the traditional 23 Roman letters, this language is no longer Latin but rather something new, looking at first glance like Spanish. Not only have most of the words changed from their Latin counterparts, but the pronunciation of certain letters themselves has changed, pointing the way to modern pronunciations of French and English. For example, a sound "v," the voiced fricative, which the ancient Romans never knew in Latin speech, is probably the sound being signified in the words *salvament* and *avant*. Within a few centuries of the Strasbourg Oath, Old French words and pronunciations would be forcibly imported to England (see below), where they would become building blocks of modern English.

• *New and important letter shapes.* As part of wider educational and administrative reforms, the Frankish king Charlemagne in about A.D. 789 initiated the creation of a new Latin handwriting, to replace various illegible business hands then in use. The new script was to be easy to write and read and would be made standard throughout Charlemagne's extensive kingdom; the project was headed by the English cleric Alcuin, master of Charlemagne's palace school at the Frankish capital of Aachen (now

continued

in western Germany). Probably by selecting and refining one of the better semi-uncial scripts then in existence, Alcuin created the new official hand, known to modern scholars as Carolingian minuscule—"Carolingian" being an adjective relating to Charlemagne and "minuscule" traditionally meaning "smaller" or "lesser." The new script was smaller than other business hands, yet more legible, and smaller also than book hands like uncials or square capitals. It was *lesser* insofar as a business hand naturally fell below uncials and other book hands in the hierarchy of scripts.

Of all Charlemagne's civilizing achievements, Carolingian minuscule has arguably been the most permanent, for it has supplied the lowercase letter shapes that we use today. Where uncial had introduced about seven modified letter shapes and semi-uncial about seven more, the Carolingian script drew on this tradition and perfected it, giving to almost all the letters the distinctive, legible shapes destined for lowercase type.

During the 800s, Charlemagne's new script proved highly successful on its own merits. Economical of space and materials, it was pleasant to write—most of its letters could be inked in one continuous pen motion— and to read, with enough dignity to recommend it also as a book hand. Soon it had supplanted uncial as the main Latin book hand of Western Europe. (Our earliest extant book in German, a rhyming translation of the Gospels from around 865, happens to be penned in Carolingian letters.)

Carolingian script fell aside, in its turn, for newer styles during the 1000s and 1100s. But dramatically, it was rediscovered in old manuscripts during the early 1400s in Italy and then inspired a whole new Italian handwriting style, called the humanist school, which emerged about 30 years before Gutenberg's printing press. In the late 1460s, early printers in Italy chose humanist letter shapes as models for the first lowercase type designs of the newly created "roman" print.

Thus was Carolingian minuscule resurrected to become the prime book hand (so to speak) of the print era. The old letter shapes are now the daily conveyors of our books, newspapers, and magazines. A Carolingian-style manuscript page is illustrated and discussed just ahead, on page 156.

• *The birth of English.* Between about A.D. 450 and 500, Germanic peoples called Angles, Saxons, and Jutes invaded Roman Britain and captured most of the territory south of the Firth of Forth, leaving only some defended enclaves in the mountainous west. The invaders spoke a Germanic language, distantly related to modern Dutch, German, and Danish, among other tongues. Dating from the moment the Angles and the others set foot on British soil, their tongue becomes known for historical purposes as Old English. It can be imagined as the "German grandfather" of modern English.

Whereas the Germanic Franks who invaded Roman Gaul (modern France) in the 500s A.D. became assimilated and adopted the defeated inhabitants' Latin dialect (the future language French), this was not so for the Anglo-Saxons; their newcomer language became that of England. One reason for this linguistic takeover was the overwhelming evacuation of the Roman British population after defeat: They sailed to Gaul or withdrew into the western uplands now known as Wales, where their Celtic element is today preserved in the traditional Welsh language, still the first tongue spoken in many homes and public places of North Wales.

The Anglo-Saxons—or English, as we may now also call them—may have brought along their own alphabet: the runes of old Northern Europe. Not necessarily magical or evil (despite treatment in modern movies and computer games), the runes comprised about 24 letters, keyed to the sounds of Germanic speech and shaped angularly for easy carving into wood (the "scrap paper" of forested Europe). Each letter was a "rune"—a Germanic word interpreted by modern scholars as meaning either "secret" or "scratchings." It is theorized that runic script may have been born from an adaption of the Etruscan alphabet by an Alpine people around 300 B.C. Runes seem to have been used for commerce, cor-

continued

respondence, and occasional magic, much like other early alphabets. For modern study, nearly all runic writing has been lost due to the perishability of wood. About 5,000 inscriptions survive, mainly memorial-stone carvings and ownership declarations scratched onto metal objects, dating between from about A.D. 100 to 1600. The majority come from Sweden; 1,000 from Norway; about 700 from Denmark; and the rest mainly from Germany, the British Isles, and Ireland. Anglo-Saxon England has contributed 70.

Alongside the Anglo-Saxon runic alphabet—and soon overshadowing it—was the Anglo-Saxon Roman alphabet, beginning around A.D. 600. Although Roman letters had been used by the Roman British inhabitants, the Anglo-Saxon conquerors seem to have learned their ABC's only with the arrival of Christian missionaries from the continent. (The Anglo-Saxons in England originally were pagans.) This earliest Roman alphabet of England had about 27 letters, including four or five supplemental signs for certain English speech sounds beyond the scope of traditional Roman letters. Two of the extra letters were runes: One was called *thorn*, denoting the English sound "th," and the other was *wyn*, for the sound "w" (there being as yet no W in the Roman alphabet). Thus *thorn* and *wyn* showed up in both the runic and the Roman alphabets of Old English; and they would become entwined in the histories of other letters, such as Y and W.

The oldest extant English writing comes from around the year 600: a few biblical passages in Roman letters, translated at that time from Latin. There follow some religious and legal writings and poetry of the late 600s. The flower of Old English literature, the 3,182-line epic poem *Beowulf* (meaning "Bear," the hero's name), was evidently written down in around 725—although the story is set in the early 500s and our single extant manuscript dates from about 1000.

The Norman Conquest of 1066 changed forever England's society and language. England received a French-speaking Norman ruling class; Normans and their descendants held wealth and power while being far outnumbered by the Anglo-Saxons, who supplied the peasantry, laborers, and some of the middle class. Old English did not die under such circumstances, nor did it continue unchanged. It gradually mixed with aspects of Norman French to become, starting in the 1100s, a substantially new tongue, which we call Middle English. This was the language of the London poet Geoffrey Chaucer (around 1380). Middle English would evolve into Modern English, generally dated by scholars as beginning in 1500 and reaching maturity in about 1660.

Middle English combined English and French vocabulary and English and French speech sounds; French spelling rules and French letter values dominated, as used by Norman clergy and teachers in England. Not only the words but the very letters of English underwent change, moving in a direction that we would call more modern.

For instance, the rune *wyn* disappeared from England's Roman alphabet by about 1300, dislodged by the Norman letter W. And the Old English letter U, frequently written and variously pronounced, came to be replaced in some spellings by the more Norman-looking O or OU— so that Old English *sunu* (pronounced "sun-uh") became Middle English *sone* and then "son," while *hus* ("hoos") became *hous* and then "house." Yet Old English *sunne* was left alone, to eventually yield "sun."

Meanwhile, Norman French had introduced into English a few sounds that were unknown to the original Anglo-Saxons. These included certain French shadings of vowel sounds (the A and O gained in repertoire, for example) and the Romance sound "j" (as in English "jolly," from Old French *jolif,* meaning "lively" or "pretty"). Middle English wrote the sound "j" with the letter I (consonantal) or G (soft), but in a future century "j" would inspire a brand-new letter of the alphabet, J. Alongside J, another new letter would emerge: V. Together J and V, arriving after W, would provide the final letters by which the 23-letter alphabet of ancient Rome grew into our own 26 letters. The W entered our alphabet during the late 1500s, but for J and V full recognition would wait until mid-19th century.

continued

Modern English contains, in theory, some 500,000 words, of which about 50,000 appear at least periodically in modern print. While the 50,000 include borrowings from many tongues—Japanese, Yiddish, ancient Greek, and others—the two biggest components are Old English and Old French, at about equal size. During the Middle Ages, the vocabulary of early English roughly doubled through French admixture, from about 12,000 to 24,000 words at that time. Most of our modern words of Latin origin were delivered through medieval French, although a few (momentum, apparatus) represent later borrowings for scientific or other technical vocabulary.

(A footnote: Within the Old English category here, a minority of words are not "pure" English but were borrowed from Old Norse into Old English, around A.D. 800 to 1000, amid Viking settlement and trade in England. This *Sc*andinavian group includes many of our own "sk" words, like "skill," "skin," and "bask.")

A comparison of French- versus English-derived words offers insight on the social setting of Middle English. As the Scottish novelist Sir Walter Scott observed in *Ivanhoe* (1819), livestock often have English names on the hoof, as being tended by English peasantry, but French names on the table, as being eaten by Norman lords. Thus English "sheep," "cows," "calves," and "swine," once slaughtered and cooked, became French "mutton," "beef," "veal," and "pork." Robert Claiborne gives other examples in his book *Our Marvelous Native Tongue* (1983). Anglo-Saxons lived in "cottages." Normans lived in "mansions," "manors," "castles." Anglo-Saxons sharecropped on a "croft." Normans owned a "farm," whose fields they might "lease" for "rent." Anglo-Saxons did the "work." Normans took the "profit." Yet Normans, too, might "labor" in "appropriate" "pursuits," like "war," "government," or "study."

With some exceptions, Old English words tend to supply our vocabulary for necessities and other basics of experience, while French-derived words may reflect activities that are more intellectual, leisurely, specialized, or lucrative. Old English gives us: heaven, hell, life, death, love, hate, day, night, food, sleep, summer, winter, mother, father, husband, wife, earth, and home, among many others. French gives us, for example: president, parliament, council, rule, and state. The baker and shepherd are English; the banker and doctor are French. The advantages of French cuisine are acknowledged in words like boil, broil, fry, grill, roast, sauce, soup, stew, toast, dinner, and table (while "cuisine" and "menu" are postmedieval borrowings).

Some French words in English have the same meanings as certain Old English words; linguists call such pairings "doublets." It has long been observed that the French word in a doublet operates usually at a more detached or general level than the Old English one. Compare the following pairs, Old English first: freedom and liberty, love and affection, lust and desire, glee and joy, insight and vision, truthfulness and veracity, and (as above) work and labor. The English word may be better suited to physical conditions ("deep water"), the French one to a mental climate ("a profound essay"). With its more personal or visceral effect, Old English has been preferred statistically in poetry and oratory. For instance, in President Franklin Roosevelt's 1933 statement to America in the Depression, "The only thing we have to fear is fear itself," every word comes from Old English.

Doublets contribute to one of the greatest strengths of English: its richness (a French word) or wealth (an English word) of vocabulary. With its choice among words that *preexist* at different levels, English often can quickly capture shadings of meaning. And it can vary its word use to avoid repetition.

The two different roots of English affect its speech sounds and letters, too. Uniquely, our tongue combines factors of both major Western European language groups: the Germanic and Romance. A Germanic tongue, English nevertheless employs certain Romance-derived sounds like "j," which no Germanic language shares. (Most Germans might at first have trouble saying English "Germany," tending instead toward

continued

"Chermany.") Or there is the issue of letter K versus C. German and Scandinavian spellings greatly prefer the uncomplicated K and they downplay C. In Romance spellings, just the opposite: The C provides French or Italian with most of what's needed, and K is nearly superfluous, being used mainly for foreign-borrowed words. But English *k*isses both *c*amps. We favor spelling with C and we use a soft C before letters E, I, or Y, as taught to us by medieval French. Yet we depend, too, on K, for, unlike French, we have many words where a "k" sound precedes E, I, or Y—kennel, kin, picky— and K is the only way to show it.

• *The spread of printing.* The invention of a practical method of printing, by the goldsmith Johann Gutenberg of Mainz, in Germany, around A.D. 1452, is a landmark of world history. Along with the capture of Constantinople by the Ottoman Turks in 1453, the Gutenberg breakthrough is normally used by historians to mark the end of the Middle Ages and the beginning of the mature Renaissance or the modern era. The topic of early printing is addressed in a historical section on pages 179–83.

The creation of modern English can be traced back to the bloody welter of an October afternoon in A.D. 1066, on the southern coast of England. At the Battle of Hastings, about 30 miles east of Brighton, a French-speaking invasion force of perhaps 5,000 men led by Duke William of Normandy defeated 7,000 English defenders under England's King Harold and won for William the English throne. It was the only major battle of the invasion and would prove one of the most consequential in all history: From the en-

suing mixture of two societies, Norman French and Anglo-Saxon, a transformed nation and language would emerge.

Here, in a scene from the famous Bayeux Tapestry, Norman knights on horseback bear down on the English shield wall at the battle's start. The English, although disadvantaged in equipment and general readiness, would lose the day only after feigned Norman retreats had induced them to break ranks and be lured to ambush, and after King Harold had been killed in the melee.

The tapestry—technically not a tapestry, since the images are embroidered on, not woven in—was created within a generation of the battle and has traditionally been housed at Bayeux in northwestern France, once a Norman center. On a linen band 231 feet long, over 70 vivid scenes, in dyed wool fibers, depict the invasion's background and main events, primarily the battle; the borders, top and bottom, contain decorative or supplemental images; and running lettering provides a simple Latin narrative. In the scene shown, the Latin words are contra Anglorum exercitum (the final letter M denoted by the horizontal bar inside the V-like U); they represent the final words of a sentence, which in translation would be the last four words: "Duke William urges his men to prepare with courage and prudence for battle against the English army."

A charming, ornate capital H opens

the book of Exodus in the Grandval

Bible. See sidebar, pages 158–59.

SLIGHTLY ANEMIC H

ow narrowly H qualifies as a letter! H, our eighth letter, is our "least" letter, too. Its problem is its sound.

All other letters represent sounds created by expelled breath interacting with elements like the vocal cords, throat, tongue, teeth, or lips. Think of the sounds of A, K, or M. The H can lay claim to the expelling-of-breath part but nothing else; uniquely, its sound involves no other pronunciation.

Due to its weak phonetics, H has a history of fading out of words in English and other languages over time. And H has been the subject of humiliating debates by grammarians down the centuries, as to whether or not it even belongs in the alphabet. Although we classify H as a con-

A charming, ornate capital H opens the book of Exodus in the medieval, handwritten Latin Bible known as the Grandval Bible (after a Swiss abbey to which it once belonged). Penned sometime around A.D. 840 at the abbey of St. Martin at Tours, in west-central France, and now housed in London's British Library, this treasured manuscript is a prime example of Carolingian minuscule, Western Europe's foremost Latin handwriting style between about A.D. 800 and 1050. Carolingian minuscule was created under the Frankish king Charlemagne and it was destined, in a future century, to help inspire our modern print lowercase letter shapes. (See also pages 147–49 and 179–83.)

Not all of the page is in Carolingian style; rather, it presents a hierarchy of scripts. The three-word headline—"Here begins the book of Exodus"—is in traditional Roman square capitals, imitating the look of ancient Roman letters carved in stone. Below that and following the initial H, Verse 1 of Chapter 1 appears in the uncial pen style (on which see pages 142–43).

The opening words are *Haec sunt nomina filiorum Israhel qui ingressi sunt in Aegyptum,* "These are the names of the sons of Israel who entered Egypt." (In medieval Latin writing, a final letter M could be signified by a bar over the preceding vowel.) The word *Israhel* contains an uncial H, looking different from the square-capital opening H. The uncial h shape represents the earliest step toward our modern lowercase h.

Below the brief uncial passage, the text switches to Carolingian minuscules for Verse 2 and following. The lettering is wonderfully clear, although tiny in size (economical of space and materials). Note the difference between certain Carolingian and uncial letter shapes, such as B, G, and N, with the Carolingian shapes generally closer to modern lowercase print. (One exception is the long-

sonant, it could alternatively be treated as something that's not a letter: an "aspirate," or phonetic breathing.

Nor is H's marginal status helped by its oddball name. Why *aitch*? Most letters of English are named for their sounds; a con-

style Carolingian S, which confusingly resembles an f shape.) Note, too, the systematic use of a dot and space to end a sentence, with an enlarged letter beginning the first word of the next sentence.

The enlarged letters fall into three categories. Most are Carolingian minuscules "writ large"—the same lettering as the other text, penned slightly bigger. However, a sizable minority (the second category) are uncial letters, stuck among the minuscules. And a couple (the third category) are square capitals. In Bibles of this era, a single square capital was normally written as the initial letter of the first word of each new biblical chapter: Indeed, the words "chapter" and "capital" are related. Similarly, an uncial letter was used for the start of each new biblical verse, within a chapter.

Thus, here, Verse 2 of Chapter 1 (just under the big H) opens with an uncial R for *Ruben*—different-looking from the Carolingian-minuscule r of *Issachar,* four words later. Over to the right and up, at the right-hand column, a large capital E stands out to announce the first word of Chapter 2: *Egressus.* Directly two lines below, there is an uncial E, marking Verse 2 of Chapter 2. The uncial E looks different from both the square capital and the Carolingian e shapes nearby.

The three levels of hierarchy are reflected in the letters' sizes. Uncials are bigger than Carolingian letters. Bigger yet are the square capitals, of which the biggest of all is the book's opening letter—an H, in this case.

We see in such hierarchy the beginning of our modern treatment of text: Each letter is thought of as commanding more than one shape and/or size, to be used variously on a page, according to certain rules. Modern print uses mainly two categories: upper- and lowercase. The large Carolingian or uncial letter that begins sentences in the Grandval Bible has given way to the uppercase letter that opens our modern sentences.

---

sonant's name typically involves the sound itself plus a vowel sound: *bee, jay, en, ar.* Logically, H should be called "hee" or "hay." Instead, the name *aitch* doesn't even have the sound "h." Only one or two other letter names lack the relevant sounds: W's name is at least visually descriptive and Y's name, while missing the consonantal "y," does capture the letter's vowel sound, "i." What's the point of H's name?

First, the question of classification. Around A.D. 500, in the majestic city of Constantinople, the authoritative Latin grammarian Priscian judged H to be not a true letter. In the opus titled *Principles of Grammar,* drawing on the accumulated Latin scholarship of prior centuries, Priscian defined H as merely a symbol that announces a breathy pronunciation for the letter next to it, either before or after, in word spellings. Priscian (and his sources) had cottoned on to H's most intriguing trait: H seems to be as much about the sound alongside it as about its own sound.

All consonants rely to some extent on the letter next door. Consonants typically display their sound against a vowel. The sound of T, for example, is indistinct by itself, but it rings clearly when put next to a vowel or an agreeable consonant (as in the words "put next to"). H is the most extreme case: It is virtually inaudible alone. To be heard, H needs the A of "hat" or the E of "adhere" or the W-E of "when" (a word that in Old English was written and pronounced as *hwenne,* showing more clearly the H's function; most modern English WH- words originally were spelled HW-).

Yet in "hat" or "adhere" or "where," you could say the H is only coloring the pronunciation of the other letter, giving it some breath. By that notion, H wouldn't have to be treated as a letter itself. In an alphabet slightly different from ours, H could easily be shown as an accent mark, over the other letter.

Take the word "hill." We might find no disadvantage in turning the H into an accent, to go over the I. We'd still pronounce the word as "hill" but spell it as something like "îll." Similarly, the word "rehab" could be "reâb." And "when" could be "ŵen" or "wên."

That's pretty much how modern Greek does it. Greek writing denotes the sound "h" not as a letter but an accent mark, placed atop or alongside another letter that is to be pronounced breathily. The accent is routinely used, even in Greek words that English transliterates with the letter H, such as "Heracles" or "Rhodes." The Greek lettering of such words has no H letter, just the accent mark.

Once upon a time, ancient Greek did have a letter H, which became the grandparent of our H. But the ancient Greeks eventually saw they could economize by dropping that sound from their letter list and reassigning the symbol H to a different sound.

Not surprisingly, H's inferior status among the Romans and Greeks served to shape the thinking of later centuries, particularly among European enthusiasts of Greek and Latin. One such was the French Renaissance scholar and type designer Geofroy Tory (introduced on page 46 here). In his wonderful 1529 book on the alphabet, *Champ Fleury*, Tory deals gently but firmly with H: "The aspirate is not a letter; nonetheless, it is by poetic license given place as a letter."

That sentiment was still current 200 years later, at least for old-fashioned thinkers like Michael Maittaire, an English scholar of Greek and Latin who wrote a 1712 *English Grammar*. Remarkably, Maittaire does not include H among the other letters discussed in his introductory chapter; instead, he delegates H alone to a later chapter. As he explains loftily, "H is not properly a Letter; and its use will be taught among those marks which belong to Syllables."

Still, H has had its defenders. One was English playwright-poet-scholar Ben Jonson (heard from already on page 86 here). Jonson's 1640 *English Grammar* treats H evenhandedly. On one hand, Jonson ducks the issue of whether H is a letter or not: In his introductory run-through of the letters, Jonson does not discuss H at its alphabetical place but holds it till the very end, after Z, thus acknowledging a question or problem about H. Yet what he has to say is supportive: By any name, H is essential for our proper pronunciation of other letters—all the vowels and some of the consonants.

"H, whether it be a letter or no, hath been examined by the ancients, and by some of the Greek party too much condemned, and thrown out of the alphabet as an aspirate merely. . . . But, be it a letter or spirit, we have great use of it in our tongue, both before and after vowels. And though I dare not say she is (as I have heard one call her) the 'Queen-mother of Consonants,' yet she is the life and quickening of c, g, p, s, t, w, or also r when derived from the aspirate Greek *rh*."

Jonson here refers to H's role in seven pairings with other consonants—CH, GH, PH, SH, TH, WH, and RH—occurring mostly in words derived from Old English, otherwise from ancient Greek, for instance: cheat, sigh, telephone, shape, that, what, and rhapsody. These seven pairings have varied and complex histories; in olden days, the "h" sound was more in evidence among them generally than today. Regarding our modern English pronunciations, we can say that the H enriches the accompanying consonant (what, rhapsody), falls silent with it (sigh), or combines with it to create a new sound entirely (enough, cheat, telephone, shape, that).

Ideally, a sound like "sh" would have its own, single letter. (It does in Hebrew, for example, while "ch" has its own letter in Russian.) However, a reliance on two-letter combinations like SH, CH, or OI is an essential trait of written English, one way by which English is able to "save" on letters. Even with 26 letters, our alphabet is thinly stretched to cover the large number of English speech sounds.

*Th*anks to su*ch* letter pairings, H ranks *high* in rate of use, being about our nin*th*-most-often-used letter in Engli*sh* print, some*whe*re around R and just above D. Yet in an analysis of spoken English, the sound "h" ranks low, accounting for less than 1.5 percent of English speech sounds. Clearly H sees most of its action in written letter pairings.

H wasn't always so complicated. In the Phoenician alphabet of 1000 B.C., the eighth letter had a guttural sound like the German "ch" in "Bach." As with all Phoenician letters, the sound was demonstrated in the start of the letter's name. The letter was called *khet* (pronounced something like "kate" with a breathy, juicy K). The name perhaps meant "fence" in the Phoenicians' Semitic tongue.

Meanwhile the Phoenician speech sound "h" was covered by a different letter, named *he* (pronounced "hay"), at alphabetic place number 5. Today *he* has become our letter E, still the fifth letter, while *khet* has supplied our H, still the eighth letter.

When the Greeks copied the Phoenician alphabet around 800 B.C., both *he* and *khet* became Greek letters, with modifications. The Greeks transformed the subtle *he* into their vowel E, called *epsilon*. Then, to supply the "h" sound, the Greeks turned to the Phoenician eighth letter, *khet,* whose sound was at least similar to "h." The Greeks reassigned *khet* to the sound "h," and they altered the foreign name to a more Greek-sounding name. The ancient Greek letter is traditionally called *eta* (pronounced "eight-a"), yet undoubtedly its very earliest name was *heta* ("hate-a"), demonstrating the "h" sound. Either name was meaningless in Greek, aside from denoting the letter. In shape, the early Greek letter looked just like Phoenician *khet*.

This Greek *heta,* meaning the sound "h," at alphabetic place number 8, would reach Italy in the 700s B.C., destined for the alphabets of the Etruscans and Romans. Meanwhile, changes would occur in a distant branch of Greek writing, among

"East Greeks" of the Asia Minor west coast: Here the *heta* would be reassigned as a vowel letter, *eta,* denoting the Greek long E. Gradually the East Greek alphabet, with its vowel *eta,* would become general throughout Greece, after being adopted by the dynamic cultural city of Athens in about 400 B.C. Greek dialects that employed an "h" sound would then show such through an accent mark. This system has been inherited by modern Greek.

The West Greek "h" letter of the 700s B.C. took the shape ⊟. Reaching Italy, it was copied into the Etruscan alphabet, still at place number 8. The Etruscan letter, in turn, was copied into the newborn Roman alphabet around 600 B.C. Over time—and probably in imitation of a development being observed in the Greek alphabet, in the shape of the letter *eta*—the Roman letter shape shed its horizontal bars top and bottom, to look like H. The

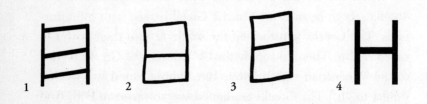

(1) Phoenician khet, *the "fence," from an inscription of about 1000 B.C. The eighth letter of the Phoenician alphabet,* khet *took a hard "ch" sound, as announced in the start of its name. The letter shape may have suggested a section of fencing, as for livestock: two poles with cords strung between. (2) By 900 B.C., Phoenician* khet's *shape had grown simpler. (3) Early Greek* heta *or* eta, *from an inscription of about 725 B.C. As part of the Greeks' copying of the Phoenician alphabet around 800 B.C., this letter kept the boxy shape and number-8 place of the Phoenician* khet *but took a new sound: "h." (4) Athenian Greek* eta *of about 400 B.C. In the "classical" Greek alphabet as written by the philosopher Plato and others,* eta *looked like our H but was sounded as a vowel, the Greek long E (pronounced like our long A). Three such* eta *vowels can be seen, for example, in the marble-carved "King Alexander" inscription of 334 B.C., on page 69. In modern Greek,* eta *takes a vowel sound rather like "ee."*

Romans called their letter something like *ha* (please don't laugh) and made good use of it.

The Romans' Latin language contained a fair percentage of words beginning with the sound "h." But in addition, the Romans began the practice of inserting H as a symbol for "thickening" the letter alongside; they did this specifically in transliterating Greek loan words into Latin—a consideration of increasing importance in the centuries leading up to the time of Christ, when Greek technology and cultural ideas were shaping Roman society.

Certain Greek letter sounds had no Latin equivalent. For four such Greek letters, the Romans felt they could approximate the Greek sound by writing the nearest-equivalent Latin letter with an H following, symbolizing a throatier or breathier pronunciation. Thus the Greek letter *khi,* sounding like a breathy K or C, came to be written in Latin not as a C alone but as C plus H. That was the birth of our hard CH (chrome, chronic, psychic), which in modern English almost always occurs in words from ancient Greek.

Similarly, the Romans used T plus H to approximate the Greek letter *theta,* which carried a sound (foreign to Latin) demonstrated in the start of the letter name. The Greek letter *rho* in certain breathy uses came to be written as a Roman RH. And the Greek letter *phi* became PH. Today in "Philip," "photo," or "Anglophile," the Greco-Latin PH is pronounced just like F, but in ancient times this must not have been the case, otherwise the utilitarian Romans would have written it as F, a letter they possessed. Rather, the sound of Greek *phi* fell between P and F, combining P's puff and F's hiss, in a way now lost to us.

Equipped with these four equivalents of Greek letters, a Roman gentleman of Cicero's day could attend a lecture on *philosophia* or a contest in *rhetorice,* see a performance at the *theatrum,* walk out and admire some *architectura,* or partake of any of a hundred other Greek-derived activities (and words)—and write about it in Latin.

Fast forward to about A.D. 1200. In Norman-ruled England, Norman-ethnic clergy and teachers, faced with the task of transliterating native English words into purely Roman letters, would borrow the old Roman H trick. They added H to another letter in word spellings, to signal a "thickening" of sound.

Traditional Anglo-Saxon writing employed about four special letters, beyond the received Roman letters, for showing certain sounds of English. Norman authorities, working to discourage and eradicate those English letters, relied heavily on H in substitutions. Thus the abundant English sound "th" (as in "thus," "the," etc.), previously written often as a single English letter called *thorn,* came to be represented by the two letters TH, exactly as in a Greek-to-Latin situation in ancient Rome.

Similarly, the breathy English "g" or "y" sound (once denoted by the English letter *yogh*) came to be spelled as GH, instead. However, it was GH's bad luck to be left behind by subsequent, general changes in English pronunciation. Originally, in words like "sight," "although," "cough," or "enough," the Norman GH-spelling mirrored the medieval pronunciations. Yet these pronunciations later changed, variously, and today the whole family of English GH words is notoriously unphonetic in spelling—to the frustration of purists like Irish author George Bernard Shaw (see page 138).

Our other written H combinations, SH, WH, and soft CH, were likewise created in the Middle Ages. Soft CH (cheese, latch) symbolizes an Old English sound originally written as a variant form of C. Norman authorities threw in an H, to bring the English spelling into line with French spelling, as in French *char* (cart). This Norman CH was destined, in both English and French, to admit confusion between the soft CH (cheer) and the hard CH of words with Greco-Roman backgrounds (choir, chorus).

The ambiguous CH is among the most irksome features of English spelling. For example, how do you pronounce the aeronautical term "Mach number"? (Hint: A hard question.)

Probably H's most distinctive trait is a tendency to fade from pronunciation, particularly at the start of words. This has happened dramatically in Romance languages: Once abundant in early Latin, the sound "h" has fairly drained away from Latin's descendant tongues. In modern Spanish and French, H is an empty shell, still written in words like *honor* and *honneur,* but never pronounced—although an "h" sound (as we would call it) has emerged in the Spanish pronunciation of J and soft G. Italian spelling omits H entirely (foreign terms excepted), hence Italian words like *orribile, onore,* and *eròico.* One hallmark of a French or Italian accent in English is the omission of the sound "h" or difficulty pronouncing it.

Evidently, such opening "h" sounds evaporated long before the Romance tongues were even born, amid general shifts in the spoken Latin of common folk under the later Roman Empire. Modern scholars, by studying variant word spelling in inscriptions, have traced the dropping of "h" back before A.D. 200.

English has experienced loss of opening "h" to a lesser and greater degree—lesser in official pronunciations and spellings, and greater in everyday speech. An "h" at the start of words was a strong element of Old English. Today the Old English legacy survives in countless words like "happy," "heart," and "hearth," where H is permanently at "home." Among words of Franco-Latin origin, however, English has inherited a sometimes-weaker H. All of our official silent-initial-H words come via medieval

French: heir, honest, honor, hour, and (in the United States) herb and homage.

During one medieval era, initial H was actually dropped from Old French spellings, a trend affecting Norman-ruled England, too, where French words were being spoken and written. Although the H's generally were put back later, a handful of modern English word spellings are still missing their original opening H. These include "able" (derived ultimately from Latin *habilis*), "ostler," meaning a stableman (from the "hosteler," or host at a hostel or hotel), and "arbor," meaning a kind of garden, derived from Old French *herbier* (and not from Latin *arbor,* meaning "tree").

In *spoken* English, meanwhile, H has suffered rather more hits. For example, many of us speak naturally of "an historian who has written a history book," pronouncing the H of "history" but not "historian." We do so because we unconsciously feel doubt about the "stopping power" of an H at the head of a syllable that's not accented (as in "his*tor*ian"): We tend to think of that H as not there, and the question is tested if the H-word is preceded by a vowel like the article "a." In print, the correct form is "a historian."

Certain American regional accents tend to swallow an initial H, especially in words of the H-plus-long-U-plus-M variety: human, humid, humor. A New York City–area accent can reduce "I saw him" to "I soaw'm," or "I said to her" to "I sed doer."

Of course, spoken English's best-known loss of initial H occurs in the London working-class accent traditionally called "Cockney," associated with the city's East End. As documented in print by British writers starting with elocutionist John Walker (1791)—and as embodied for most Americans in the Eliza Doolittle character of George Bernard Shaw's 1913 stage comedy-satire, *Pygmalion,* and its musical adaption of stage (1956) and screen (1964), *My Fair Lady*—the dropping of an initial H ("'ello") was the most striking aspect of the Cockney accent as opposed to that of a middle-class Londoner. Also, certain Cockneys were heard to overcompensate by placing H in front of vowels where it didn't belong. An anonymously written piece of about 1900 has the letter H complaining to the Cockneys that it has been banished "from 'ouse, from 'ome, from 'ope, from 'eaven; and placed by your most learned society in Hexile, Hanguish, and Hanxiety."

In class-bound Britain of the 19th and 20th centuries, the spoken H provided a small indicator of larger social divides. How you used H in your speech was a sign of which side of the railroad tracks you belonged to. As the unabridged 1933 *Oxford English Dictionary* explains under its "H" heading: "In recent times, the correct treatment of initial *h* in speech has come to be regarded as a kind of shibboleth of social position." (For the term "shibboleth," meaning "password," see page 293 here.)

Consequently, there arose a British adjective "H-less" or "aitchless," referring condescendingly to a labor-class Londoner or one of labor-class background, regardless of income. A published letter to the London *Times* of March 1894 sniffs at the political activism of a wife who "brings 'h-less' Socialists as guests to her husband's house." And a piece in the London lawyer's *Temple Bar Magazine* of July 1893 contains the memorable phrase, "Millionaire cheesemongers who dwell *h*-less in the feudal castles of the poor."

Shaw's *Pygmalion* concerns a scheme to remake the "guttersnipe" Cockney flower vendor Eliza into a refined lady and pass her off in polite society as a duchess, by first tutoring her to speak upper-class style—a process requiring much work on her H's. In the 1938 *Pygmalion* movie version (although not in Shaw's original script), Eliza must repeatedly and laboriously practice to pronounce the sentence "In Hampshire, Hereford, and Hertford, hurricanes hardly ever happen." A similar detail appears in *My Fair Lady.*

1   2   3   4   5

(1) Early Roman H, from a carved inscription of about 500 B.C. As copied from the Greeks by the Etruscans (700 B.C.) and from the Etruscans by the Romans (600 B.C.), this letter stood at place number 8 and took the sound "h." (2) By the late 200s B.C., Roman H had shed its horizontal bars top and bottom. In shape, sound, and alphabetical place, this Roman letter was now our H. (3) Roman carved H from the 100s A.D. This shape enjoys the pleasing effects of serifs and of a crossbar set slightly above midlevel—details maintained in modern type design. (4) An uncial H from a Latin Gospel penned in northern England around 700. This shape still suggests that of the capital, just shorn of its upper right bar, yet the uncial also looks ahead to our lowercase h. (5) A Carolingian minuscule h, from the first half of the 800s, clearly anticipates our lowercase form.

Outside of this lively literary corner, H seems to have had little impact on modern culture, perhaps due to its being claimed by the hemorrhoid medicine Preparation H (a product name always good for a laugh in teen-movie dialogue and similar). On chemistry's elemental chart, H stands for hydrogen: You can remember that easily, if troublingly, through the existence of an H-bomb.

As to H's peculiar name. Like most letters, H takes its English name from the medieval French version, introduced to England after the Norman Conquest of A.D. 1066. The Old French name was *hache* or *ache*—written both ways but in either case pronounced as something like "ah-cheh," with a soft "ch" sound. Today that old pronunciation and the spelling *ache* survive in H's name in Spanish.

Where did Old French "ah-cheh" come from? One modern theory claims that since the minuscule h looked like an upside-down hatchet, it was called in French the "hatchet" (*hache,* pronounced in olden days as "ah-cheh"). Yet a more plausible explanation traces the French name back to some name for H in late Latin, a name spoken in common parlance but nowhere recorded in writing.

As mentioned, H's official early Latin name was probably *ha.* By the early centuries A.D., however, that name probably shifted unofficially to something like *ahha*—a process described on page 127. Later still, the Latin name may have reached the form *accha* ("ah-cha"). In Old French of the 800s A.D., it emerged as *ache* ("ah-cheh"). Arriving in England after the Norman Conquest, the name became anglicized to the pronunciation "aitch."

*The shape of little i is charmingly incorpo-
rated in a French engraved scene, one of an
alphabetical series, of 1865.*

[INDEFATIGABLE I]

Imagine the I as a pillar, supporting its substantial share of English in writing and print. Now count the I's in the preceding sentence (12 in 16 words) and you'll see what I mean—and what I can do, and how busy I may be, no, not me, I'm referring to I . . . Ah, skip it.

One of our five main vowel letters, I is by some counts the fourth-most-often used letter in English print, below E, T, and A. (Other counts put it sixth, below O and N also; all three letters hover in the same range.) I's strong showing is due partly to its place in the verb "is" and in the "-ing" ending of English participles and gerunds. Also, the I shows up frequently in combinations with other vowels, especially E.

The pronunciation of I and E together is notoriously varied, as in the words: varied, sieve, dried, friend, rein, receive, height. By itself, I has two main English sounds, short and long, as in "tin mine."

While short I is pronounced much the same from language to language, our English long I is a maverick: Long I means something different in English from what it means in any other European tongue. Spanish, German, or Czech, for instance, would pronounce long I as rhyming with "sea" (as in Spanish *si*), not with "sigh." While such languages may contain the vowel sound of "sigh," they don't spell it as "I" but usually as "EI" combined. Example: German *drei* (pronounced "dry"), meaning "three."

The "ee" pronunciation of long I is the original and proper one, dating back to the ancient European tongues of Greek, Etruscan, and Latin. English stands apart, due to the mysterious vowel-pronunciation shift in England during the 1400s and 1500s A.D. Prior to that time, the medieval English long I was evidently pronounced closer to "ee." The word "life," typically spelled as "lif," would have sounded like "leaf." Likewise, the medieval English name for I—derived from Old French and imitative of the vowel's long sound—was more like "ee" than "eye." In modern French, the name is still pronounced "ee."

This continental "ee"-for-I has snuck into modern English in words borrowed mainly from Italian or French since the Middle Ages: pizza, piano, clique, liaison, to name a few; also ski (Norwegian) and Fiona (Gaelic). Among I's other variant sounds are the interesting effects in front of R. In words like "fir" and "nadir," the short I reduces to an indistinct vowel sound, a schwa; yet long I before R will stretch dramatically to almost two vowel sounds: "hire" and "fire" rhyme with "liar." In certain positions before another noun—million, union—the I may take the consonantal sound "y," about which more will be said in the next chapter.

But probably I's most distinctive feature is visual: the starkness of its shape. It is the skinniest and simplest of our letters. Traditionally, capital I has been essential to type designers, as the starting point for the creation of a typeface. The designer's I supplies the typeface's basic straight line, to be incorporated into most other letters: A, B, N, etc. As none less than German master artist Albrecht Dürer wrote, in a 1535 treatise on letter design: "Almost all the other letters are formed after this letter, although always something has to be added to it or taken away."

The I being all straight, some designers recognize a *second* essential type-design letter—that one that's all curved, O. "Given an O and an I of any alphabet, we can make a very good guess at the forms of the other letters," the famous British designer Edward Johnston observes in his book *Writing and Illuminating, and Lettering* (1906).

Lowercase i is the alphabet's smallest letter. In legibility, this creates a potential shortcoming (pardon the pun) that has affected i's fortunes through the centuries. For example, the medieval i originally had no dot but acquired one because the letter as a hatless stroke was hard to distinguish on a crowded page of handwriting. By about A.D. 1000 the custom had arisen of perhaps topping the minuscule letter with a slanted mark, at the writer's discretion: í. With the spread of printing in the late 1400s, the stroke was generally reduced to an economical dot in many typefaces, although the stroke still shows up today in cursive-print wedding invitations and similar. The i's dot, meanwhile, has become proverbial for any small detail, in our expression "to dot the i's and cross the t's."

Another way in which medieval writers solved the "i-legibility" problem was to substitute a minuscule letter y, as it was easier to read. Thus, "his" might be spelled as "hys," for example. This expedient led to the increased popularity of letter Y and to its rise as a challenger to I in medieval and Renaissance English spellings (about which, more in Chapter Y).

Uppercase I, too, can be a headache, at least for modern graphic designers. For instance, at the New York City–based magazine *Vanity Fair* in the mid-1980s, editors were requested not to allow the text of their finalized articles to begin with any word opening with the letter I. The reason: An opening letter in the magazine would normally be rendered as a drop capital, and a capital I in the sans-serif fonts favored at *Vanity Fair* would look like: I. That shape, stuck in the upper left margin of a text page, was not easily recognizable as a letter of the alphabet but seemed rather to be a design ornament. Hence the editorial embargo against a starting I.

More recently, the letter has turned some of its shortfalls into gains. Today little i, meaning "computer connection," his joined e, X, and a handful of other letters as a brand mark of the digital revolution. In 1998 Apple Computer introduced its sleek iMac model. The "i" signified Internet, for which the iMac was specifically designed, but the real message was in the styling—the way the i stood stuck against the M, announcing some special feature within a superb organic composition. The name sent the message of "high tech and groovy"—and iMitation began immediately. Today brand names like iVillage, iHome, iTime, iPower, iPlane, and dozens more all promise to harness the power of computer search or remote control for your convenience.

Unlike most letter shapes through history, I's shape, from its earliest stages, grew *less* distinctive, not more so. In around 1000 B.C., the tenth sign of the Phoenician alphabet was called *yod*. Like all Phoenician letters, it was a consonant whose sound was demonstrated in the opening sound of its name: "y" in this case. The name *yod* meant "arm and hand" in ancient Semitic speech, and the letter's shape, a bit like a Z with crossbar, did suggest a jointed elbow-wrist-hand extension.

By about the mid-900s B.C., Phoenician *yod* had been copied into the newly created Hebrew alphabet, for the writing of that language. Today the tenth Hebrew letter is still called *yod* and takes the sound "y." But the letter shape has changed considerably, shrinking to a mere pen stroke—so that *yod,* for its part, is the smallest of today's Hebrew letters.

When the Greeks took their turn copying the Phoenician letters, around 800 B.C., they reassigned a handful of Phoenician letters to be the vowel letters needed for the writing of Greek. Presumably because *yod*'s "y" sound naturally suggested the vowel sound "i," the Greeks made *yod* their I vowel. The Greek letter's sound was "i" short and "ee" long.

Having no tie to a Phoenician word for "arm and hand," the Greeks altered the name to *iota*—more Greek-sounding although otherwise meaningless in Greek. They soon straightened the letter's shape to an austere vertical stroke, probably in order to distinguish *iota* from their S letter, *sigma,* which was a zigzag.

Greek letters of the day had only one shape, no minuscule versus majuscule. But the *iota* stroke was simple enough to suggest a metaphor, and eventually the word *iota* took on a second meaning in Greek—anything small in size or, particularly, the least element in a bigger group. Our familiar phrase "not one iota" comes from Greek, specifically from the biblical book of Matthew (5:18), written in Greek in the 1st century A.D. In the King James Bible of 1611, the word *iota* is translated as "jot." Our word "jot" derives from Greek *iota,* with the same metaphorical meaning.

Meanwhile, in ancient Italy, the Greek alphabet was copied by the Etruscans (700 B.C.) and the Etruscan one was copied and

1   2   3   4   5   6

(1) Phoenician yod, *whose name meant "arm and hand" (800 B.C.). Like all Phoenician letters,* yod *was a consonant; it took the "y" sound, demonstrated at the start of its name. (2) The early Greek* iota—*this example from an inscription of about 740 B.C.—loosely imitated the* yod*'s shape. The Greeks had copied* iota *from the Phoenician letter but had reassigned it to be the vowel I. (3) By about 725 B.C.,* iota*'s shape had become an austere line. The Greeks straightened it perhaps to avoid confusion with their zigzag letter* sigma. *(4) Serifs have never looked better than on this Roman capital I, from Trajan's Inscription of A.D. 113. In marble-carved inscriptions, the Romans gave weight and dignity to the letter shape. The Romans also narrowed the letter's shape in the middle, to avoid the illusion of bulging created by a perfectly straight vertical bar. (5) An inked letter in the Carolingian minuscule style, from a manuscript of the 900s. The shape makes reference to the Roman capital but also looks ahead somewhat to our lowercase i. (6) A dotted minuscule* i *from a handwritten Latin prayer book from Italy, early 1500s. The scribe's accentlike jot would later be finalized as the printer's dot.*

adapted by the Romans (600 B.C.). The I-stroke entered the Roman alphabet as the ninth letter, where it remains for us today. The Romans called it something like "ee" and employed it as both short "i" and long "ee." After Rome's fall (A.D. 500), this Roman I passed into the alphabets of new European tongues like French, Spanish, and, eventually, English.

"I" meaning "me" emerged in English starting around 1150, from an Old English pronoun *ic,* related to the modern German pronoun *ich* (meaning "I"). This English pronoun "I"—gradually shifting in pronunciation from "ee" to our long-I sound—could be written as "i," "y," or "Y." With the spread of printing in the 1500s, it settled down as "I."

Among Other Vast Effects, the Advent of Printing Would Finalize Our Alphabet

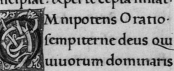

It looks like print, but look again. This page of handwritten Latin, from a prayer book penned by a monk in Naples in A.D. 1477, is a superb example of humanist script. Aside from the dotless i's and the "long" s (shaped like an *f* and appearing at the beginning and middle of words), the letter shapes are not too different from those in this morning's newspaper.

The term "humanist" or "Humanist" indicates a post-medieval spirit of enlightenment, including a reverence for non-Christian ancient Greco-Roman literature, evident in Renaissance Italy especially. Humanist handwriting, emerging at Florence in the early 1400s, married together two different lettering traditions: the capital letter shapes of ancient Roman stone-carving, whose surviving relics were visible at many Italian sites of the day, and the small letter shapes of the Carolingian minuscule ink style of the 800s to 1000s, as discovered by humanist scholars in old manuscripts. (On Carolingian minuscule, see pages 147–49 and 158–59.) Humanist capitals were copied from old Roman capitals; humanist minuscules were based, somewhat more loosely, on Carolingian letters; in a text, the two tiers operated much like our upper- and lowercase letters today.

With the advent of print, the humanist shapes would be copied into the earliest typefaces of the style called "roman," which today supply our favored typefaces for books, newspapers, and magazines.

continued

The invention of a practical means of printing, in Germany in the mid-1400s A.D., changed the world. By allowing for quick and relatively cheap reproduction of writings, printing revolutionized literacy on a scale comparable with the original spread of the alphabet in the second and first

A print shop scene, from an engraving by one J. van Velde, in a Dutch book of 1628. The three workers, in chronological order of the printing process, are the typesetter, seated at right; the inker, at left; and the pressman, center. The typesetter is arranging metal blocks of type on a composing board, having selected them from the compartmentalized trays at his right. His arrangement creates (in mirror image) the words of a page to be printed. He works from a model page, handwritten or printed, lying on his desk. Meanwhile, the pressman is lowering a long sheet of paper onto perhaps two sections of prepared type. The type has been locked into a frame, face-up, on the printing press's "bed" (lower surface) and has been swabbed with ink. Next the paper will be clamped evenly against the inked type by the descending "platen" (upper surface) of the press. The printed sheet will be replaced by a clean sheet, and so on, perhaps hundreds of times. Later the same sheet will be printed on the other side, and the later still it will be woven into the produced book, providing two two-sided pages.

millennia B.C. Thanks to printing, whole segments of society below the wealthy classes gained a chance to own or borrow books. In 1400 a single handwritten copy of a book might represent two months' work by a scribe; in 1500 a printing press could run off 500 copies in a week, with a commensurate difference in retail price.

Not just books were involved. Printing brought the true beginning of journalism, advertising, and public notification. In 1776, for example, the Declaration of Independence was handwritten but then printed for distribution through the thirteen colonies, to be read aloud and posted in town squares. By empowering the middle classes, printing contributed to huge social changes in early modern Europe, of which the Protestant Reformation (1500s) was but the first.

One of printing's strongest effects was on individual languages. Like television, but less so, print worked toward homogenizing a language, by strengthening the influence of commercial centers like Paris, London, Cologne, Rome, and Venice. Through print, the vocabulary and usage of Parisian French or London English began to bear more heavily on other dialects. England's first printer, William Caxton, set up shop in London (1476) because that was where the business was. But the London market determined much of Caxton's choices and treatment of books: The English language in a Caxton book would need to be an English that London could understand. Thus, London English circulated in books through the country. We hear of one incident, around 1495, when Caxton's business heir reprinted an older English book, having edited the language to bring it into line with current London speech; he might have changed *twey* to "two," *wend* to "go," and so on. Changes like those in print hastened the development of a standard English. Gradually regional dialects were leveled, much as regional accents have been leveled by the effects of radio and TV since the 1920s.

The mechanics and early history of printing can be dealt with only briefly here. The general notion of printing onto paper is much older

continued

than Johann Gutenberg. For centuries prior to 1400, China and Korea had been printing text from inked blocks of wood, the carved wood surface being perhaps an entire page. Similarly, European artisans since the early 1400s were printing illustrations from woodblocks or engraved metal sheets. (Today we still call a reproduced image a "print.") But there was no versatile way to print text. For this, some kind of movable lettering would be needed.

The theoretical solution—obvious probably to many at the time—was to create individual letters on little blocks. (The letter would be presented as a mirror image in relief.) You would need many letter blocks, so as not to run out of any letter in preparing multiple pages at once. For durability and precision, the blocks would have to be metal, not wood. There were four challenges: (1) to find the right metal to combine toughness with malleability for casting; (2) to find a casting method to make all the letter blocks exactly the same size; (3) to find a nonsmear ink; and (4) to find a way to press the inked letters evenly to the paper.

These problems were solved in about 1450 by a middle-age goldsmith in Mainz, in western Germany: Johann Gensfleisch, called Gutenberg (good mountain) from the name of his wealthy family's estate. The metal he chose was an alloy of lead, tin, and antimony; and his pressing method, as the world knows today, was a wooden machine, a screw-operated press, inspired no doubt by the grape presses of the Rhineland vineyards near Mainz.

Details of Gutenberg's life and work remain murky. After printing a masterpiece—his Latin Bible of about 1455, of which 47 copies survive today—Gutenberg lost his press shop in a lawsuit brought by his investor, Johann Fust. Fust, probably using Gutenberg's equipment and plans, soon produced one of the most beautiful books ever, the Mainz Psalter, illustrated here on page 64.

Meanwhile, Gutenberg's equipment and process were copied by other metalsmiths, who became Europe's first generation of printers.

Within 15 years of Gutenberg's Bible, printing presses were operating in Strasbourg, Cologne, Basel, Rome, Venice, and Paris.

The move to Italy had great consequences for the alphabet, for in Italy the market demanded different letter shapes from those of German print (which were based on German medieval handwriting). Italian readers wanted letter shapes like those of the lovely humanist handwriting of Rome and Florence. (See page 179.) Humanist shapes thus got finalized in print, in typefaces known as roman and (a slanted, thinner variant) italic—the names reflecting their 15th-century Italian origins and their partial legacy from ancient Rome. The perfection of early roman type was achieved in about 1470 by a French printer, Nicolas Jenson, working in Venice. Today roman shapes are what most people think of as our letters.

The arrival of print finalized the alphabet in other ways, too. The little i now got its dot; the use in England of Old English letters *yogh* and *thorn* became greatly reduced, as these shapes did not exist in continental-made letter casts; and so on. Most important, print mechanics demanded that letter shapes be uniform in size and consistent in style within a typeface. Variant or fancy letter shapes had to be used sparingly, for an obvious reason: Letters now came from laboriously produced metal casts, not from the tip of a pen.

The new value on consistency helped call into question certain ill-defined uses of letter shapes. For example, the shapes J and I were being used interchangeably to mean either a vowel sound or a consonant sound (which in English was "j"), and similarly, shapes U and V were used interchangeably for a vowel or a consonant, "u" or "v." In the hands of printers of the 1500s and 1600s, shapes J and V gradually became assigned exclusively to the consonant sounds. Later J and V would officially join the alphabet as our final two additions, letters 25 and 26.

This elegant J was penned by the famous American type designer Frederic W. Goudy (1865–1947), based on ornamental forms found in European manuscripts of the 1200s A.D. Our J shape originated in medieval handwriting styles, as a hook-tailed version of the letter I.

THE BIRTH OF A LETTER

Just as flowing water follows gravity, letters follow language. Their job is to show sounds of speech. If sounds change, so will letters, in some way, eventually.

If a language evolves new sounds, its alphabet has to catch up, probably by adding sounds to existing letters or (a step further) by inventing a brand-new letter or two.

Such is the story of J, our 10th letter in alphabetical order but historically one of two last letters (with V) to join the Roman alphabet. Ancient Romans of A.D. 100 had 23 letters only: no J, V, or W. Ancient Latin had no sound "j," hence no letter for it. The "j" sound arose later in European speech, amid tidal shifts that transformed Latin into the medieval Romance tongues.

Even after the sound became common, the letter was slow to emerge. Not until the 1500s A.D., amid the standardizing effect of printing, did J start to appear systematically in spellings of French and other European languages.

In English spellings, J had arrived by 1640. Nevertheless, over the next 200 years, J was not recognized universally as a separate letter but (for reasons explained below) was viewed by some as a variant of letter I. Only in the mid-19th century, under influence of new dictionaries by Noah Webster (1828) and others, did J and V gain full acceptance and follow W into our alphabet.

J was born from I, the preceding letter in alphabetical order. The pregnancy and birth labor took 1,000 years, from about 500 to 1500, the entire Middle Ages. Prior to that, the affair began in language, in spoken and written Latin of the Roman Empire.

With no sound "j," the closest that ancient Latin came in sound was the consonant "y." This sound was written with letter I. Latin I could thus be either a vowel or a consonant. Comparison may be made with our English Y, which is a vowel in words like "fly" and "cycle" but a consonant in "yes" and "canyon"— and practiced readers have no trouble distinguishing the two roles. If Y precedes a vowel letter, Y is probably a consonant, sounded as "y." Latin I worked much the same.

Latin consonant I occurred only in front of a vowel letter, usually A or U, as in the word *iam* (now), pronounced "yahm" or perhaps "iy-yahm." Even in front of a vowel, the letter I might not always be a consonant. A Roman name like Claudia treated I as a vowel, forming a separate syllable: "Cloud-i-ah."

The name Claudia shows how consonantal I could be considered a natural facet of vowel I. Say the name carefully and you'll hear a faint "y," riding uninvited between the I and A: Cloud-i-(y)ah. That's because vowel I can create a "y" sound in front of a following vowel. You hear it in English: triad, I am, lazier, lion.

No doubt this factor recommended the letter I to the earliest Roman adapters of the alphabet, circa 600 B.C., for part-time work as a consonant symbol. The Greek and Etuscan writing systems, models to the Roman, were already employing their letter I that way.

Many modern uses of English J go back to Latin consonantal I. The Roman gods whom we call Jupiter, Juno, and Janus actually had Latin names Iuppiter, Iuno, and Ianus (pronounced "Yupp-piter," "Yoono," "Yahnus"). Janus was patron god of the doorway (*ianua*), connected also to the Roman word for doorkeeper, *ianitor*, whence our janitor. The Roman calendar opened with the month of *Ianuarius*, January.

Julius Caesar was actually named Iulius (Yoolius). The emperor Trajan was Traianus (Trah-yahn-us). In Rome, if you caused someone an *iniuria* (injury), you might be hauled before the *iudices* (judges) in a court of *iustitia* (justice). There you'd swear innocence by the emperor's *maiestas* (majesty) and you'd call witnesses: your *coniunx* (spouse) and your brother, the one who's *iunior* (younger). Whatever future claim the letter J might have on these words in English, they began in Latin with rather different sounds and spellings.

Nor did the sound "j" sneak in under letter G. Latin G was always hard, no matter what letter followed. A Roman jewel was a *gemma,* the G pronounced as in English "gum."

But changes in spoken Latin were under way during the centuries prior to the Roman Empire's collapse in around A.D. 500, and they accelerated after. As Latin broke into regional dialects that grew into French and other Romance tongues, pronunciations shifted beneath traditional Latin spellings that were slower to change. Modern scholars trace pronunciation shifts by analyzing variant spellings in late Latin writings and general spellings in early Romance writings, such as the Old French Strasbourg Oath

The consonantal I of ancient Roman writing is dramatically recalled in the crucifixion story, in the detail of the lettered plaque that Roman officials posted on the cross—here included in a Lamentation-scene woodcut by German artist Albrecht Dürer (about 1496). Jesus during his lifetime probably bore the Hebrew name Yeshua *(Joshua), which the Romans pronounced as "Yay-sus" and transliterated as* Iesus. *Jesus' ethnic group called themselves* Yehudim *(Jews), a word approximated in Latin as* Iudaei, *pronounced "Yewd-eye-ee." At Jesus' execution, the Roman letters INRI formed the initials of a sarcastic Latin title:* Iesus Nazarenus Rex Iudaeorum, *"Jesus of Nazareth, King of the Jews."*

of 842. (See page 147.) Studies show how the "y" sound of consonantal I slurred gradually to new sounds, involving a more relaxed tongue position.

In medieval Spanish, the new sound was "h." In medieval French, Italian, and Portuguese, the consonant reached a sound very like our J. For example, ancient Latin's word for justice, *iustitia* (yus-tih-ti-a) turns up in early Spanish writing as *iusticia*, pronounced something like "hoos-tee-see-a." The same Latin root produces Old French *iustice*, pronounced something like "joos-tee-seh."

These changes affected the sense of letter I. No longer were its vowel and consonant sounds logically linked, as in ancient Rome. Now they were two unrelated sounds. Letter I had become really two sounds sharing one written shape: a first step toward its eventual split into a second shape.

Developments in Old French would prove highly relevant to the story of English after 1066, when the Norman invasion of England brought Norman French vocabulary and spelling rules (and much else, besides) to the Anglo-Saxons. Old English apparently had no native sound "j." That sound now entered the English stream as a French borrowing.

As mentioned, Old French "j" was pronounced like our modern English J—in fact, more like ours than like modern French J, which is pronounced like the S in English "measure." Modern English preserves the Old French sound, while in France itself the sound continued changing, growing smoother through the Middle Ages.

Like other of our consonant sounds, "j" is phonetically more complex than we might think. You place your tongue behind your upper teeth, as if about to say "d" or "t," but then you blow forward, buzzing, as with a fricative like "sh" or "f." The process has saddled sound "j" with the ponderous title of voiced palatal-alveolar affricate—in which "palatal-alveolar" refers to your starting tongue position and "voiced" to your use of your vocal cords, while "affricate" denotes a consonant sound that ends in a fricative release, a tightly channeled expulsion of air. English uses only two affricates: "j" and "ch." The two are closely akin phonetically, "ch" being the unvoiced counterpart of "j."

Many modern languages lack the sound "j," just as ancient Latin and Old English did. German and the Scandinavian tongues have no "j." When speakers of these languages are learning English, they may substitute the sound "y" for "j"—hence expressions like "*Yum*pin' *Yim*minny" from jovial Swedish-immigrant characters in 1940s and '50s Hollywood films.

In Geoffrey Chaucer's England, around 1380, sound "j" occurred all over Middle English, in words borrowed from French, derived mainly from Latin. Two different letters represented the sound: consonantal I, as in Middle English *maiestie* (majesty) and *iustice* (justice), and soft G, as in "gem" and "Geoffrey." The use of these letters, like the sound "j" itself, was a French feature that had passed to English. The sound as yet had no letter of its own.

But it needed one. Europe's spoken languages were settling down as written forms in their own right, alongside literary Latin, and the part-time use of letter I had come to seem inadequate for the frequent sound "j" in English and French or "h" in Spanish. The need was felt for a new letter, to symbolize more authoritatively the new sounds.

Meanwhile, there existed in European writing a variant shape for minuscule letter i. Scribes working within certain handwriting traditions—typically in medieval Latin, for religious or legal documents—had for centuries been drawing an elongated i, with a tail hanging below the baseline. The tail might point straight down or hook leftward (the preferred form over time). If the handwriting style normally capped the i with a dot or stroke, then the tailed i would likewise be capped: j.

The Latin word iusti, *"righteous men," is framed in two i letters with tails, in the uncial pen style, from a Psalter of the 400s A.D. The tailed letter shape of this era was an embellishment only, with no meaning for pronunciation. A thousand years would pass before the J form came to be reserved for a certain sound—although not the same sound—in Spanish, French, English, German, and other European tongues.*

The tailed form originally meant nothing for pronunciation: The tail was purely visual, an ornament to distinguish little i on a crowded page of handwriting. Like any other i of the era, the form j could be either vowel or consonant. Often it was chosen to begin or end a word. The Latin word *filii* (sons) might be written as filij, the word *iusti* (righteous men) as justj. But most handwriting traditions avoided the tailed form in a capital position, such as the start of a proper name or of a book chapter, where a capital I form would be used instead.

A tailed minuscule i begins the Latin phrase ignis in aqua *(fire in water), from the celebrated Grandval Bible, written in France around A.D. 840. (See pages 158–59 for a description of this Bible, a splendid specimen of Carolingian minuscules.) The words are from the Apocryphal book of* The Wisdom of Solomon *(19:19).*

What happened next, starting by 1500, was that the variant letter shape and the variant letter sound gravitated toward each other. Gradually the j became reserved exclusively for the consonantal sound "j" in French and English (or "h" in Spanish), even though that wasn't the shape's original meaning.

The marriage was prompted by printing's spread through Western Europe, after about 1470. In general, the mechanics of print ordained that letter shapes be clearly distinguished and limited in number. A printer's box could hold only so many letter blocks, which were small metal casts. Where once a variant letter shape had seemed a token of a penman's skill, it now became impractical. If the shape j were to be included as a letter block, it would need a specific job—an assignment that cried out to be matched with the consonantal I sound.

The earliest fixed use of j was in Spain. Here, soon after printing's arrival in the 1470s, we find the shape j for the consonant and the shape i for the vowel, in all lowercase uses in the Spanish language. A capital shape J followed, appearing in Spanish print before 1600. Thus, with no change of pronunciation, the holy name Iesus ("Hay-soos" in Spanish) came to be spelled as Jesus. The word *iusticia* (hoos-tee-see-a) became *justicia*. Modern Spanish still uses J to mean the sound "h," Spanish H being silent.

Publication in Spain helped promote J for other languages. In German lands, where consonantal I took the native sound "y," that I eventually became replaced by J in spellings. Thus, German J got the job that in England had already been assigned, for other reasons, to letter Y. German J still denotes sound "y": Swiss psychologist Carl Jung stays "young" forever.

In France, where consonantal I meant the "shj" sound, this sound was now pursued by letter shape J. The J began to replace consonantal I in French print and handwriting after about 1570. With no pronunciation change, French *iustice* became *justice*;

maiesté became *majesté*; and the French name Iules, derived from imperial Roman Iulius, was now spelled Jules.

Italian, meanwhile, rejected J after early experimentation and instead denoted the sound "j" with a soft G—either G in front of the old I when followed by A or U, or G *instead of* I before other vowels. Today, among Italian words starting with the sound "j," Jesus is Gésu, justice is *giustizia,* and Julius is Giulio (from which the surname Giuliani derives). Italian uses letter J only for foreign words already in print, like "jazz."

In England, the changeover from I to J was guided partly by examples of similar French words, like "justice." Still, the English transition was slow and irregular, taking from about 1580 to the 1630s. The two printed masterpieces of the age, the King James Bible (1611) and the First Folio collection of Shakespeare's plays (1623), use I in the old way and don't use J—except that the Folio does have J capitals in the table of contents and other secondary text, a sign apparently of the publishers' ambivalence about J. Other English print of the time might show the consonant as I for capitals but j for lowercase. And there was flux between J and soft G, in spellings like *maiestie, magestie,* and *majesty,* all for the same word.

Even after J became standard to English-language print, many people considered it a facet of letter I and not a letter unto itself. (Similar controversy attended V in relation to its mother letter, U.) The English alphabet of about 1640 had 24 letters. Scholars debated for generations afterward whether J and V should be admitted officially as two letters more, to stand next to their respective vowel letters in alphabetical order. London schoolmaster Thomas Dyche's grammar book, *A Guide to the English Tongue* (1707), lists 26 letters, but Samuel Johnson's monumental *Dictionary of the English Language* (1755) stands fast at 24, handling J as a variant of I and V as a variant of U.

The life and death of King Iohn.

Actus Primus, Scæna Prima.

Enter King Iohn, Queene Elinor, Pembroke, Essex, and Sa-
lisbury, with the Chattylion of France.

King Iohn.

Ow say *Chatillion*, what would *France* with vs ?
Chat. Thus (after greeting)speakes the King
of France,
In my behauiour to the Maiesty,
The borrowed Maiesty of *England* heere.
Elea. A strange beginning : borrowed Maiesty ?
K.Iohn. Silence (good mother)heare the Embassie.
Chat. *Philip of France*, in right and true behalfe
Of thy deceased brother, *Geffreyes* sonne,
Arthur Plantaginet, laies most lawfull claime
To this faire Iland,and the Territories :
To *Ireland, Poyctiers, Aniowe, Torayne, Maine*,
Desiring thee to lay aside the sword
Which swaies vsurpingly these seuerall titles,
And put the same into yong *Arthurs* hand ,

Which none but heauen, and you, and I, shall heare.
Enter a Sheriffe.
Essex. My Liege, here is the strangest controuersie
Come from the Country to be iudg'd by you
That ere I heard : shall I produce the men ?
K.Iohn. Let them approach :
Our Abbies and our Priories shall pay
This expeditious charge : what men are you?
Enter Robert Faulconbridge, and Philip.
Philip. Your faithfull subiect, I a gentleman,
Borne in *Northamptonshire*, and eldest sonne
As I suppose, to *Robert Faulconbridge* ,
A Souldier by the Honor-giuing-hand
Of *Cordelion*, Knighted in the field.
K.Iohn. What art thou?
Robert. The son and heire to that same *Faulconbridge*.
K.Iohn. Is that the elder, and art thou the heyre ?
You came not of one mother then it seemes.
Philip. Most certain of one mother, mighty King,

---

*Early 17th-century English ambivalence toward the J (a letter invented on the continent,
after all) has left a mark on the First Folio collection of Shakespeare's plays, published in
London in 1623, seven years after his death. Letter J never appears in the main text,
which uses old-fashioned I and i. Above: On the opening page of the tragedy* King John,
*"John" and "majesty" are "Iohn" and "Maiesty." Yet J does appear in italicized secondary
text such as page headlines—but only in capital form, not lowercase, and never in Shake-*

Johnson uses J and V in spellings throughout his dictionary—
including the J to spell his own last name—but in editorial comments he rejects the reform of actually placing them in the
alphabet. He gives neither J nor V a dictionary heading; his headings run "H, I, K, L" and "T, U, W, X." Words beginning with

What woman poſt is this? hath ſhe no husband
That will take paines to blow a horne beforeſher?
O me, 'tis my mother : how now good Lady,
What brings you heere to Court ſo haſtily ?

Enter Lady Faulconbridge and Iames Gurney.

Lady. Where is that ſlaue thy brother? where is he ?
That holds in chaſe mine honour vp and downe.
Baſt. My brother *Robert,* old Sir *Roberts* ſonne :
Colbrand the Gyant, that ſame mighty man,

Scæna Secunda.

Enter before Angiers, Philip King of France, Lewis, Daul-
phin, Auſtria, Conſtance, Arthur.

Lewis. Before *Angiers* well met braue *Auſtria,*
Arthur that great fore-runner of thy bloud,
Richard that rob'd the Lion of his heart ,

---

62   *The Tragedie of Romeo and Juliet.*

French ſlop : you gaue vs the the counterfait fairely laſt
night.
Romeo. Good morrow to you both, what counterfeit
did I giue you ?
Mer. The ſlip ſir, the ſlip, can you not conceiue?

Nur. Out vpon you: what a man are you ?
Rom. One Gentlewoman,
That God hath made, himſelfe to mar.
Nur. By my troth it is ſaid , for himſelfe to, mar qua-
t ha: Gentlemen, can any of you tel me where I may find

The Tragedie of Romeo and Iuliet.   79

I married them; and their ſtolne marriage day
Was *Tybalts* Doomeſday : whoſe vntimely death
Baniſh'd the new-made Bridegroome from this Citie :
For whom (and not for *Tybalt*) *Iuliet* pinde.
You, to remoue that ſiege of Greefe from her,

And then in poſte he came from *Mantua*
To this ſame place, to this ſame Monument.
This Letter he early bid me giue his Father,
And threatned me with death, going in the Vault,
If I departed not, and left him there.

---

speare's stage directions, even though italicized. Notice King John *versus* Iames Gurney
(above, top). *Even the italicized headlines can be inconsistent, as in* Juliet *versus* Iuliet *on
the* Romeo and Juliet *pages* (center and bottom). *Apparently the publishers wanted the
Bard's own words kept clean of newfangled J, which they used inconsistently otherwise.
But within a generation after the Folio, the J would be standard to English spelling, in
place of consonantal I.*

J are distributed under heading "I," and ditto for V and "U."
Johnson's first entry under heading "I" is the pronoun "I," followed immediately by entries for "Jabber" and "Jabberer," which
are followed eventually by "Jackal," "Jam," "Iambick," "Jangle,"
"Ibis," "Ice," "Idiot," "Jealous."

1   2   3   4

(1) Letter I of late Roman handwriting in ink, about A.D. 450, in the uncial style. (2) Tailed i from the Grandval Bible, written in about 840, in the Carolingian minuscule style. Although the tailed i meant nothing special for pronunciation, the shape would later be chosen by European printers to help create our letter J. (3) A lowercase French print j of about 1615 shows the type designer's debt to a tradition that included the Carolingian inked shape. (4) Uppercase J in the popular Helvetica typeface, designed in Switzerland in the late 1950s to mirror the enthusiasm of the Jet Age. With its extended hook, the letter seems to balance pleasingly on its bottom.

The authority exerted by Johnson's dictionary helped to delay J and V's official arrival by at least 75 years. Their wait ended only after *another* landmark publication: *An American Dictionary of the English Language* by Connecticut educator Noah Webster (1828). Webster, who took a questioning attitude generally toward British spellings and usage, treated J and V as full-fledged letters and thereby, through the influence his work was to have, delivered a 26-letter alphabet to the young United States. Holdouts remained in Britain, where Charles Richardson's *New Dictionary of the English Language* (1836) omitted J and V. But by midcentury, acceptance was complete.

J has a secret to divulge now: Its name didn't always rhyme with K. As natural as the "jay, kay" jingle may seem in recitation, J's name originally rhymed with I, prior to the late 19th century.

That's logical in light of J's origin: It was "the j-I." Eventually, however, J's name became attracted to K's through the stronger appeal of the long-A rhyme. In Scotland and some other parts of Britain, the name "jye" stayed in common parlance until about the 1950s.

The name "jye" must have come to English from medieval French, as did most of our letter names. The modern French name for J, pronounced *shjee,* represents a development from medieval "jye."

J's names in other tongues reflect the letter's diverse use. In Spanish, where J takes sound "h," the letter is called "hota," spelled *jota,* a name that means the "h-sound iota" (*iota* being letter I: see the preceding chapter). In German, where J takes sound "y," its name is "yot," spelled *jot,* meaning the "y-sound iota."

J's distinctive shape has contributed little to English vocabulary, due no doubt to competition from the word "hook." We have a J-curve and J-bend and that's about all, mainstream-wise. The "J" fountain pen mentioned in some-20th century American writing did *not* involve a hooked shape; the model J was simply an inexpensive but well-regarded product of the Esterbrook pen company, from 1948 to 1955. The J's specific meaning (if any) remains obscure. The oddly pleasant term "jaywalk," first documented in American print journalism in 1917, uses "jay" in a very old sense of "simpleton," a meaning inspired by a garrulous, intrusive kind of bird.

Most of our letters take their shapes from ancient Roman capitals carved in stone, but J is one of a very few to have emerged in lowercase, via medieval penmanship. Uppercase J is basically a European printers' invention of the 1500s; there were no ancient models to work from. Consequently, capital J has been disesteemed by some. The alphabet scholar David Diringer calls it "inferior in design to other letters, lacking the balance, boldness, and dignity of the classical Roman monumental letters." Yet for many of us, J large or small has a jolly shape that sweetly evokes fishing and Victorian field hockey.

English poet, journalist, and scholar Samuel Johnson (1709–84)—shown here in an oil portrait of about 1772 by his friend Joshua Reynolds—was a Litchfield bookseller's son. Johnson's vast learning and mercurial wit went to produce, in 1755, the best dictionary the English language had yet seen. His 40,000-entry Dictionary of the English Language *combines liveliness and remarkable precision in its prose, and is the earliest English dictionary to include literary quotations illustrating word use. The work made Johnson famous, though not rich.*

The dictionary presents a conservative 18th-century alphabet of 24 letters, in which J and V are used in spelling but are denied places in the letter row. Instead, J is treated as a variant of letter I, and V as a variant of U. Johnson chose this interpretation after deliberating and in spite of some contrary scholarly opinion at the time. His decision would, through his posthumous influence, serve to delay J and V's final admission to the alphabet until the mid-19th century.

K is for Komunismus? *The K becomes a symbol of industry and perhaps repression in a 1980s image by Czech graphic designer Oldrich Posmurny, from the final years of that nation's communist regime. Among English-speaking readers, too, in the 20th century, the K might have a sinister look, suggesting the foreign languages and totalitarian regimes of Eastern Europe and Germany.*

K AND ITS KOMPETITORS

indred in sound to both C and Q, the good-hearted K has to fight for its market share of English spelling. This book's chapter on letter C has already mentioned the rivalry of C, K, and Q, a rivalry unique in scope within our alphabet. Generally, our letters are too few: We could use more, to represent sounds like "sh," "th," or the schwa vowel (as in "mentəl"). Yet we extravagantly allocate three letters for one sound, the unvoiced velar stop, "k."

The big loser in the three-way turf war is Q, nearly the least-used letter in English print. K fares badly too, standing at about number 22 or 21 in frequency of use, fourth or fifth to last.

C stands at around number 13. From K's viewpoint, C hogs the limelight and quite undeservingly—for C is far less consistent in sound than K (or Q). The C turns to "s" before E, I, or Y, while K is always "k."

Indeed, K saves C's skin in some spellings, as in the change from "panic" to "panicky" or "shellac" to "shellacking," where K is inserted to denote the "k" sound that could never be shown with the word ending "-cy" or "-cing."

Since K is more dependable than C, why, logically should we use C for "k" at all? Why not substitute K? We could spell "contract" as "kontrakt" and "convector" as "konvektor" (German does). And jettison Q while we're at it: God save the Kween.

Recommendations like these have been put forward by thinkers through the ages who have sought to simplify English spelling by making it more purely phonetic. K is a traditional darling of spelling reform, an ugly duckling turned swan to replace the problematic C and moribund Q. From the writings of Englishman John Hart in the mid-16th century through the British-American New Spelling movement of the 20th, K has been advocated as the one symbol for the one sound. New Spelling, for example, writes "queen," "collide," "discover," and "kick," as "kween," "kolyd," "diskuver," and "kik."

In real-life spellings, K is vastly favored over C among Northern European languages and those of Eastern Europe that use the Roman alphabet, including German, Dutch, Swedish, Czech, and Hungarian. Hence, German words like *Katalog, Dokument, kompakt, effektiv, Nomenklatur,* and *Kommandotruppe.* In German, you might meet a *dekadenter Theaterkritiker.* Or a *Musiker* in a strange *Kostüm.* The German affection for K is exemplified in the proverb of a bygone era that said a married woman's domain is exclusively the four K's: *Kinder, Kirche, Küche, Kleider*—children, church, kitchen, and clothing.

German C, meanwhile, is the lesser letter, relegated to letter combinations like the soft SCH of *deutsch* (the German word for "German") or the hard CH of Sachs (a surname referring to Saxony, often anglicized by 19th-century emigrants as "Sacks"). Similarly, in Czech, in Croatian (a language that calls itself Hrvatska), and in several other Eastern European tongues, C mainly helps convey "ts" and soft "ch" sounds; the "k" sound belongs almost exclusively to K. Only in a few foreign words like "California" does C show up alone to mean "k."

Regarding the odd rivalry of C, K, and Q, history is to blame. Chapter C has sketched already how the Etruscans of ancient Italy, to meet peculiarities of their language, maintained three different letters for the "k" sound. These were the ancestors of our C, K, and Q, and, after being copied into the alphabet of the ancient Romans—who didn't need three any more than we do but who nevertheless preserved them—the C, K, and Q were bequeathed to alphabets of medieval European languages, including English.

However, the full story begins earlier, in Egypt of 2000 B.C. Among Egyptian hieroglyphic symbols was the stylized picture of an outstretched hand. For Egyptian writing, the hand might contribute to various meanings in combination with other pictures, but alone it meant the word "hand." Alternatively, the hand picture could denote the sound "d," for it was one of about 25 hieroglyphs that Egyptians employed at times as alphabetic letters. The symbol's "d" sound corresponded to the opening sound of the Egyptian word *drt,* "hand."

Around 2000 B.C., certain Semitic foreigners in Egypt, probably soldiers or laborers, invented the world's first alphabet: perhaps 27 letters, keyed to Semitic language sounds. As described in the introductory chapter, pages 19–28, the earliest Semitic letters were pictures—a human head, an ox's head, a throwing stick, an eye—all copied from Egyptian hieroglyphic pictures, but with the Egyptian pictures' names and meanings discarded. Undoubtedly, the whole Semitic alphabetic concept was prompted by the example of Egyptian picture writing, particularly those 25 pictures that doubled as Egyptian letters, showing tiny speech sounds.

Simple and distinctive, the Egyptian hand symbol was a likely choice to be copied into the new Semitic system. The Semites created their own "hand" letter: a picture of an upright hand, called by the Semitic name *kaph,* "palm of the hand," and signifying the "k" sound that began the name. This *kaph* was the direct ancestor of our K. Today the fingers of the early letter shape survive, distortedly, in the diverging strokes of our shape K.

As usual for the early Semitic letters, *kaph* is better known to us from a later stage of its use, the Phoenician alphabet of about 1000 B.C. Under the Phoenicians, the letter shape changed to a rather abstract hand, easier to write as a letter. The earliest Phoenician *kaph* showed three spread fingers; later the Phoenician shape evolved to something like a backward K.

Kaph came 11th in the Phoenician alphabet, just as K comes 11th in ours. Following *kaph* in sequence were the L, M, and N Phoenician letters, at places 12, 13, and 14, where our L, M, and N fall today—a reminder of how much of the Phoenician alphabet still lives with us.

The Phoenicians had two letters for the "k" sound: *kaph* and *qoph,* the ancestor of Q. The point of the distinction was that the Phoenicians and other Semites pronounced their "k" in two slightly different ways, involving slightly different tongue positions. Thus, each "k" sound had its own letter for writing. No doubt valuable for the Phoenicians, this distinction between K and Q would prove basically useless for the Indo-European–

speaking peoples who were destined to inherit the alphabet: that is, the Greeks, Romans, French, English, and others. They all would pronounce only one "k" sound. As for the letter C, it was never part of the Phoenician alphabet but would be invented later.

Around 800 B.C., *kaph* and *qoph* passed to the newborn alphabet of the Greeks, who renamed them *kappa* and *qoppa*. Today *qoppa* has long since dropped from Greek as superfluous. But *kappa* remains as the Greek K, the 10th letter of that alphabet.

In modern English, *kappa* plays a modest role in scientific terminology (representing something 10th in sequence, for example) and among U.S. college fraternity names, also in the names of academic societies like Kappa Mu Epsilon and Phi Beta Kappa. Kappa Mu is the national college mathematics honor society: The three Greek letters abbreviate the core words of the fellowship's

(1) Egyptian hand hieroglyph, 2000 B.C. This writing symbol apparently inspired Semitic foreigners in Egypt to invent a "hand" letter for their formative alphabet. (2) The Semitic letter kaph, *meaning "palm of the hand," from inscriptions carved in central-west Sinai, about 1750 B.C. Not resembling the Egyptian model but nevertheless portraying a hand, the* kaph *represented the "k" sound that began its name. (3) Phoenician* kaph, *about 1000 B.C. This "three-fingered" shape took less care and time in writing. (4) Phoenician* kaph, *about 800 B.C. The shape now suggests three fingers on a wrist extension. The letter shape projects leftward, as used in right-to-left Phoenician writing. (5) Early Greek* kappa, *from a right-to-left inscription of about 740 B.C. Although copied from the Phoenician letter, the* kappa *less resembles a hand. The Greek name did not mean "hand" and indeed had no Greek meaning aside from the letter.*

Greek motto, translatable as "Learn to appreciate the beauty of mathematics." The three letters of Phi Beta Kappa represent the words of *its* Greek motto: *Philosophia biou kubernetes* (Love of wisdom is the helmsman of life).

By 700 B.C., *kappa, qoppa,* and the other Greek letters were being adopted by the Etruscans, who soon created their letter C out of the Greek *gamma,* at place number 3; the C became the third Etruscan "k" letter. Like the Phoenicians but more so, the Etruscans pronounced C, K, and Q slightly differently from each other: Each was used only with certain following vowels. The distinction can be glimpsed in the spellings of the three letter names. The Etruscans probably called their C by the name "kay" (spelled C-E); their K they called "ka" (K-A); their Q was "koo" (Q-U).

The Romans, who spoke Latin, a tongue far different from Etruscan, copied the Etruscan alphabet in about 600 B.C. Included in the package were the Three Stooges—er, rather, the three "k" letters: C, K, and Q, highly redundant for Roman language needs. Eventually the Romans imposed order. They made C their prime "k" letter and relegated Q to a specialty use: always alongside U to denote the Latin sound "kw," as in *quantum* (how much).

K drew the short straw of the arrangement: It came to be almost entirely neglected by the Romans. By about 300 B.C. it was used only for a handful of Latin words where it had taken hold prior to the primacy of C. One such K-word was the name of Rome's detested enemy city of North Africa, often written in Latin as Carthago (Carthage) but sometimes as Karthago. The unusual K must have looked extra creepy to Roman eyes.

Even with the influx to Roman society of Greek technical and cultural vocabulary in the centuries after 300 B.C., the Roman K was not called up, as logically it might have been, to transliterate the *kappa* letters of Greek loan words. Instead, the honor went to the Roman C (pronounced always as hard C, in that era). For instance, the mythical witch whom the Greeks called *Kirke* (hawk lady) became the Circe of Roman poets, still pronounced as in Greek (kir-kay) but with C's instead of K's. The large, copper-rich, Greek-occupied, eastern Mediterranean island known in Greek as Kupros came to be spelled in Latin as Cyprus, yet (again) pronounced much as in Greek—a pronunciation that has created our English word "copper," the Cypriot metal. Similarly, Greek names and words like Arkadia, Perikles, *komma, krokos, kolossos,* and *basilike* were transliterated to Latin as Arcadia, Pericles, comma, crocus, colossus, and basilica. The Romans were damned if they'd use their letter K for any such words; they just preferred C.

In modern English, the Roman C for Greek *kappa* can be found in hundreds of Greek-derived words, whether related to ancient Greece or to modern technology (microscope, cinema). The earliest layer of Greek-derived words to reach English did so in latinized form, during the Middle Ages, delivered mainly via Old French. Subsequent borrowings from Greek into English, during the 16th through 20th centuries, stuck to the prior rule of using latinized spellings: C for *kappa,* Y for the Greek U letter, and so on. Thus, English "acanthus," not "akanthos," and "cybernetics," not "kubernetics" or "kubernetiks." Only in very recent borrowings like "kudos" (from Greek *kudos,* "praise, glory") have *kappa* and other Greek letters been more accurately represented.

Miraculously, Roman K survived more than 1,000 years, roughly 600 B.C. to A.D. 500, in its shunned position as the least-used letter of Latin writing. That it didn't just fall out of the letter row is surprising, a tribute to the strength of tradition. But K's day would come later, after Rome's fall (500) and the emergence of new European nations at the start of the Middle Ages. In that era, mainly through church missionaries, the alphabet of old Rome came to be fitted to newer languages, like English, German, Norse, and Polish. These tongues would need a K for their writing, in ways that old Latin didn't.

By the Middle Ages' start, C was a problematic letter (and remains so today). As used in Church Latin and the nascent Romance tongues, C before the vowels E, I, or Y was customarily pronounced as soft: either as "ch" or "s." The spelling rule reflected vast changes that had occurred in the pronunciation of late Latin over prior centuries. A changeable C was fine for a Latin-derived language like Spanish, which shared in the conditions that had created the spelling rule. But not so a Northern European tongue like English or German, with non-Latin origins and its own pronunciation patterns. A German root like *ken,* meaning "to know," needed to show a "k" sound before the vowel E: How else to write it but with K? A spelling with C, "*cen,*" would invite the misreading "sen." Accordingly, when early German began to be written in Roman letters, just before 800, scribes and teachers seized on the uncomplicated K. Neighboring tongues like Danish and Czech followed suit.

Today K and C rule different sectors of the map of Europe. The "K languages," favoring K over C in word spellings, lie mainly in the north and east, as mentioned: They include the Germanic and some of the Slavic tongues, also Finnish and Hungarian (which together belong to a third language family). C's province lies generally farther south: Spanish, Portuguese, French, Italian, and, in the east, Romanian. These languages rely almost exclusively on the old Latin C and use K almost never, typically only for foreign borrowings. Among a handful of French K-words, for example, the most mainstream one is *képi,* denoting the round, flat-topped, visored French military and police cap. The word comes from Swiss German *kappe,* "cap."

English, as often, straddles both traditions, Germanic and Romance, and combines their elements. We use K to supplement the preferred C in our spellings, at a ratio of about one to five. Our unusual custom of using both to this degree stems from the centuries after the Norman Conquest of England in 1066. Amid the burgeoning vocabulary of Middle English, generated from a mix of Old English and Old French, Norman scribes and authorities in England favored Norman French–style spellings with C, which worked fine for appropriate-sounding words like "cat," "cease," "city," "cow," and "cut." But, as in German, the scribes also faced English pronunciations that didn't work for C, pronunciations with a "k" sound before an E, I, or Y, as in "king," "Kent," "speaker," "rocky." How to spell those? Answer: what you've just seen, K. A phrase like "mackerel cakes and kegs of cider" suggests how English spelling developed K to hold the hard sound amid E, I, or Y.

Simplicity of use may be the reason why K became favored over C in transliterating foreign words that have flooded into English since the 1600s, often as by-products of British colonialism. These aren't just words like "ketchup" and "kiosk," with problematic vowels, but also: kangaroo, koala, karma, karate, kung fu, karaoke, kow-tow, kumquat, skunk, polka, mazurka, and many others that could have taken a C.

K-words arose even where older English words had used C. The title of Islam's holy book, meaning "recitation" in Arabic and originally transliterated as Coran, became Koran in the late 1700s (now often Qur'an). In North America, the one-paddle, sealskin boat of the Inuit entered 18th-century English as "kayak" despite what might have been a precedent for C: "canoe" (from a Spanish transliteration of a Caribbean native word in the 1500s).

Sharing a sound with two other letters, K routinely gets used nowadays in the sort of deliberate, eye-catching misspellings that

As an accessory to many deliberate misspellings in English, K may be partly responsible for the creation of our most American expression, "okay." Printed as "O.K.," the term is first documented in a Boston newspaper article of March 1839. According to the current *Oxford English Dictionary*, the best-documented theory is that "O.K." began as abbreviating the jocularly incorrect written notation "orl korrect" ("all correct"). Other theories—that "O.K." was the phonetic rendering of a word from the Choctaw language or from a West African tongue of Southern slaves—lack support, the dictionary says. Regardless, "O.K." became the 1840 presidential campaign slogan of incumbent Martin Van Buren, nicknamed "Old Kinderhook" after his birthplace of Kinderhook, New York. Van Buren got K.O.'ed in the election, losing to William Henry Harrison, but meanwhile he had helped to popularize "O.K."

marketing people love. Consider: Kool cigarettes, Kool-Aid fruit drink, Krispy Kreme doughnuts, Kwik Sew patterns, Kidz Korner website, Klean-Strip paint removers, Kwest management consultants (not to be confused with Qwest long-distance provider), Kandy Korn, Krazy Kat (George Herriman's affronting newspaper cartoon series of 1915 to 1944), and the Pontiac Aztek sports utility vehicle, to name a few. Although visually a bit clunky, the K spelling can suggest a hip, subversive style, too kool for skool.

A more sinister misspelling has been "Amerika," from 1960s political protest banners and graffiti in the United States and elsewhere. The word—which is the German rendering of "America" and the title of a novel written around 1912 by Franz Kafka (an author preoccupied with political repression)—succinctly evoked the totalitarian nightmares of Nazism and communist

Eastern Europe, applying them to American foreign policy and law enforcement. So Richard Firmage observes in his enjoyable book *The Alphabet Abecedarium* (1993).

K was Kafka's own initial, of course, and that of his most famous protagonist, Joseph K., of the novel *The Trial* (1925). Kafka viewed his personal letter with typical pride and confidence. As he wrote in his diary: "I find the letter K offensive, almost nauseating."

Today K's menacing aspect lives on in the Ku Klux Klan. Formed in the American South after the Civil War, and now more diverse geographically while demographically much more of a fringe group, the KKK pursues white supremacy and the terrorizing of people of color and other minorities. The name derives perhaps from the Greek word *kuklos,* "circle," plus "clan." Alternatively, *ku-klux* was said to imitate the sound of a pistol hammer being cocked.

Elsewhere, K is a benign initial. From Greek *khilioi,* it can mean a thousand of something, as in "She earns a hundred K." A 10K race is 10 kilometers, about six miles. K represents the element potassium, from the medieval Latin word for potassium, *kalium,* related to the Arabic-derived word "alkali." Kellogg's Special K breakfast cereal is named simply for the Kellogg Company. K2, the world's second-highest mountain, on the China–Pakistan border, is so called from having been the second peak surveyed in the Karakoram Range. But a police dog K-9 unit is just a pun, a phonetic rendering of "canine."

The U.S. servicemen's K rations of World War II were named for Ancel Benjamin Keys, the scientist who developed them. These lightweight, compactly packaged, no-cook emergency meals, officially called "Field Rations, Type K," were a small triumph of American technology, superior in nutrition and convenience to anything available to other combatants. Introduced in

1   2   3   4

(1) Roman K from a right-to-left inscription of about 500 B.C. The Roman shape had been copied closely from the Etruscan K, which had been copied from the Greek. (2) Mature Roman K from the 100s A.D. Nearly 13 centuries later, in Italy, this shape would be copied as the capital K of early printers' roman typefaces. (3) An inked k in the handwriting style called Carolingian minuscule, from a German-language manuscript of about 865. During the Middle Ages, the K proved essential for the adaptation of Roman letters to non-Romance tongues like English and German. (4) A debt to the Roman past is evident in Baskerville Old Face, a typeface based on Englishman John Baskerville's classic design of about 1768.

1942, the K's quickly displaced the inferior C rations of that day—K versus C again—although an improved C version would make a strong comeback in the postwar armed forces. (The C of "Field Rations, Type C" was not an initial but an ordinal, meaning "number 3 in development.")

Speaking of the 1940s . . . "The K" is a mysteriously titled poem by American writer Charles Olson, penned in 1945, a few months before the end of World War II. In "The K," the 34-year-old Olson announces his decision to be a career poet, not a bureaucrat, having recently quit his job at the Office of War Information. Perhaps alluding to the Allies pressing toward victory after earlier years of disaster and frustration, the poet describes himself in terms of sexual arousal or rearousal, climbing forward from a trough of failure or exhaustion:

Take, then, my answer:
there is a tide in a man
moves him to his moon and,
though it drop him back
he works through ebb to mount
the run again and swell
to be tumescent I . . .

The verses continue, yet the poem's title may perhaps here be explained. The K would be that "tumescent I." In other words, the K, symbolizing Olson, is a stick man, with two legs and an erection, moving forward. To judge from the K's proportions—it's a capital K, no less, not even a lowercase k—we can safely call poet Olson an optimist.

A curious drawing from Champ Fleury—*the 1529 book about the letters by French type designer and calligrapher Geofroy Tory—presents L's shape in cosmic or mystical terms. Tory claims (apparently seriously) that the ancient Romans designed the ideal L through reference to the shadow cast by a human body shortly after the autumn equinox, in late Sep-*

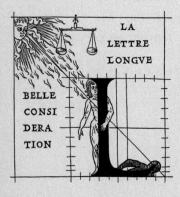

tember, when the sun is in the zodiacal sign of Libra, the balance scale. Libra, as well as being the emblem of balance and harmony, possesses the right initial. Tory here illustrates the design concept, with the man's shadow (lower right) supplying the guideline for the letter's foot bar. The titles in French, from left, translate as "grand deference" and "the long letter," that is, the L. Tory—who would become the official printer to King François I through the credit of having written Champ Fleury—*normally employed letter-design methods that were more scientific.*

THE LURE OF L

ateral emission of breath, that's the secret to L. L's sound comes from using your vocal cords while you push air past the sides of your tongue as it partly blocks your mouth with its tip at the palate. (Seem complicated? We do it countless times a day without thinking.) If you sound a continuous L, then drop your tongue free and slightly purse your lips, the L turns to R. The two consonants in English make up a small category called "liquids"—meaning consonants that can be sounded continuously and with minimum friction in the mouth but that are distinct from our semivowels, W and Y.

L and R's kinship is demonstrated in Japanese pronunciations of English. As has been much observed, Japanese speakers, without practice, cannot say the sound of L, a sound absent in their tongue. Instead, they naturally substitute R. The expression "No problem" becomes "No probrem." "Flying" becomes "frying."

The sounds of L and R are considered among the loveliest of human speech. The expression "cellar door"—which has gained recent attention due to its mention in the teen film *Donnie Darko* (2001)—is said to possess a combination of sounds particularly sweet to the ear; of its five consonant sounds, three are liquids. Admiration for "cellar door" goes back at least to 1963, to an essay titled "English and Welsh" by medieval languages scholar and *Lord of the Rings* author J. R. R. Tolkien. "Most English-speaking people," Tolkien writes, "will admit that *cellar door* is 'beautiful,' especially if dissociated from its sense and spelling. More beautiful than, say, *sky,* and far more beautiful than *beautiful.*" Tolkien explains that for him, as an Oxford undergraduate in 1911, the study of medieval Welsh offered a whole language full of cellar doors.

For pure ability to soothe, the letter L probably tops all other English consonants, edging out another contender, M. The L's calming effect is heard in "lull," "lullaby," "lollipop," "lotus land," and "la-la land"—the latter two sometimes referring to fanciful atmospheres of the Pacific Northwest and southern California, respectively. Even the term "loss leader" (as in a sales item) may suggest some mildly narcotic effect.

L's delicate sound has been appreciated and exploited by wordsmiths through the centuries. Ben Jonson, in his 1640 *English Grammar,* said of L that "It melteth in the sounding, and is therefore called a liquid." In many languages' poetry, L has conveyed softness, calm, flux, childishness, slipperiness, departure, or gradual release or surrender, including sexual. Remarkably, most of these nuances are honestly advertised in the title of Vladimir Nabokov's sensationalist 1955 novel, *Lolita*, about a 40-year-old man in love with a girl of 12.

L helps to paint a picture of biblical Eden in John Milton's *Paradise Lost* (1667)—

Hill, dale, and shady woods, and sunny plains,
And liquid lapse of murmuring streams. . . .

—and of evening's fall in Thomas Gray's "Elegy Written in a Country Churchyard" (1750):

The curfew tolls the knell of parting day,
The lowing herd wind slowly o'er the lea . . .

Let's not forget the opening line of a well-known Latin poem, written in about A.D. 130 by the Roman emperor Hadrian, reflecting sadly on the soul's flight from the body at death: *Animula vagula blandula* (Gentle little soul sent wandering . . .), in which the L's seem fairly to slip from your grasp. One hopes the emperor produced his ghost poem without benefit of a ghostwriter.

L's history flows smoothly, too. Two letters that are probably primitive L's appear separately in the world's oldest known alphabetic writing, the stone-carved inscriptions at Wadi el-Hol in central Egypt, from about 1800 B.C. One of the letters seems to be part of the written ancient Semitic word *el,* meaning "god" (see the photograph on page 39). However, as with other letters, our best information on the early L comes from a later stage of the ancient Semitic alphabet, namely, the Phoenician alphabet of 1000 B.C.

The Phoenician letter had a crowbar shape and was called *lamed,* pronounced "lah-med," meaning "ox goad." (A goad was a strong stick, typically with a crook handle, for poking livestock in herding.) *Lamed* took the "l" sound that began its name. It came 12th in the Phoenician alphabet, the same position our L holds today.

When the Greeks copied the Phoenician letters around 800 B.C., they made *lamed* their own L letter, at alphabetic place number 12. As with all Phoenician letters, the Greeks adjusted *lamed*'s name to make it more Greek-sounding. They called their letter *lambda*. The meaning "ox goad" had vanished in transition; the name *lambda* had no meaning in Greek aside from signifying the letter.

The Greeks also made one change to the letter's shape: They reversed it, so it faced the opposite direction from the Phoenician

(*1*) *Semitic letter from the Wadi el-Hol inscriptions, about 1800 B.C. On the basis of later Semitic letter shapes, we believe this letter is L in its earliest known form.* (*2*) *The same letter, 1,000 years on: Phoenician lamed, the "ox goad," from an inscription of about 800 B.C. Lamed came 12th in the Phoenician alphabet and denoted the "l" sound that began its name. The letter shape's hook probably represents the crook of the goad, which would hang on the herdsman's arm. As used in right-to-left Phoenician writing, the lamed points "backward" toward the letter preceding it.* (*3*) *Greek lambda from a right-to-left inscription of about 725 B.C. The Greek letter faces the opposite way, toward the end of the word or line. Our modern L maintains the tradition, the only difference being that we write exclusively from left to right.* (*4*) *The early Roman L—this example from right-to-left writing of about 500 B.C.—closely imitated the Etruscan L letter, which closely imitated the Greek.* (*5*) *Roman L of the late 200s B.C. had reached the right-angled shape familiar to us. Also, Roman writing had by then settled at left to right.*

Greek lambda, *the L letter, in capital and lowercase forms in modern Greek. Both come from letter shapes of classical Athenian writing of about 400 B.C.*

Like *delta, eta,* and other Greek letters, *lambda* continued evolving in shape within the Greek alphabet, after being handed off to the Etruscans of Italy for their alphabet in about 700 B.C. Within Greek writing tradition, *lambda*'s shape eventually stood up on two legs *(above, left)*. It's still possible to see in it the basic aspects of our own L shape.

This mature *lambda* would have adventures of its own. For reasons obscure, the lowercase form λ became the early 20th century's scientific symbol for any kind of wavelength, often used in regard to shortwave radio. With this background, λ in about 1970 became a symbol of gay identity—the connection being that, in that era, a homosexual lifestyle might typically require a degree of secrecy and discreet signaling; individuals would look for others on the same wavelength. Today, although the concealment issue is in many locales obsolete, *lambda* and λ remain emblems of gay pride. For example, on a college campus, the name Lambda Society can mean only a homosexual interest group. The U.S. national lesbian sorority is called Lambda Delta Lambda; the national gay fraternity is Delta Lambda Phi.

version. Where Phoenician *lamed* had pointed its foot or handle toward the preceding letter in the writing, Greek *lambda* pointed the other way, toward the letter that followed. The change brought *lambda* into line with most other asymmetrical early Greek letters, whose bars and projections pointed in the direction of the writing flow, not against it. Early Greek writing itself could run either right to left or left to right; therefore *lambda* might face either way, but according to the direction of the flow.

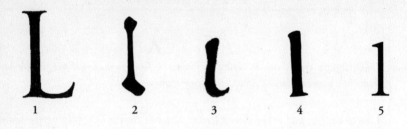

(1) Imperial Roman L of the 100s A.D. *Enhanced by handsome serifs and tapering, this shape would become the general model for our modern print capital.   (2) Ink L in the so-called rustic Latin handwriting style, from a manuscript probably of the 500s* A.D. *Very similar to the rustic I shape, the L was distinguished only by a slightly larger "foot."   (3) Ink l in the Carolingian minuscule style, from a Latin religious text from southern England, about 970. This pleasantly legible letter was distinct from the Carolingian i shape, being both taller and marked by its foot.   (4) Our lowercase l shape emerges in the minuscule letter of the Italian Renaissance humanist handwriting style—this example from a Latin manuscript of about 1540, from Rome. Based on Carolingian minuscules of centuries prior, humanist letter shapes provided the models for lowercase letters of the earliest roman typefaces, around 1470.   (5) The humanist shape lives on in the print l of today's Garamond type, based on type designs of the 1500s.*

Lambda with other Greek letters was carried in Greek trading ships to western Italy (700s B.C.), where the letter was quickly copied into the Etruscan alphabet. The Etruscan L letter, in turn, was copied into the newborn Roman alphabet (600 B.C.). The Romans modified the letter's shape further and bequeathed it to us.

Visually the L has won less applause than phonetically. Capital L looks fine, but lowercase l has the distinction of being our least-recognizable letter form of all 52, as analyses of modern reading tests have shown. When separated from the contexts of familiar word spellings, the l invites confusion with capital I or numeral 1. On manual typewriters—the laptops of yesteryear—the lowercase l doubled as the numeral 1.

The lowercase l also demonstrates the superior legibility of serif typefaces (which employ letter shapes with tiny finishing strokes, based on ancient Roman models; the typeface on this page is such a one). Tests show that serif lettering can be read more quickly and at smaller sizes than sans serif (the type style that omits serifs). Such advantages are embodied in the lowercase l, which offers three little nibs to catch the reader's eye for recognition, versus the starkness of its sans-serif counterpart: l. This l for sans-serif lowercase l is very nearly the same shape as the sans-serif uppercase I. The word "Ill" at the start of a sentence—no joy to read even in serifs—would in sans-serif type look like Ill, a figure that might be a Roman numeral 3 or three sans-serif lowercase l's. Such ambiguity is perhaps the low point of modern mainstream typography. It's Enough to Make You Ill.

Imperfections like these will slow a reader down, but they are not fatal, for one important reason: As adults, we don't read by letter; we read by word. Our eyes sweep along the page, instantly recognizing the word shapes and taking meaning from them, with little thought to individual letters. The optimum word shapes for this purpose are lowercase—preferably in serif type around one sixth of an inch tall. On the other hand, text printed in all capitals deprives us of familiar word shapes and makes for slower reading. Mention that to your office mate who likes to send out all-capital "URGENT" memos.

Like other letters, lowercase l does its bit by contributing generally to the familiar word shapes in our texts. In that sense, its shortcomings in shape are more theoretical than practical. By standing in place in our word spellings, it earns its pay.

Not surprisingly, the indistinct lowercase l shape came very late to the alphabet: It was the last to arrive. All our lowercase letter shapes were created as forms in ink, amid handwriting styles of late antiquity and the Middle Ages. The shapes of d or h, for example, emerged in the uncial pen style probably in the 300s A.D. But the shape of lowercase l became finalized in ink only in the 1400s, in the humanist pen style of Italy. (Some letters never developed a different lowercase form, such as O and X.)

The 12th letter of our alphabet, L ranks about 11th place among the letters in frequency of use in printed English—slightly above U and either below or above D. A silent L before a consonant in words like "should" and "walk" commemorates a sound once pronounced in Old English, according to scholars. This slow vanishing act can be glimpsed in "palm," a word listed in modern dictionaries as having two possible pronunciations: without the L sound or with it.

In print, an "ell" may be a building's extension, at a right angle to the main structure, so that the whole thing would resemble an L from a bird's-eye view. Or an "ell" can be a right-angled pipe. But in Shakespeare and other earlier English writers, an "ell"—unrelated to the letter shape—might mean a measure of length, about 45 inches, dating back to an Old English word, *eln*. An "el" with one L is short for "elevated subway line," as in Manhattan's old Third Avenue El, dismantled in 1955.

One L, the title of Scott Turow's 1977 memoir of his first year at Harvard Law School, refers simply to the first-year student, designated as "One L," versus "Two" or "Three L." In measurements, L may abbreviate "length," "longitude," and (in lowercase only) "latitude." Surprisingly, the Roman numeral L, meaning 50, does not abbreviate a word (the Latin for 50 was *quinquaginta*) but rather is thought to commemorate a primitive Roman symbol, a numeral, that became standardized as the letter L shape. The same holds true for the puzzling Roman V for 5, X for 10, and D for 500, none of which stands for a Latin word. However, M for 1,000 did abbreviate the Latin word *mille,* while C for 100 evidently began as an abstract symbol that over time became "attracted" to the appropriate letter shape for abbreviating the Latin *centum*. Meanwhile, Roman I for 1 and II for 2 speak for themselves. Roman IV means "1 less than 5." And as we all know by now, Roman III means "ill" (just joking).

The traditional symbol £ for British pound sterling is an L in the medieval black letter ink style. It stands for Latin *libra,* the old Roman pound weight, also commemorated in our abbreviation lb. (*Libra* could otherwise mean "balance scale," as immortalized in the name of the constellation Libra; see page 214.) In England by about A.D. 1280, the word meant a pound weight of silver, the standard large monetary unit, equivalent to 240 silver pennies (later, copper ones, eventually devalued and refigured at 100 per pound). If Britain should ever move to join the euro currency system, the £ will sadly lapse—slipping, lost, while the bell tolls farewell. And so farewell to L.

ONE L OR TWO?

The Creation of American Spelling

George Bernard Shaw once defined the British and Americans as two peoples separated by a common language. Not just in accent and vocabulary but in spelling, too, is this true.

Like the spelling of "honor" versus "honour" and "defense" versus "defence," the use of one L versus two in certain positions in words is a sure sign of American English. Classic examples include American "traveled," "jewelry," "counselor," and "woolen" versus British and Commonwealth "travelled" "jewellery," "counsellor," and "woollen." Yet American spelling may sometimes take two L's, not only in obvious cases like "hall" but in "controlled," "impelled" (from "control" and "impel"), and elsewhere.

Most of our specifically American spelling rules come from Noah Webster, the Connecticut-born educator and lexicographer whose magnum opus was his 1828 *American Dictionary of the English Language,* granddaddy of all "Webster" dictionaries today. Webster's two-volume, 70,000-entry tome became the authority for 19th-century American vocabulary and spelling, and set American English on a confident course away from British usage.

An American patriot, Webster had interrupted his undergraduate study at Yale to serve briefly in the American Revolution, and he personally knew George Washington, Benjamin Franklin, and, on unfriendly terms, Thomas Jefferson. Webster envisioned a distinctly American language, to help unite the new nation and make it independent of Britain's printing presses and other cultural influences. This American language he sought to engineer, personally, through his writings and lectures.

At a time when English-language spellings were still fluid, Webster compiled his dictionary with an eye toward establishing consistent spelling rules that would *create* differences between American and British English. The British authority of the day was Samuel Johnson's 1755 dictionary (on which see page 199). Many of Webster's spellings differ from Johnson's.

Some Webster spellings can claim to be more authentic than the British ones: Webster's "color" and "favor" (versus "colour" and "favour") return the words to their original Latin spellings, with no intervening influence of medieval French. Other Webster spellings could fall back on the claim of being, in the 1820s, the existing, prevalent Americanisms, like "racket" for British "racquet" and "jail" for "gaol." But other of his choices look more willful—like "mold" instead of British "mould," from an Old English word—and seem prompted by his ulterior motive, to separate American from British. And a few 1828 Websterisms were so eccentric, such as "aker" for "acre" and medieval-style "tung" for "tongue," that the American public rejected them, and they disappeared from subsequent dictionary editions.

Webster would generally, where feasible, choose the shorter form of a word for American English, thus "program" not "programme," "plow" not "plough," "ax" not "axe." A favorite target of his was the double consonant, to be condensed to one consonant: from British "waggon" to American "wagon," for instance. Consonant doubling often occurred where a word, ending in one consonant, became a derivative form, as in the British change from "focus" to "focussed."

Webster decreed an American spelling rule that a final consonant in an unaccented syllable would *not* be doubled in derivatives, usually. Thus "focused" (one S) was to be the American form. This rule knocked the second L out of many prominent words, of which the American versions became "traveler," "channeled," "marvelous," "duelist," and so on, where British spelling would keep two L's. But Webster did allow consonant doubling in *accented* syllables, which is why we have "appalling," "distiller," "beginning," and others today.

An abrasive personality with a brilliant mind and missionary zeal, Noah Webster (1758–1843)—here in a painting of about 1796 by James Sharples—worked 60 years to help forge a distinctly American language. He was the son of a West Hartford, Connecticut, farmer who, to send the boy to Yale, mortgaged and then lost the family farm. But Noah, who became a schoolteacher and lawyer, would achieve lifelong income at age 25, with his American Spelling Book *(1783). Published as the Revolutionary War was ending, the "Blue-backed Speller" answered the need of American schools and the public for an authoritative spelling guide not distributed from Britain, and the book succeeded spectacularly. It went through some 400 printings during Webster's lifetime and became a cornerstone of 19th-century American schooling.*

Ironically, Webster would later reject and change many of the spellings in his speller. Soon after its publication, he was seized with the vision of reforming American spelling, thereby to contribute to American unity and identity. A distinctly American spelling, he argued, would encourage American publishing (versus importing British books and printer's plates) and more generally would help break America's lamentable cultural subservience to Britain. "A national language is a band of national union," he wrote. "Every engine should be employed to render the people of this country national . . . and to inspire them with the pride of national character."

Where the 1783 speller had systematized the British-received forms, Webster now set out to create a purely American system. He started by writing A Compendious Dictionary of the English Language *(1806). Although later dwarfed in importance by his famous* American Dictionary, *this earlier work introduced spelling innovations and was possibly the first English dictionary anywhere to observe a 26-letter alphabet: That is, it* treated J and V as sovereign letters, the 25th and 26th. Prior lexicographers, particularly the influential Samuel Johnson, had admitted only 24 letters, giving no dictionary heading to J or V but treating them as variants of I and U. (See pages 193–96.)

Webster's masterpiece and legacy was his 70,000-entry American Dictionary of the English Language (1828), published when he was 70. For it, he spent about 22 years in study and writing, including delving into over 20 modern and ancient languages in pursuit of English word etymologies, plus a voyage to visit libraries of England and France at age 66. Comprehensive and up to date, if innovative in spellings, the dictionary supplied the authoritative reference to liberate American English from British dictionaries. It sold well but was not lucrative, and the aging Webster mortgaged his home to finance a second edition (1841), which was unsuccessful. When Webster died in 1843, his family sold the book rights to brothers George and Charles Merriam, of Springfield, Massachusetts, whose company produces the familiar Merriam-Webster dictionary to this day.

"... the last time she saw them, they were trying to put the Dormouse into the teapot." The final words of the "Mad Tea-Party" chapter of Lewis Carroll's Alice's Adventures in Wonderland are illustrated in one of the classic John Tenniel pen-and-ink drawings that accompanied the original edition of 1865. Assisting the Dormouse here are the March Hare and Mad Hatter. Is it our imagination, or does the position of the three characters suggest the shape of an M? As well as having a prominent place in the chapter title and two characters' names, M receives a mysterious mention in the chapter's dialogue.

PRIMORDIAL M

Ma-ma-ma-ma-ma. How many parents remember that sound of baby talk? Numerous studies confirm that *ma* is among the earliest rudimentary speech noises made by infants the world over. Like B and P (which also have a place in baby vocabulary), the M belongs to the category of consonants known as labials, from the Latin word for "lip." Formed at the lips, with no tricky use of the tongue and no need of teeth, the three labial sounds are simple enough to be spoken by infants as young as age two or three months. By contrast, sounds like "j," "v," or "sh" may not emerge consistently until much later, for while a child learns to recognize many adult-language sounds during her first six months, she can manage at the start to imitate only a few. (See below.)

When a baby says *ma-ma,* that doesn't have to mean "mother." It may be prattle or it may mean something in the child's personal language: This writer had a year-old daughter who would say *ma-ma-ma* to communicate, "I'm hungry." (Her mother meanwhile was called *da,* and I was *da,* too.) Yet because of its powerful kiddy connection, the syllable *ma* or similar has denoted "mother" in diverse languages through the centuries. That is to say, the *ma-ma-ma* of infant speech has imposed itself—partly through its pleasant association—on adult speech around the world.

THE BABY LANGUAGE OF GROWN-UPS

Aspects of World Languages May Be Colored by Baby Talk

Babies in their first year of life learn to speak—first in baby talk, then with the rudiments of a genuine vocabulary—by imitating the speech sounds they hear around them. (Often these sounds are addressed to the baby in an exaggerated, singsong form—"How did you sleeeep?"—which apparently helps the child to learn.) But some scholars have long theorized that language in the nursery is partly a two-way street and that certain family-related words of English and other tongues were formed originally, perhaps prehistorically, in imitation of baby talk. Such words are easy for babies to pronounce, perhaps at parental prompting—"Say *dada*"—and so the words retain a secure place in the language.

What are these words? While they vary from language to language, in English they would be some of the "ba," "da," "ma," and "pa" words.

The earliest speech sounds out of an infant's mouth, sometimes as early as the second month of life, might typically be pure vowels: The sounds "ah," "ee," and "oo" are said to predominate among babies the world over, with "ah" earliest and most frequent. The infant's next

Just look at the "mother" words in a handful of languages that have nothing to do with each other, that are linguistically and geographically separate. There's Mandarin Chinese *ma,* Hindi *maa,* Vietnamese *me,* Malay *emak,* Hawaiian *makuahine,* Swahili *mama,* Finnish *emo,* Hebrew *ema,* Basque *ama,* and Quechua (aboriginal Peruvian tongue) *ma*—all of which would seem a re(ma)rkable coincidence, were there not a suspected common cause.

Of the above-mentioned languages, Hindi belongs to the large Indo-European language family, which includes English. Within the Indo-European group, *ma* meaning "mother" is pervasive. Modern scholarship has long theorized that the original

step, usually begun before four months of age, is to float a consonant sound in front of the vowel: *ma-ma-ma* or similar, the sound of pure baby talk.

But not every consonant is within the baby's reach: Certain pronunciations like "sh" or "j" may take years to master, even for a child who perfectly understands them. In English, as in many other tongues, the earliest consonant sounds to be uttered consistently might belong to the labial, alveolar, or velar categories—"b," "m," "p," "d," "t," "g," or "k"—floated on vowels like "ah" and "oo."

Here some linguists find the ultimate origins of such adult English words as "mama," "papa," "daddy," and (in Ireland) "da." Our word "baby" derives officially from medieval French *bébé,* probably from late Latin *baba.* But where did Latin *baba* come from? Surely from an imitation of baby talk. Meanwhile, similar-sounding words in other languages have their own family connections. A *baba* in Russian is a grandmother; in Swahili, a father. A father in Arabic is *abu,* not so different-sounding from *baba.* And in the language of the Eastern European republic of Georgia, a father is our old friend *mama* . . . while a mother is *deda.*

Indo-European tongue of around 4000 B.C. had a word for "mother" that was something like *mater* (mah-tair). From this root come similar "mother" words in dozens of Indo-European descendant languages through the ages—including English, with its word "mother."

Compare, for example, ancient Sanskrit *matr*, ancient Greek *meter* (may-tair), modern Farsi *madar*, Irish *máthair*, Russian *mat* (mat-eh), Polish *matka*, Czech *matka*, Dutch *moeder*, Danish *moder*, and ancient Latin *mater* (mah-tair). From the Latin are derived such modern Romance words as Spanish *madre*, Portuguese *mae*, and French *mère* as well as the English adjective "maternal." Our word "mother" comes from Old English *modor*, related to the above-mentioned Dutch and Danish words and to German *mutter* (moo-tair). The German version may perhaps bear on a quip by the 1920s and '30s American author and Algonquin Round Table wit Dorothy Parker: "A girl's best friend is her mutter."

The origin of the Indo-European word *mater* may lie in the related Indo-European word *mamma*, meaning a mother's breast. Where *that* word came from, we can guess—prehistoric Indo-European babies who said *ma-ma-ma-ma*, perhaps meaning "mother" or even "I'm hungry." From this root word *mamma* come similar words for "breast" in Greek, Russian, Lithuanian, Irish, Welsh, and other Indo-European tongues. But the most influential derivative has been the ancient Latin *mamma* (again, meaning a mother's breast), which supplies our words "mammary" and "mammal." A mammal is an animal of the class that suckles.

You have to marvel at the strength of the association of *ma* with mother. True, all of the Indo-European "mother" words come from the same root, which might suggest they're bound to sound similar; yet most words don't remain so much alike, from one Indo-European tongue to another, down the millennia. Words for "water" or "home" today tend to differ among Hindi, Greek, German,

Spanish, etc. Words for "mother," by contrast, have stayed in line with the sound *ma* or *mat* and have even spawned duplicates like French *maman* or English "mommy," "mamma," and "ma"— words that obviously are based on baby talk.

The letter M, thus representing a primordial sound of human speech, has been a member of the alphabet from the start. Letters believed to be M's appear as vertical wavy lines in the world's oldest extant alphabetic writing, the two rock-carved Semitic-language inscriptions at Wadi el-Hol in central Egypt, from about 1800 B.C. Scholars think this letter was called *mem,* meaning "water" in the users' Semitic tongue, and that it took the "m" sound with which its name began. Like all early letters, *mem* was also a picture, the wavy lines clearly suggesting water. The styling of the letter shape as *vertical,* rather than horizontal, is an unlikely choice that offers a clue to the date of the first Semitic alphabet's invention: See pages 36–40. Today, nearly 4,000 years later, the waves of the original *mem* survive in the zigzags of our capital M.

The Phoenicians, heirs to the ancient Semitic alphabet, had a *mem* that was more condensed in shape (1000 B.C.). Extant Phoenician letter lists show *mem* as their alphabet's 13th letter, just as M remains our 13th letter today.

Inscriptions from later dates show the Phoenician *mem* shifting in shape: The waves now run horizontally, the letter more resembling our modern M but standing on one long, vertical "leg." Probably the change helped give *mem* a more distinctive look.

Sometime shortly before 800 B.C., the Phoenician letters were copied by the Greeks. *Mem,* representing a sound just as basic to the Greek language as to the Phoenician, was ushered into the newly made Greek alphabet, keeping its zigzag shape, "m" sound, and 13th alphabetical place, but now with a Greek-styled name: *mu.* As with all early Greek letter names, the name *mu* meant nothing in Greek, aside from signifying the letter. The "water" reference was left behind in the Semitic alphabets.

Carried to Italy in Greek merchant ships in the 700s B.C., *mu* and the other Greek letters were soon copied by the Etruscans (700 B.C.) and, from the Etruscan alphabet, were copied by the Romans (600 B.C.). Under the Romans, the zigzag letter eventually settled down onto two even legs: our familiar M shape. In this form, it was bequeathed to European writing after Rome's fall (A.D. 500).

The letter's name during the late Roman Empire was probably something like "emmay," much the same as in modern Spanish. In passing from late Latin to Old French to medieval English

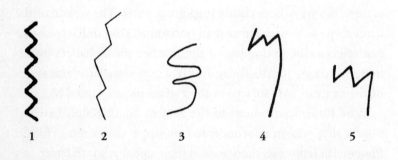

1   2   3   4   5

(1) Egyptian hieroglyph depicting water, 2000 B.C. In Egyptian picture writing, it meant the word "water" or the sound "n" or had other meanings when used in combinations with other pictures. Normally drawn horizontally, the water symbol instead appeared vertically during one Egyptian era, around 2000 B.C. At that time, Semitic foreigners in Egypt copied the symbol to supply the letter M for their newly created alphabet. We believe the inventors called their letter mem, *meaning "water" in the Semitic tongue. (2) A* mem *from the Semitic inscriptions at Wadi el-Hol, the world's oldest known alphabetic writing, from about 1800 B.C. While imitating the Egyptian hieroglyph in appearance, the* mem *had its own, different meaning: It denoted the "m" sound that began its name. (3) Phoenician* mem *of about 1000 B.C. The compact, curly shape slightly resembles our script m lying on its side. The name* mem *was still understood as meaning "water." (4) Another Phoenician* mem, *of about 800 B.C. The Phoenicians had by now changed the letter shape, to make it simpler and more distinctive. (5) Greek M letter, the* mu, *from an inscription of about 725 B.C. Mu copied the Phoenician* mem *in shape, sound, alphabetic place, and name.*

M & M

The candies called M&M's—chocolate pellets in thin sugar shells—are named for their inventor, Forrest Mars (around 1940), and for the Mars candy company that he founded. A phonetic respelling gives us "Eminem," name of the controversial white rap star who was born as Marshall Mathers. While the name obviously refers to the rapper's childhood initials, it may also betoken a sincere belief by him that essentially, like the candy, he is brown (in other words, Black) on the inside.

(with the Norman Conquest of England in 1066) and thence into modern English, "emmay" became shortened to "em."

Our lowercase m derives simply from the letter's rounded shape in the late Roman pen style known as uncial, emerging around 300. During the Middle Ages, this m shape contributed to a religious idea that God has written the human name upon our face: The nose, eyebrows, and cheekbones form an m, and the eyes form two letters o within the m. Our face is thus readable as "omo" or Latin *homo*, "human being."

As mentioned, M belongs phonetically to the category called "labials." But, like most consonants, it falls also into some second category. M's other classification is as a "nasal"—to pronounce M, you send air up into your nasal cavity from the inside and use your nose as a sound box. (In English, M and N are the only two nasals.)

M's flowing sound has been attractive to the poets. John Milton's phrase, quoted back on page 217, "liquid lapse of murmuring streams," relies equally on M and L for effect. A more sonorous M contributes to the famous opening words of Vergil's epic poem in Latin, the *Aeneid*, concerning the adventures and battles of the hero Aeneas, legendary founder of the Roman race: *Arma virumque cano* . . . (I sing of war and the man).

1   2   3   4

(1) Early Roman M, from about 520 B.C. The letter shape had been copied from the Etruscan version, which had been copied from the Greek. (2) Roman M from the famous Trajan Inscription of A.D. 113. This mature shape would become the model for the capital M's of the "roman" typefaces of early print, around 1470. (3) Ink M from a Latin manuscript in the uncial handwriting style, from Italy, around 450. Reducing the angular capital to rounded humps, easier to pen, the uncial shape also anticipates our modern lowercase m. Along with d, h, and q, this was one of the earliest future-lowercase letter shapes to emerge from European handwriting of the first millennium A.D. (4) An m in the Carolingian minuscule pen style, from a Latin manuscript from southern England, around 975. Derived from the uncial, the Carolingian shape would later help to inspire early printers' lowercase m shapes.

Vergil's M conveys danger and grandeur. Elsewhere, M has conveyed danger and mystery, perhaps due to the word "mystery." No movie title is more grabbing than *Dial M for Murder,* Alfred Hitchcock's 1954 classic thriller about a husband's plot to kill his innocent wife. Sue Grafton's alphabetically titled detective novels have contributed not only *M Is for Malice* (1996) but also their heroine's name Kinsey Millhone. The evil antagonist in J. R. R. Tolkien's *Lord of the Rings* fantasy trilogy (1954–55) inhabits a dark realm of power called Mordor—a word that, not coincidentally, means "murder" in Old English.

Arthur Conan Doyle, in his Sherlock Holmes tale "The Adventure of the Empty House" (1903), characterizes M as the letter of villains. Holmes, hot on the trail of murder and perfidy, sits in his study with the loyal Dr. Watson and consults a self-compiled "index of biographies," a catalog of bad guys. Chief among the indexed M's is Holmes's nemesis, evil genius Professor James Moriarity. But tonight's antagonist is someone else, "the second most dangerous man in London." Watson narrates how Holmes

> *turned over the pages lazily, leaning back in his chair and blowing great clouds of smoke from his cigar.*
>
> *"My collection of M's is a fine one," said he. "Moriarity himself is enough to make any letter illustrious, and here is Morgan the poisoner, and Merridew of abominable memory, and Mathews, who knocked out my left canine in the waiting-room at Charing Cross, and finally, here is our friend of tonight."*
>
> *He handed over the book, and I read . . .*

Ah, but enough said.

In the 1950s and '60s, long before anyone had thought up the parodistic Austin Powers, the fictional British super-spy James Bond was the hero of Ian Fleming's novels of intrigue and adventure. Bond has a crusty boss known only as M, although somewhere identified as one Sir Miles Messervey. The use of the initial creates cloak-and-dagger secrecy and a hint of ennobling symbolism: Motherland? Mission? Mankind?

But the most enigmatic M in literature appears toward the end of the "Mad Tea-Party" chapter in Lewis Carroll's *Alice's Adventures in Wonderland*, where the yawning Dormouse tries to tell a goofy tale about three little sisters learning to draw. " 'And they drew all manner of things—everything that begins with an M—'

" 'Why with an M?' said Alice.

" 'Why not?' said the March Hare.

"Alice was silent."

Letter N gets the imperial treatment on the bottle-neck label of Newman's Own salad dressing, a line created and owned by movie star Paul Newman. The letter is framed by two olive branches, appropriate to salad oil, yet referring, too, to the ceremonial garlands worn by rulers—also by victorious athletes, honored poets, actors, etc.—in ancient Greece and Rome. Fitted to the person's head, a garland consisted of leaves of laurel or oak or of other trees or plants (olive, myrtle, celery, ivy) sacred to the gods. The Newman N seems deliberately to recall Napoleon Bonaparte, Emperor of France (1804–15), whose court imagery included paintings and relief carvings showing a large N bordered with a Caesar-like garland.

[NASAL N]

Noses are needed for pronouncing the N. To prove the point, say that phrase while plugging your nose with your fingertips. You'll hear something halfway to "Dozes are deeded for prodowsing. . . ."

Like M, the N is classified as a "nasal," a consonant pronounced through the nose. M's nasal component is demonstrated in an experiment mentioned back on page 72: Plug your nose for "My mommy meets me," and it comes out a bit like "By bobby beets be."

N and M are the only nasals in English. To say N or M, you actually drop your uvula to divert airflow up into your nasal cavity from the inside, so that your nose acts as a sound box.

You may do this hundreds of times a day, without ever thinking of it: It's one of the tricks your brain learned while you were an infant in the cradle, preparing to imitate the speech sounds you heard around you.

The "m" sound is formed at the lips, so simple that four-month-old babies can say it. "N," more complex, sets the tongue against the palate. The tongue position for N is surprisingly close to that for L, yet N's sound is far more like M's, due to the nose factor.

Since ancient Rome, scholars have noticed how certain letters in the alphabet seem to pair off, resembling each other in shape, name, and/or sound. Such pairs today include C and G, B and P, and S and Z. Typically, these couplings can be traced as developments within the ancient Greek and Roman alphabets; they seem to reflect a human need for association (visual or verbal) as an aid for memorizing a list like the alphabet.

Two letters could hardly be closer than N and M, fraternal twins in shape, name, sound, and positioning. Together they form our alphabet's center, with 12 letters on either side. The resemblance in shape is noteworthy: Basically, N is a three-quarters M,

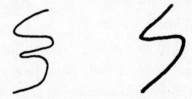

The Phoenician letters mem *and* nun, *"water" and "fish," the ancestors of our M and N, from an inscription of about 1000 B.C.*

and the two letters have had this sort of visual kinship since at least ancient Phoenician times, 3,000 years ago.

Most of N's life has been lived in relation to M. As the prior chapter recounts, the 13th letter of the Phoenician alphabet of 1000 B.C. was the wavy-lined *mem,* ancestor of our M. The name *mem* meant "water." The Phoenicians' 14th letter was their N, called *nun,* meaning "fish." Yet the shape of *nun* was a serpentine undulation, not at all suggesting a fish, aside from an eel.

Modern scholarship has determined that N was invented (by Semitic soldiers or laborers in Egypt) through copying of an Egyptian hieroglyphic picture of a snake. The shape of the Semitic N looked like a snake. (See page 243.) The attested letter name "fish" therefore becomes problematic.

In ancient Semitic language, one word for snake was *nahash,* which began with the sound "n." By the rules of ancient Semitic letter names, this would have been a perfect name for a snaky-looking letter that took the "n" sound. So why didn't the early alphabet users just call their wiggly N letter by the name "snake"?

The answer may be: They *did.* They did perhaps call the letter *nahash* at the start, around 2000 or 1900 B.C., but later the name got changed—for the sake of M. Perhaps, in the centuries after 1900 B.C., a need was felt to bring the letters M ("water") and N ("snake") more into line with each other, on account of their unique nasal factor. The two letters had been placed together in sequence probably at the alphabet's invention; now they would develop even closer associations. In these centuries, the N letter grew more to look like the M letter. And if N's name had been "snake" (as is theorized), then it now changed to "fish," to better fit *mem*'s "water." The purpose of such associations would have been to supply a memory aid for Semitic children learning the alphabet: In the letters' sequence, "fish" would follow "water," the two letters looking and sounding rather similar.

The Phoenician letter dalet, *meaning "door," about 800 B.C.*
Not much of a door: Was the letter shape at one time a fish?

If the Semitic N letter did undergo a name change from *nahash* (snake) to *nun* (fish) during the second millennium B.C., that fact might shed light on another mystery of the early alphabet—namely, why the Semitic D letter, named "door," had such an undoorlike shape. As theorized back on page 96, the Semitic D letter might have started out being named *dag* (another Semitic word for "fish"), around 2000 B.C. But the letter's documented name, in the late first millennium B.C., is *dalet,* "door." Possibly the D letter lost the name "fish" when the N letter took the name "fish," perhaps around 1600 B.C. The alphabet's users didn't want two "fish" letter names, even though the exact words differed.

When the Greeks copied the Phoenician alphabet, around 800 B.C., they maintained the close relationship between N and M. Phoenician *nun* became a Greek letter called *nu,* taking the sound "n," while Phoenician *mem* became Greek *mu,* with the sound "m." Although the Semitic-language "water-fish" connection was necessarily lost on Greek ears, the Greeks forged their own link between the two letters by giving them rhyming names. (Greek *mu* seems to have been named for *nu;* otherwise, why not just convert the Phoenician letter-name *mem* simply to a Greek form like *mema?*) And so ancient Greek children, learning their alphabet, had the advantage of an associative jingle between the M and N letter names.

After the Greek letters reached Italy in the 700s B.C., the use-

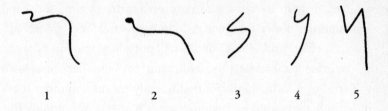

1   2   3   4   5

(1) *Egyptian snake hieroglyph, 2000* B.C. *As used in Egyptian writing, this picture meant the word "cobra" or had other meanings in various contexts. The snake figure would be copied by Semites (for its look, not its meaning) to supply one of about 27 picture letters of their newborn alphabet. (2) Semitic snake letter of perhaps 1750* B.C., *from a stone-carved inscription in western Sinai. It took the sound "n." Logically, Semitic users would have called this letter* nahash, *"snake," yet puzzlingly, its only documented name, from a later century, is* nun, *"fish." (3) Phoenician* nun, *the 14th letter of the Phoenician alphabet, about 1000* B.C. *Descended directly from the earlier Semitic letter,* nun *took the "n" sound that begins its name. Here the letter shape has begun to resemble our N—the more so when you consider that this example faces leftward, in right-to-left writing. Today N remains number 14 in our own alphabet. (4) Phoenician* nun *from an inscription on the island of Cyprus, about 800* B.C. *This was roughly the time and place at which the Phoenician alphabet would be copied by the Greeks. (5) Early Greek N letter, from a right-to-left inscription of about 740* B.C. *Called* nu, *the Greek letter imitated the Phoenician in name, shape, sound, and alphabetic position.*

ful *mu* and *nu* passed into the Etruscan alphabet and thence into the Roman. In Etruscan and in early Latin, the two letters were perhaps called *me* ("may") and *ne* ("nay"). By the late Roman Empire, their names in everyday Latin were probably being pronounced as "emmay" and "ennay"—the forerunners of their modern English names. (For the Romans' naming of liquid and fricative consonants generally, see pages 126–27.)

In modern English, the humble-seeming N is a surprisingly high performer: It is among our most frequently used letters in print, placing about fifth or sixth, after E, T, A, and O or I. Being a common sound in words from Old English, N benefits particularly from its standard use in our verb forms (seeing, seen) and as a euphonic buffer alongside A, as in "an ostrich" or "anaerobic." Also, uses like "and," "not," and "-n't" put added wind in N's sails.

Because it abbreviates the Latin word for "number" (*numerus*), the symbol n in mathematics traditionally means a number that's indefinite, that could be any number: $0 \times n = 0$. We employ this

1 2 3 4 5

(1) An early Etruscan N letter, about 660 B.C. It completely imitated the Greek nu in shape, sound, and alphabetic sequence. This letter faces leftward, in a right-to-left inscription. (2) An early Roman N, also facing leftward, from an inscription of about 520 B.C. The Roman letter had been copied from the Etruscan but soon grew simpler in shape. (3) Roman N from the marble-carved Trajan Inscription, A.D. 113. As used in mature Latin left-to-right writing, the letter was essentially our capital N. (4) N in the uncial handwriting style, from a Latin Psalter of the 400s A.D. It was basically the Roman capital shape adapted to pen and ink. (5) The shape of our lowercase n was one of the last to arise from medieval handwriting, being introduced only around 800, as part of the Carolingian minuscule style. This example comes from a Latin legal document from England, dated 1018. Although the old N shape had been both distinctive and simple (two reasons for its longevity), the Carolingian form required only two pen strokes, not three. Unfortunately, its pleasant shape did allow possible confusion with minuscule h, m, or r. Today, in many people's handwriting, even with print-shape letters, the n remains hard to distinguish.

in common parlance when we speak of something "to the nth degree."

N: A Romantic Mystery is an enjoyable 1997 detective novel by an African American author, Louis Edwards, set in New Orleans. The title plays intelligently on our ugliest N-word as well as on "noir" (as in film noir) and "new." "Make it new," says a well-known verse and a book title (1934) from American poet Ezra Pound. To make it new, let's now move on.

The letter O's inviting shape is well served

in this illustration from an 1845 fiction col-

lection by French author Honoré de Balzac,

titled Petty Annoyances of Married Life,

published in Paris.

THE STORY OF O

O Jerusalem. O Canada. Oh, say, can you see? O for a Muse of fire. For centuries, the robust O has conveyed emotion and demanded attention in verse and oratory. It is perhaps our most expressive letter, and one of our hardest working. While all five of our full-time vowels are essential for writing English, O ranks near the top, as a letter heavily relied on and individually esteemed.

Among O's feature points are: (1) its many shades of pronunciation in English; (2) its uses as a word unto itself; and (3) its beautiful written form—a circle, a ring, intriguing and satisfying to the eye. O is the only letter whose name creates its shape, however imperfectly, on the speaker's lips.

According to certain analyses of English-language print, O averages fourth place in frequency of use, below the letters E, T, and A. A disadvantaged world without O is amusingly imagined in James Thurber's 1957 children's book, *The Wonderful O*, about pirates who land on an island called Ooroo and, offended at the inhabitants' lack of treasure to steal, tyrannically expunge their patron letter. "And so the locksmith became a lcksmith, and the bootmaker a btmaker ... Books were bks and Robinhood was Rbinhd." The island's language and society are shaken—"A swain who praised his sweetheart's thrat, and said she sang like a chir of riles or a chrus of vices, was slapped"—until, finally, good prevails.

Theoretically, our alphabet could use a few more vowel letters, to better show shades of sound. This need is clear with O. The *Oxford English Dictionary* lists seven possible O sounds, as in: no, got, glory, north, do, son, and word; plus others in combination with a second letter: boy, now, good, fool, favor, and (depending on where you live) cough.

Vowels carry most of a speaker's regional accent. O is particularly impressionable this way. To an outsider, an Ulsterman's "now" sounds like "nye," an Ontarian's "about" like "abewt," an Australian's "notes" like "nayts," a New Yorker's "dog" like "doawg." There's also George Bernard Shaw's unforgettable phonetic rendering of the word "don't" as pronounced, circa 1900, by a London Cockney: "daownt."

O's many pronunciations hark back to our language's development in medieval England after the Norman Conquest of A.D. 1066, when new vowel sounds arose from the brew of Old English and Norman French. Adding to O's duties at the time was a Norman preference for spelling with O in place of U, so as to give written English a more Norman French look (although not necessarily with any change in pronunciation). Among many examples, Old English *sum* eventually became "some" (while Old

French *summe,* a different word, supplied our "sum"). Old English *sunu* (pronounced "sun-uh") got changed to *sone* (still "sun-uh"), later shortening to "son." And Old English *lufu* ("luv-uh") eventually made "love."

To understand the medieval Norman thinking here, compare the spellings of two modern words—our "bun" and modern French *bonne* (a form of the adjective "good"), pronounced exactly the same. Such overlaps in sound provided a rationale for substituting O for U in many (not all) medieval English spellings.

This Frenchified O has contributed to one of the most confusing aspects of English spelling, namely, our regular use of O or U for several of the same vowel sounds. The classic example is son/sun, yet there's also loot/lute, cost/caustic, and word/curd/bird/herd—all multiplied by hundreds or thousands of occurrences. O's dilettantism here has troubled many thinkers, including the English educator Richard Mulcaster, whose 1582 grammar book, *The First Part of the Elementarie,* contained the first-ever English spelling dictionary. "O is a letter of great uncertainty in our tongue," Mulcaster notes, for "it soundeth as much upon the u, which is his cousin, as upon the o, which is his natural."

Strictly speaking, O's proper English sounds are the short O of "bob" and long O of "bone." Linguists call these the low, back vowel and high-mid, back vowel, respectively, in reference to the tongue's position in each case. The short O of "son," meanwhile, is the low, front vowel, a sound equally belonging to U.

Our interjection "O" (always capitalized) is a variant of "oh," normally reserved for expressing a wish or calling on some concept or ideal entity, not a real person.

Shakespeare was perhaps overfond of it: "O curse of marriage" (*Othello*); "O brave new world" (*The Tempest*); "O that this too too solid flesh would melt" (*Hamlet*). The word entered medieval English in literary imitation of an interjection "O" that existed in ancient Greek and Latin writings. (The Romans had copied it from the Greeks.)

Prior to Shakespeare, probably the best-known O of Western literature occurs in a famous speech by the Roman statesman Cicero, delivered to a packed Senate chamber in November 63 B.C., for the purpose of exposing a plot, by a senator then present, to overthrow the republic, murder Cicero, and seize supreme power. The bad guy's name was Catiline, and Cicero's speech, one of four in the course of several days, is sometimes called the First Catilinarian. Among its opening words is a deathless phrase of controlled outrage: *O tempora, O mores* . . . (O the times, O the customs.)

The one other famous O of Western lit belongs to Shakespeare, although in use not an interjection but a description. The martial history play *Henry V*, which premiered in London's Globe theater in spring or summer 1599, features an opening speech, addressed to the audience by a narrator character named Prologue. He begins with the words "O for a Muse of fire," but that actually isn't the point right now; Prologue then urges the audience to use their imaginations to fill out the on-stage scenes of royal courts, army campaigns, and the famous Battle of Agincourt (1415). Referring to the theater building around the stage, Prologue asks rhetorically:

> . . . *Can this cockpit hold*
> *The vasty fields of France? Or may we cram*
> *Within this wooden O the very casques [helmets]*
> *That did affright the air at Agincourt?*

Among its other virtues, the passage supplies modern scholars with evidence (more recently corroborated by archaeology) that the Globe Theatre was an "O," that is, it was shaped like a short stack of doughnuts. The center, open to the air, was partly the stage platform, partly ground seating for some of the audience; around the center, the tall wooden structure held galleries of seats and (behind the stage) the stage house. The whole "wooden O" business is well handled visually in the opening sequence of Laurence Olivier's 1944 *Henry V* film version. Today an O-like replica of Shakespeare's Globe stands in south London, 500 yards from the original site.

The story of O's distinctive shape begins in ancient Egypt, with the painted image of a human eye. An eye was one of the symbols of Egyptian hieroglyphic writing. There were several variations, the simplest being a long, horizontal oval with an interior circle. This hieroglyph denoted the word "eye" or other words relating to vision, and might have other meanings besides.

Around 2000 B.C. Semitic soldiers or workers in Egypt invented the world's first alphabet by copying about 27 hieroglyphic pictures and giving them the meanings of tiny speech sounds. The distinctive eye symbol became one such letter: The Semites apparently called it *ayin,* meaning "eye" in their language.

Like all ancient Semitic letters, *ayin* was a consonant: It took a guttural sound, a harsh throat catch, used in Semitic speech and existing today in spoken Arabic. The sound actually occurred at the start of the name *ayin,* but this fact is awkward to show in English transliteration (we have no letter for it) and is usually omitted from our spelling of the name.

Over the next millennium in the Near East, 2000 to 1000 B.C., the *ayin*'s shape simplified: from an oval eye to a circle with a central dot, then to a circle merely. In the Phoenician alphabet of 1000 B.C., *ayin* stood as the 16th letter. In shape, it was a simple circle, basically the same as our O.

When the Greeks copied the Phoenician alphabet sometime around 800 B.C., they had no need of the *ayin*'s guttural sound, foreign to their speech. As with certain other extraneous Phoenician letters, the Greeks held on to *ayin* in regard to its shape and alphabetic place, but they reassigned it to one of the vowel sounds (which were not shown in Phoenician writing but which Greek writing needed to show so as to be comprehensible). The circular *ayin* received the Greek vowel sound "o." Just possibly, this marriage of shape O and sound "o" was prompted by the letter's shape, which suggested the shape of a speaker's mouth saying "o."

Representing both long- and short-O sounds, the Greek letter stayed at place number 16 in the alphabet. For its first 150 years or so, the letter was called probably just *o*.

Around 660 B.C., Greek writing invented a second O letter, to specialize as the long-O sound; its shape was an O "broken open" at the bottom: Ω. Placing the newcomer at the very end of their letter row, the Greeks called it *o mega* or *omega*, meaning "big O." Their 16th letter, now confined to the short-O sound, became known as *o mikron*, "little O." (In English, the name is usually spelled *omicron*.)

Today *omicron* and *omega* live on in the modern Greek alphabet. Both names have also gone into English-language marketing and name-branding, but of the two, *omega* thrives especially. With its elegant shape and its suggestion of "the last word" or "ultimate craftsmanship," *omega* has been put to work representing a line of expensive Swiss watches, as well as camping gear, nutritional supplements, and paintbrushes.

The other O. Being the last letter invented by the ancient Greeks, omega *(meaning "big O") stood at the very end of the Greek alphabet. Its place as the "Z" of the Greek letter list is commemorated in the biblical book of* Revelation, *in a phrase cited back on page 53, "I am Alpha and Omega, the beginning and the ending, saith the Lord." Since the days of the Roman Empire, the paired Greek letters* alpha *and* omega, A Ω, *have comprised a Christian religious symbol.*

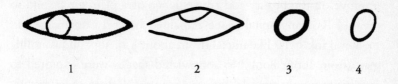

1   2   3   4

(1) Egyptian hieroglyph of an eye, 2000 B.C. In hieroglyphic writing, this picture denoted the word "eye" or other possible words. Memorable in appearance, the eye symbol would inspire the Semitic invention of an alphabetic picture letter, with a Semitic name and a new, phonetic meaning. (2) The Semitic letter ayin, *the "eye," from a sandstone-carved inscription at Serabit el-Khadem in western Sinai, from perhaps 1750 B.C. One of our oldest extant examples of* ayin, *this letter clearly shows its debt to the Egyptian hieroglyph.* Ayin *represented a harsh throat sound, a consonant, which was also the first sound in the letter's name but is usually omitted in English transliteration. (3) Phoenician* ayin *from an inscription of 1000 B.C. The letter name still meant "eye" to the Phoenicians, but the shape had by now been reduced to a circle with no iris.* Ayin *was the Phoenician alphabet's 16th letter. (4) Greek letter O, later to be known as* o mikron *(little O), from an inscription of about 725 B.C. Although the Greek letter copied the Phoenician shape and number-16 place, the Greeks had revalued the symbol to mean the vowel sound "o."*

Meanwhile, in the 700s B.C., before *omega* was born, the Greek alphabet had reached Italy, with only one O letter. The Etruscans of Italy copied this alphabet to create their own (700 B.C.). The Etruscan letters, in turn, were copied and adapted by the Romans (600 B.C. and following). The single O, representing both long and short sounds, became a Roman letter and eventually was bequeathed to us. Today, O is our 15th letter. Like most vowels, it takes its English name from its basic long sound.

O's simple, pleasing shape has barely changed in 3,000 years, since the early Phoenicians. During the century before Christ, the Romans, in monumental inscriptions carved in stone, found ways to subtly taper and widen parts of the letter, giving it a suave, ribbonlike look that we often use today. During the Middle Ages, certain handwriting styles made O more square or diamond shaped or (for a fancy initial capital) gave it ornamental crossbars. But these variations didn't stick. No alternative could improve on the beauty and convenience of a plain circle, and so the old Roman capital shape remained basically unchanged in medieval ink styles like uncial (from about A.D. 300) and Carolingian (from about 800). No abbreviated shapes were explored to eventually supply a model for early printers' lowercase letters; instead, capital O supplied the lowercase shape. Today, C, S, V, W, X, and Z share with O this distinction of having closely the same shape for upper- and lowercase in most typefaces.

O resembles our zero symbol, 0, but that's by chance. The zero, as first written in Hindu and Arab lands during the early Middle Ages, was a tiny circle or dot, smaller than other numerals and used for holding place in computation. A larger zero emerged in European handwriting by about 1400, through the custom of keeping characters at roughly equal size; this letter-size zero became a print form by the late 1400s. In modern typefaces, zero's sign tends to be more elongated than O.

With its inviting visual associations—doorway, porthole, offered lips, push button—O has enjoyed a prime place in product names, signposting, and the like. At the "Tunnel of Love" amusement park rides of the 1920s to 1960s, you might be conveyed into the dark interior through the huge letter O of "Love." The celebrated early 1980s Manhattan restaurant Odeon (familiar from the cover painting and storyline of Jay McInerney's 1983 novel, *Bright Lights, Big City*) surely owed some success to the look of its name on its Art Deco neon sign, with two beckoning O's. Other examples include the appliances Veg-O-Matic ("It slices, it dices") and Ice-O-Matic, with names that verbally mimic the word "automatic" but visually use O to suggest push-button ease.

By far the best example of a recent commercial O is in the remarkably successful women's lifestyle magazine copublished by TV talk-show personality Oprah Winfrey. Officially titled *O, The*

MAP

OF

VILLA SITES

OFFERED FOR SALE

by the

Rutherfurd Heights Association

RUTHERFURD PARK

N.J.

By its placement and design, the O of "Offered" seems to invite a bid, or at least a look, in this sales poster from an 1870 American collection, Copley's Plain & Ornamental Standard Alphabets. *Note the different type styles: the traditional "roman" lettering of "Rutherfurd Heights Association" and the early sans-serif forms of "Offered for Sale."*

Oprah Magazine, but more casually known as "O magazine" or "Oprah's magazine," this monthly has hit a steady paid circulation of nearly 2.3 million since its launch in the year 2000. Without doubt, one small ingredient of its appeal has been its O—that is, its clever name and logo, drawn from Oprah's fortuitous initial but deftly handled, visually, by the magazine's designers. The cover logo is a large, white O, in the classic but emphatic Bodoni typeface (see page 256), set against a solid rectangle of color, the color changing each month. Dignified yet friendly—like Oprah's image, which appears in a different photo on every cover—the O seems to invite the reader through a portal of (self) discovery.

Which brings us to the hidden source of O's commercial

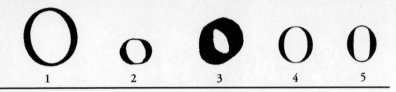

strength: its subliminal vaginal reference. Oprah's O appears to send at least a "women's own" message. Further along in this direction is the unabashed title of the women's how-to book *The Big O,* subtitled *Orgasms: How to Have Them, Give Them, and Keep Them Coming,* by sex educator Lou Paget (2001). The lettering on the book cover features a big O that—but you get the idea.

O likes male attention, too, of course. This writer won't soon forget the T-shirt message "Dyn-O-Mite," associated usually with expensive denim shorts and cork-heeled sandals, as worn by young women during Manhattan summers of the 1970s and early '80s. For me, the lettering could have said "tOrment."

The mother of such sexual O's is the 1954 French pornographic fantasy novel *The Story of O,* by Pauline Réage. With a despairing view of female destiny, the story follows a young female Parisian fashion photographer known only as O, who cooperates in being systematically degraded by her boyfriend and others. Her name is meant to illustrate a woman's sexuality, a slave's fetter, and, finally, a worthless zero. The novel, once respected as a kind of feminist wake-up call, is now more often seen as exploitative trash. Yet we still talk about it.

The Story of O has a theme of male-to-female sadism, which today colors the letter O, at least potentially. In certain circles, O can be a coded symbol for bondage, fetishism, and similar dark preoccupations. Among several examples is a German magazine named *O*, subtitled (in translation) *The Art, the Fashion, the Fantasy*. Distributed also in the United States, this *O* magazine focuses on fashion aspects—leather garments, high-heeled boots—of what might be called the fetish or bondage scene.

What makes German *O* noteworthy is that (at this writing) it is on a deliberate collision course with the ocean liner of Oprah's *O*. The German businessman who publishes the fetishist *O* has sued the corporate publishers of Oprah's magazine for trademark infringement, on the grounds that through prior publication he owns the U.S. trademark for a magazine named *O*. When first filed in 2001, the lawsuit inspired a tickled-pink *New York Times* editorial titled "Legally, the Alphabet Isn't as Simple as A, B and C." Its opening words: "Who owns the letters of the alphabet?"

German *O*'s lawsuit has since received a tentative spanking from a Manhattan U.S. District Court judge, who in 2002 denied a motion for a preliminary injunction (namely, Oprah's *O* to suspend publication for the case's duration). The judge ruled that the two magazines are dissimilar enough to avoid consumer confusion. But a preliminary ruling is not a final verdict, and a courtroom showdown is promised for sometime in 2003.

Traditionally, in affectionate written correspondence, O's beneath the person's signature have meant hugs, complementing the X's of kisses. Taking a cue from this charming custom, let's now say OOO and go.

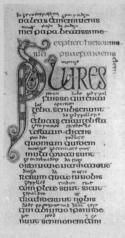

Considered among the most beautiful of all decorated letters of medieval manuscripts, an initial P begins the Latin word plures, *"many people," on a page from the famous Lindisfarne Gospels, written probably in about A.D. 695. The P, colored in amber and light green in the original, incorporates the head of a dragon and of a seagull, as well as whorl motifs of traditional Northern European art (familiar also from extant jewelry, stone carving, etc.). The page presents the beginning of St. Jerome's preface to the four biblical Gospels—that is, Matthew, Mark, Luke, and John—which follow in the manuscript. Above the P, a line of text addresses "my most blessed Pope (*papa*)."*

The Lindisfarne Gospels were produced at the monastery of Lindisfarne, on a small island near the northeast English coast. Although it is not an original composition—the text is St. Jerome's Latin version of the Gospels, from around A.D. 400—the manuscript's gorgeous painted "illuminations" make it a treasure of medieval British art. The handwriting style is called insular majuscule, the term "insular" a reference to the monastic writing traditions of the British and Irish islands. The talented scribe and painter was probably a monk named Eadrith, who later became Bishop of Lindisfarne.

PUFF DADDY P

ushing off from the lips, P exemplifies the category of consonants known as stops. Stops make sound by expulsion of breath, during which the nasal passage is momentarily stopped from within; they include also B, D, G, K (with C and Q), and T. Stops are known also as plosives, a word (related to "explosion") that is built on the forthright sound of P. Come to think of it, "stop" is half built on P, too.

One other stop consonant makes a sound through the lips: B. The two letters are closely related, nearly alter egos, not just in manner of pronunciation but also in shape and name. They form one of those intriguing letter pairs of our alphabet, such as C and G or M and

N. The kinship of P and B was summed up back in 1580 by the early English lexicographer John Baret (see pages 85–86), in his dictionary titled the *Alvearie:* "This letter p seemeth by both his name and form to be of kind to b, and as it were a b turned upside down."

As Baret's wording suggests, P comes across as the relationship's junior partner—the following or besotted one, living in awe of the somewhat better established B and trying at times to imitate him. Their main difference in sound is the vocal cords: B engages the vocal cords while P does not, therefore requiring a more effortful, audible puff of breath. Yet in some words, P may be heard to blur into B: for example, in "spill," which sounds closer to "bill" than to "pill." Or in "napkin," pronounced as "nabkin" in most North American accents.

Of course, P mimics B in shape, too. We can phrase it that way because that's how it happened: Inscriptions from the early centuries of the ancient Roman alphabet, around 600 to 200 B.C., show the Roman letter P gradually morphing in shape to reach its present form, presumably in order to resemble the existing shape of B. The purpose behind the change seems to have been memorization: The Romans apparently found the two letters easier to learn and remember if they looked alike on top of sounding alike.

P and B belong also to a second category of consonants, whose third member is M. Formed at the lips, they are the "labials" (from the Latin word for "lip"). Labials are easy to pronounce, as needing no fancy tongue work. They seem to have played a role in most human languages, and they are often among the earliest speech sounds from an infant's mouth: "Pa-pa-pa. Ma-ma-ma. Ba-ba-ba."

The baby connection of P, M, and B has been explored here in Chapter M. As mentioned, P contributes to a number of baby-related words in different adult languages; the common element may be an adult imitation of child speech. The most obvious such English word is "papa," with its abbreviated form "pa" and variants "pop" and "poppy" and alternative spelling "poppa." While these five words derive officially from Latin *pater* (father), they have thrived and multiplied by their aptness of sound: They mimic baby talk. Among other examples are "papoose" (from the North American Algonquian tongue, meaning a young child or a knapsack-style basket for carrying same), "pap" (meaning the female nipple, from Old Norse into medieval English), "pap" (meaning mushy food for babies, from a Latin word), and "pope" (a title that passed into late Latin as *papa,* from the Greek *papas,* "father" or "daddy").

P in English is basically a solid fellow with very few variant sounds, aside from the occasional yearning to be B. In words like "tempt," "redemption," and "Simpson," P has an interesting half pronunciation, made possible by the preceding, similarly labial M: The P can slide quickly between M and the following letter. Elsewhere, P has gone to silence, as in "raspberry" or in our many words with Greek roots wherein the P was pronounced by the ancients: psychic, psalm, pneumatic, etc. And as every schoolboy knows, there can be a silent P in swimming.

Our 16th letter, P descends straightforwardly from the 17th letter of the ancient Near Eastern alphabet. The world's oldest known alphabetic inscriptions, at Wadi el-Hol in central Egypt, contain examples of a large letter, shaped somewhat like a thick V or downward-pointing chevron, that experts believe is the early P. The letter's name was *pe,* pronounced "pay," meaning "mouth" in the ancient Semitic language; the V shape was a kind of smile or expression to characterize the mouth. The *pe* took the "p" sound that began its name.

But the early P is better known to us from a later stage of Semitic writing, namely, the Phoenician alphabet of 1000 B.C. The Phoenician 17th letter was the *pe,* still understood as meaning "mouth" and still taking the "p" sound, but by now its shape had changed. The mouth figure had shrunk to a mere corner of its former self: It now looked like a candy cane, with its crook, at top, facing leftward. Although the Phoenician letter shape in no way resembled a mouth anymore, it did suggest the beginning of what we would call a backward P. (As used in right-to-left writing, Phoenician letters tended to project leftward, "backward," whereas ours project rightward in left-to-right flow.)

When the Greeks adopted the Phoenician alphabet in around 800 B.C., they copied *pe* closely: The letter's shape, sound, and alphabetic place remained the same in the newborn Greek alphabet, while the letter's Greek name was tweaked to "pee"—pronounced just like our letter name but spelled *pi*. The "mouth" connection was by now completely lost: As with all other Greek letters, the name *pi* meant nothing in Greek aside from signifying the letter.

During the 700s B.C., the cane-shape *pi* traveled with other Greek letters in Greek merchant ships to Italy, where it was copied into the newborn alphabet of the Etruscans and thence, around 600 B.C., into that of the Romans. At this point, as with other early Greek letters, the road forks: The Greek-derived P letter would evolve in shape within the Roman alphabet, but so would *pi* evolve in shape within the Greek alphabet, "back home." By the 300s B.C., most Greeks were writing *pi* as a two-legged double-T figure, perhaps familiar to us from geometry class.

Today *pi,* pronounced as "pie" and shown as π, represents probably the most famous ratio in mathematics, namely that of a circle's circumference to its diameter—the number of times the diameter would fit atop the circle's circumference. This ratio π is usually approximated at 3.14 but is in fact an irrational number that begins as 3.1415926535 and has been calculated to more than 1.24 *trillion* decimal places (by Tokyo computer scientists in 2002), with no end in sight. The π owns a place in several well-known equations, the best-remembered being $A = \pi r^2$, or, the area of a circle equals π times the square of the circle's radius.

The use of Greek letter *pi* in this way dates from A.D. 1706, when Welsh mathematician William Jones published a book that

Π π

Shall we call thee "pie" or "pee"? Here is the modern Greek letter pi *in upper- and lowercase, as derived from the ancient Athenian alphabet of about 400 B.C. Taking the "p" sound, the Greek letter is a close family relation of our P. The ancient Greeks probably called it by the name "pee," as modern Greeks do. Yet the rules of anglicization—whereby we pronounce foreign words' vowels as if they were English—require this letter's English name to be "pie," with an English long-I sound.*

included π as the symbol for the circumference-to-diameter ratio (the ratio itself being long known from prior mathematics and variously shown). Jones's choice of *pi* was due to it being the first letter of the ancient Greek word *periphereia,* "circumference." In keeping with traditional scientific notation, he used the lowercase letter shape: π. And by the rules of anglicization, the Greek letter name in English was pronounced "pie." Jones's symbol caught the fancy of other mathematicians of the day, and it stuck.

Largely through *pi*'s mathematical association, the letter's shape and name have enjoyed a philosophical prestige in some treatments, as a sort of key to the universe. In the 1999 independent film titled π, a brilliant mathematician is on the verge of decoding human destiny and the stock market, while Yann Martel's 2001 novel, *Life of Pi,* winner of Britain's prestigious Booker Prize, follows 16-year-old Pi Patel, born in India, who gains wisdom through loss and fantastical adventure.

Meanwhile, back in the ancient Roman alphabet, the cane-shape P letter gradually transformed into the capital shape we know today. As mentioned, the change may have involved an "attraction" to the existing shape of the letter B: The two letters, so similar in sound, thus became paired for easier memorization.

By coincidence, the Roman letter name apparently echoed the ancient Phoenician one: "pay." The Romans would have spelled it P-E, with the long E in Roman pronunciation. This was the name bequeathed to Europe's Romance languages after Rome's fall (A.D. 500), and today the letter name remains near to "pay," spelled P-E, in French and Spanish. Passing to medieval English from Old French after the Norman Conquest of England in 1066, the name "pay" eventually changed its vowel sound, amid the general English vowel shift culminating in the 1500s. Today we maintain the spelling of the letter's name as P-E, but we pronounce it "pee."

P has the odd distinction of being the third-most-often-used opening letter in English vocabulary. (Think: Peter Piper picked a peck of etc.) Letter S starts off the most English words, with C in

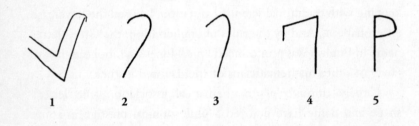

| 1 | 2 | 3 | 4 | 5 |

(1) Early Semitic letter, probably the pe, *meaning "mouth," from the Wadi el-Hol inscriptions of about 1800 B.C. Carved perhaps 200 years after the alphabet's invention, this letter shows its original aspect as a (primitive) picture of a person's mouth. (2) Phoenician* pe, *the "mouth," about 1000 B.C. The letter took the "p" sound that began its name. The written shape, by now reduced to the extreme right-hand edge of the older shape, no longer looked like a mouth but like a cane. The letter projected leftward, for Phoenician right-to-left writing. Potentially confusingly,* pe *looked like an upside-down version of another Phoenician letter, the L letter,* lamed. *(3) The early Greek* pi—*this one from a right-to-left inscription of about 740 B.C.—closely imitated the Phoenician letter in shape, sound, name, and alphabetic position. (4) Early Roman P, from a right-to-left inscription of about 520 B.C. The shape was again changing. (5) The Roman P of about 200 B.C. had reached more or less its modern shape. It faced rightward in mature Roman left-to-right writing.*

second place. Surprisingly, these three initial letters together account for one-third of all words in the dictionary. That is, a third of English words begin with an S, C, or P.

Yet, according to scholarly analysis, P was used only rarely as a beginning letter in words of Old English, during the early Middle Ages. Its proliferation since those days betokens how much our language has grown and changed, with the influx of Latin-derived French vocabulary after the Norman Conquest of 1066 and of Greek- and Latin-derived technical vocabulary in the 19th and 20th centuries. (So please remember your debt, next time you hold the parasol for a photographer at a pork parade.) Among other elements in this invasion of P-words, there has been the continually expanding number of our words with the Latin prefixes *pre-* (as in "prefix"), *post-, per-,* and *pro-,* and the Greek prefixes *para-, peri-,* and *pro-.*

Partly due to its regrettable association in English, P hasn't had much of a cultural life of its own. Unlike its neighbor O, the P will probably never give its name to a wildly successful, mainstream, English-language magazine. There are, however, *P* magazines published in Flemish, Turkish, and other tongues: The Flemish contender—a kind of Belgian *Maxim,* for young adult males—uses P benignly to stand for "panorama."

P as an abbreviation means "phosphorus" in chemistry and "softly" in musical notation, from the Italian word *piano* (softly). Our piano instrument was originally, in around 1770, called a "pianoforte," from *piano e forte,* "softly and loudly" (describing the gradation of tone available, in contrast with the monotoned harpsichord).

The PX, a kind of general store found on U.S. military bases, is named as an abbreviation of "post exchange." Rather different is the superimposed P-and-X symbol that appears on church stained glass, certain priests' robes, and other Roman Catholic and Episcopalian settings. Contrary to what is sometimes thought, this PX does not stand for the Latin word *pax* (peace)—nor are the letters even P and X. Known as the Cross of Constantine, the two letters are Greek: a *khi* (the X shape, sounded as "kh") and a *rho* (the P shape, which is the Greek R), these being the first two letters of *Christos,* Christ.

Our expression "to mind your p's and q's"—meaning to be careful in your behavior and observe all etiquette—harks back to the printer's trade of the 15th to the early 20th century. Metal letter blocks, bearing letter shapes in relief, were stored in two different cases: "upper case" for capitals, "lower case" for minuscules. Once removed from their case, the blocks with the lowercase shapes could be hard to identify and to distinguish from each other, especially for the similar-looking b, d, p, and q—and the more so since the blocks' letter shapes were mirror-image versions of the actual print shapes. In setting the type and in (finally) replacing the blocks in their case, printers had to pay attention lest they confuse p with d, or q with b, or p with q.

The P was briefly explored by American humorist author James Thurber (1894–1961), whose many works include the children's book *The Wonderful O,* cited in the prior chapter. Plagued by ailments and eventually blindness, Thurber died at age 66 from complications following a stroke. A few months before that, he

The Cross of Constantine, named for the Roman emperor who, having converted to Christianity, declared it a state religion in A.D. *324. The symbol comprises two Greek letters, a* khi *and* rho, *shaped like X and P. They are the first two letters of the Greek title* Christos, *"anointed one," which provides the name* Christ.

P p P Perpetua

1   2   3   4

(1) Roman capital P from the marble-carved Trajan Inscription, A.D. 113. This letter shape would become the model for capital P's of all modern roman typefaces, although the charming mannerism of the incomplete loop would prove impractical for early print. (2) Inked P in the uncial handwriting style, from a Latin biblical manuscript of the 600s A.D. While closely imitating the shape of the Roman carved capital, the uncial letter also descended below the baseline with the lower half of its bar, thus anticipating our modern lowercase letter. (3) P in the semi-uncial ink style, from a Latin manuscript of the 500s, from southern Italy. This P—a "descender," like the uncial shape—seems more clearly to look ahead to our modern lowercase shape. (4) The influence of the past is apparent in the letter shapes of Perpetua, a roman typeface created by eminent British type designer Eric Gill in about 1928.

published his last book while alive, the collection *Lanterns and Lances* (1961), including an essay on insomnia, "The Watchers of the Night." Poignantly, the cheerful essay betrays a physical discomfort and restlessness that, unknown to the author, would culminate soon in his death. Thurber describes how, awake in bed at 3 A.M., he counts sheep by thinking about the alphabet and one letter especially. "The letter 'P,' that broad, provocative expanse between 'O' and 'Q,' is one of the most ambivalent of all the twenty-six, for in it one finds pleasure and pain, peace and pandemonium, prosperity and poverty, power and pusillanimity. . . ." In the end, Thurber finds, the mental exercise keeps him awake: "'P,' the purloining letter, the stealer of sleep, is as hard to throw off as any addiction."

Yet, pulling free of P, we now pass on.

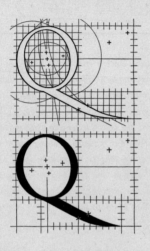

Wheels within wheels. In an illustration from his 1529 book about the letters, Champ Fleury, *French type designer Geofroy Tory demonstrates on a grid the proper proportions of his elegant, long-tailed Q. The small crosses indicate the center points of the compass strokes needed to plot the shape. The tail is Q's most distinctive feature and traditionally an object of pleasure and fastidiousness among calligraphers and type designers.*

THE QUALITY OF Q

QWERTY. Recognize that? Not a character's name from a P. G. Wodehouse novel nor the name of next Christmas's buyer-frenzy toy for preschoolers, QWERTY appears on a typist's keyboard. It spells out the first six letters, left to right, in the top row of the letter keys.

Q's extreme left-hand perch reflects a quirky fact about typing: Originally the keyboard was *designed* to slow the typist down. Letter-wise, our familiar keyboard is basically unchanged from the earliest specimens of the 1870s, exemplified in the 1874 Remington manual typewriter, the first commercially successful one. This keyboard deliberately forces the typist's fingers to stretch to find the likely letter combinations of English.

The purpose in 1874 was to help prevent jamming. The manual-typewriter key, when tapped, would operate a long, thin "typebar," which swung up to punch its letterform through an inked ribbon onto paper. Under a skilled typist's fingers, the type-bars rose and fell in chattering profusion. But the bars of the early machines were apt to jam if the typist went too fast, or if two neighboring keys were touched at nearly the same time. There-fore, on the keyboard, many of the frequent letter combinations of English have their keys separated, particularly by left side versus right, so as to be under different hands to the typist. The Q key is safely distant from the key of Q's constant companion—the letter U. In English, we almost never write Q without writing U next to it; thus, Q is a left-hand key while U is a right-hand one. And al-though technology has since banished the jamming problem, the keyboard design is too deeply entrenched ever to change.

The Q is a modern success story. Previously marginalized and disesteemed, it has, since about the 1980s, enjoyed a happy rever-sal of fortune. Today Q is the darling of certain interest groups and marketing circles, emblazoned on our signposting and brand names.

But in the old days, to start with, Q seemed exotic, foreign, potentially strange or embarrassing. This was due first of all to its low rate of use. Q is nearly the least-often-used letter of English print, falling second, third, or fourth to last, according to different surveys. (Z comes last by most counts: See the chart on page 118.) This low ranking results from Q's wasteful rivalry with C and K, as described in those letters' chapters: All three take the sound "k," but there simply aren't enough "k" sounds to go around.

In English spelling, C gets favored; K finishes a distant second; and Q specializes. Almost always, Q appears before a U and a sec-ond vowel, with the QU- usually taking the sound "kw," as in "quail," "quest," "equilibrium." Otherwise, in words derived relatively recently from French, QU- may take a simple "k" sound: mannequin, antique, and the British cheque and queue.

Q's problematic specialized role—problematic because we don't need it: We could easily drop Q from the alphabet and spell "quail" as "kwail" or "liquor" as "licor"—has earned the wrath of thinkers through the ages. Back in about A.D. 90, the Roman grammarian Quintilian dismissed Q as "redundant [Latin: *supervacua*] except for the purpose of attaching vowels to itself." And the English playwright and scholar Ben Jonson, in his 1640 *English Grammar,* points out distastefully that our use of Q in English spelling was imposed by a French-language invasion (the Norman conquest of 1066) and that previously Old English had gotten by fine with no Q: "The English-Saxons knew not this halting Q, with her waiting woman *u* after her."

Adding to Q's marginality, traditionally, has been its fancy shape, its lip-pursing name, and the fact that Q tended to stand for things considered mysterious or dicey. Q abbreviates the word "query," meaning "question mark"—as in "Q fever," so named because its origin puzzled doctors in the 1930s, and "Q-ships," which were World War I British warships disguised as helpless freighters, to lure German U-boats. (There's U following Q again.) And Q meant "queer," in senses both of "odd" and "homosexual." Such associations might be played for laughs on the 1930s vaudeville stage or in film comedies through the 1960s: A male character with middle initial Q was probably meant to signal "uh-oh" to the audience.

Caspar Milquetoast was a meek, submissive character, featured in a New York *Herald Tribune* comic strip of 1924 to 1953 by Harold Tucker Webster. The faux French name Milquetoast (which has since gone into common parlance to mean any timid soul) came from the mainstream word "milktoast," describing a dish traditionally served to invalids and babies. Although with no obvious sexual reference, the Q in his name helped to set Caspar apart: He was different from you and me—supposedly.

Today, however, the stigma of Q is a thing of the past. As our era has grown suspicious of uniformity—remember those Apple "Think Different" ads of the late 1990s—Q's offbeat aura has gained in appeal among marketing and advertising minds. Like X, Z, and a few other letters, Q is now exploited for its very rarity and eye-catching power; today Q is "quantum," "quasar," "quark," "quick," and, yes, "queer," only now as a proud badge of identity. In mainstream brand names, Q seems to promise a rules-breaking technological genius, or a cool alternative, or science fiction become reality. Witness, for instance, names like Q-Media software, Q9 website engineering, Qsound electronics, QLogic computer hardware, Q hard drives, the digital Q Phone, the British pop-music magazine Q, the rapper Q-Tip, the Infiniti Q45 and other Q's of the Infiniti auto line. And let's not forget the distinctively misspelled Qwest Communications, fourth largest of U.S. long-distance carriers, now mired in financial and legal woes.

Clearing the path for such Q's of the 21st century was none

JOHN Q. PUBLIC

In the term "John Q. Public," documented in the United States since the 1930s, the Q is unexpected, puzzling. Instead of the marginal Q, we get a Q that supposedly embraces everyone. Yet even here Q is probably negative, contributing to a likely tone of disdain: John Q. Public is someone unimpressive, the frequent dupe of the politicians and the rich. The 2002 movie *John Q.* stars Denzel Washington as an angry, financially struggling factory worker who lacks sufficient health insurance to provide a needed organ transplant for his young son.

other than Bill Gates (and company), with release of Microsoft's influential QBasic computer program back in 1986. The Q (for "quick") had been kicking around computer jargon for perhaps a decade, but at that point it seems truly to have spread its wings, language-wise, in programming and marketing circles.

Meanwhile, Q for "queer," meaning "homosexual," has passed from an offensive or underground symbol of the early 20th century to an open emblem of gay interest groups and identity. "Series Q" is the gay and lesbian studies book series published by Duke University in North Carolina. Other such Q's include the Wisconsin gay theater group StageQ and websites with names like Planet Q, QWorld, Q-Fish, Q-online, and Q-mmunity.

Q has almost always been a dark horse, running from behind. The Phoenician alphabet of 1000 B.C. had two K letters: *kaph,* ancestor of our K, and *qoph,* ancestor of Q. The reason for two Phoenician letters was their subtle difference in pronunciation: In Phoenician speech, *qoph* represented a sound where the tongue touched a different part of the roof of the mouth than for *kaph.* The name *qoph* probably meant "monkey"; the letter shape was perhaps a stylized form of a monkey face and tail: Ϙ

Qoph was the 19th Phoenician letter. Today the Hebrew alphabet has a 19th letter called *qof,* which takes a sound like "q." The Hebrew letter shape still somewhat resembles its Phoenician forebear of 3,000 years ago. Meanwhile, the 21st letter of the Arabic alphabet is called *qaf* and takes a similar sound.

The ancient Greeks, sometime around 800 B.C., copied *qoph* into their alphabet, modifying the name to a more Greek-style *qoppa.* (Phoenician *kaph,* meanwhile, became the Greek letter *kappa.*) Unlike the Phoenician language, Greek had no subtle distinction between "q" and "k" sounds and didn't need two

Kindred in sound and in lineage: the Hebrew letter qof *and the Arabic* qaf. *While not similar in shape, they both derive from the ancient Phoenician Q letter. Both these modern Semitic Q letters are distinct from the K letters of their respective alphabets, as sending the tongue tip to a different part of the roof of the mouth. In Arabic, for example,* qalb *means "heart" while* kalb, *pronounced slightly differently, means "dog."*

such letters. Eventually *qoppa* would drop out of Greek—but meanwhile it had reached Italy in Greek trading ships. There it was copied from the Greek into the Etruscan alphabet (700 B.C.) and from the Etruscan into the Roman alphabet (600 B.C.). The Etruscans called their letter *qu*, pronounced more or less as "koo," from which the letter's modern name in English and other tongues derives.

Like the Phoenicians, the Etruscans observed a difference in pronunciation between K and Q. But like the Greeks, the Romans *didn't.* The order-loving Romans wound up with three letters for the "k" sound—C, K, and Q—two of which they basically did not need. To fix the mess, they relied on C, ignored K, and confined Q to one use only: to help capture the abundant Latin consonantal sound "kw."

Thus, for "kw," the Romans wrote the letters QU-. The Q meant the "k" part and the U in that position meant "w." Because "kw" could be pronounced only before a vowel, the letters QU- were written only before a vowel. The U had many uses in Latin aside from accompanying Q, but the Q had no other role: It was written only before U and a second vowel.

Among hundreds of such Latin words were *squalor* (squalor), *aequalis* (equal), *eloquens* (eloquent), and *quinque* (five), all of which have since contributed to English words. The Latin spelling QU- can be contrasted with the CU- of Latin words like *cultus* (cultivation) and *porcus* (pig), where the sound was a simple "kuh" or "koo," without "w."

The Latin QU for "kw" was bequeathed to Romance languages such as French after Rome's fall (A.D. 500). Meanwhile, on the isle of Britain, the Anglo-Saxons were writing Old English with a modified Roman alphabet that omitted the letter Q. The Anglo-Saxons didn't need it, as Ben Jonson points out above (page 271). They were happy to write "queen" as *cwen* and "quick" as *cwic*. But that changed with the Norman Conquest of England in 1066: Not only did the invaders bring hundreds of Norman French words with QU- spellings (quart, quest, require, etc.), but

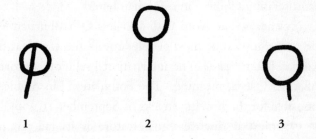

1   2   3

(1) The Phoenician Q letter, called qoph, *the "monkey," from an inscription of about 950 B.C. This letter shape—which probably evolved from a more pictorial version of a monkey face and tail—already shows the beginning of our modern Q shape. Qoph's sound was similar to that of the Phoenician K letter, called* kaph. *(2) Greek* qoppa *from an inscription from the island of Thera, around 685 B.C. Although copied from* qoph, *the Greek letter took a slightly different shape, to avoid confusion with another Greek letter,* phi. *(Phi had not been copied from a Phoenician letter.) The Greek shape shows the two elements of our modern Q: a circle and a tail. (3) Roman Q from an inscription of about 520 B.C. The Roman letter was copied from an Etruscan letter, which had been copied from the Greek. The Etruscans and Romans kept three letters for the "k" sound—C, K, and Q—which we inherit in our modern Roman alphabet.*

Norman scribes in England began spelling native English words with a French-style QU-, as well. So *cwen* became "queen" and *cwic* became "quick." Q, or rather QU-, had arrived in English.

Only in recent decades has English Q occasionally gone out without "her waiting woman" (Ben Jonson again). Most dictionaries now use Q without U to transliterate a few familiar foreign words and names, usually from Arabic, Hebrew, or Chinese. Examples include the Arabian sheikdom of Qatar, the collected Hebrew mystical writings called the Qabbala (variant of Kabbalah), and the ancient Chinese dynasty called Qin (variant of Ch'in). The change to Q for Arabic and Hebrew represents an attempt to render more loyally the Q letter of Arabic or Hebrew, that is, the *qaf* or *qof*. In prior generations, *qaf* or *qof* was routinely transliterated as a K, in order to spare English-speaking readers the effrontery of a U-less Q. In the case of Chinese, the newer use of Q reflects the Pinyin system, universally accepted since 1979 for transliterating Chinese into Roman letters.

Nowadays, one word with a U-less Q has burned itself into the consciousness of most people around the world, if they read Roman letters: *qaeda*. The international religious terrorist group called Al Qaeda, meaning "The Foundation" in Arabic, was responsible for the horrific attacks of September 11, 2001.

Q's most distinctive visual feature is its tail, an item approached seriously in calligraphy and type design. Some typefaces, aiming at elegance, make the tail extra long—a look that American type designer D. B. Updike deplores in his influential 1922 book, *Printing Types*. Yet British type designer Edward Johnston, in his classic 1906 work titled *Writing and Illuminating, and Lettering*, sees nothing wrong with a long tail, provided it has "a slight double curve to take off its stiffness."

Q has found a modest niche in modern literature. The *Star Trek* sci-fi novel series includes a recurring character named Q, a powerful being "from another continuum" who sometimes threatens, sometimes aids our heroes of the starship *Enterprise*. Q's name plays on the scientific term "quantum" (from Latin *quantum,* "how much"), which denotes a quantity of energy in certain proportions and which is the basis for a whole theory of physics. Go, Q!

Fans of Ian Fleming's James Bond novels and their movie versions know Q as the code name of Major Boothroyd, Bond's equipment officer, who usually appears near the tale's beginning to brief the superspy on the miraculous or fiendish devices being issued for his mission. The deadpan Q has a comic effect, both as a foil for Bond's playfulness and as a lower-rank duplicate of the other letter in Bond's life—his serious-toned boss, code-named M. Why Q? For "quartermaster"? Or did author Fleming, writing in the 1950s to '60s, just think it was good for a laugh?

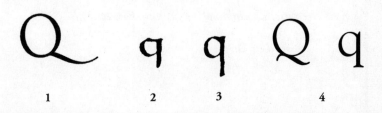

1   2   3   4

(1) Roman Q from the Trajan Inscription, A.D. 113. This handsome letter takes a prominent place in the inscription's top line, in the Roman public formula Senatus Populusque Romanus, "the Senate and People of Rome." Carved Roman letter shapes like this would inspire the capital Q's of early printers in Italy, around 1470; however, the long tail would prove impractical for standard print. (2) The inked Q of uncial handwriting—this example from a Latin biblical manuscript of the 600s—clearly anticipates our modern lowercase print q shape. In the uncial style, which developed around 300, scribes wrote the tail as a down-stroke from the circle's side, not bottom, which saved time by allowing the pen to stay always on the surface. (3) A slightly cleaner look than the uncial's distinguishes the Carolingian minuscule letter. This one comes from an English document of 1018. (4) Upper- and lowercase versions in Goudy Old Style typeface, created in 1916 by American type designer Frederic W. Goudy. These letter shapes draw from the past, but on their own terms.

The letter's shape is cleverly and even plausibly captured in this 1836 print, part of a fanciful alphabet of human figures, published in Paris.

OUR ARRESTING R

R U C.N. an I ? F Y ? U'r I's R 2 2 . Translation: Are you seeing an eye doctor? If not, why not? Your eyes are too dear to waste.

This rebus has been brought to you by R, the 18th letter of the alphabet (and the first letter of "rebus"). A rebus—as almost everyone —is a word puzzle in which pictures or symbols serve as phonetic substitutes for the sounds of certain words or syllables. Pronounced *REE-bus* in English, the name comes from the Latin phrase *rebus non verbis*, "by means of objects, not words." Rebuses can be surprisingly fun, combining brainteaser challenge with humorous wordplay. R is a favorite rebus tool, since its name approximates the words "are" and (cheating a bit) "our."

R's name displays well the letter's remarkable sound, a sound created by vibration of the palate, throat, and tongue, with the tongue approaching the palate. If you begin making the R sound, then lift your tongue tip to your palate, you'll find you've switched to L. Phonetically, L is R's sister; the two letters constitute the small category of consonants called "liquids." (See page 215.) R's open tongue position allows for more throat than L, and throatiness is R's hallmark.

R's growling sound (demonstrated in the word "growl") has inevitably been associated with dogs. Geofroy Tory observes in his 1529 book on the alphabet, *Champ Fleury*: "When dogs are angry, before they begin to bite each other, contracting their throats and grinding their teeth, they seem to be saying R." As Tory himself mentions, the dog reference dates back at least to ancient Rome: The poet Persius, in the mid–1st century A.D., called R the "dog letter," *canina littera*. Likewise, in his 1640 *English Grammar*, Ben Jonson (who certainly had read Persius and probably Tory) described R as "the dog's letter." Yet this highly accomplished and intriguing letter is by no means itself a dog.

Phonetically, the two liquids, R and L, are known to have an effect on a vowel sound that precedes them in a word: The R or L draws out the vowel's pronunciation, usually making it stronger. Listen carefully to "Al," "pole," "pure," "fire," versus words where the same vowels have no L or R following: an, poke, duke, fine. (Still, the trick may not work if the L or R itself is followed by a vowel sound: The A sound of "carol" falls short of "carnal.")

Pronunciation-wise, R ranges widely. The sound represented by the symbol R means different things to various speakers, not only from language to language but within English itself.

Parisian French pronounces R as a demure gargle along the throat and palate—a sound whose exact pronunciation is nigh on impossible for most English speakers. (Can you say *regarder*? We want to begin the R at the tongue tip and bring in the throat afterward.) In Croatian, a written R may include a vowel sound; thus the city name Trieste is spelled as *Trst*, for example. In Spanish and Italian, the R is trilled; you say it by vibrating the tongue tip against the palate: *misericordia*. Scottish R is trilled, too, providing the famous Scots burr.

Ask an Englishman of a certain social class to say "earl" and you'll hear "euhl," the R flattened into a brief tightening of the throat, very unlike the earnest R of a North American or Irishman. Or maybe not: People of Brooklyn or Queens might diminish R to the point of omitting it in some words. *Meet ja's at Toidy-toid Street at tree o'clock.*

Together, the Brooklyn accent and the cited British accent point to a more general principle—namely, R is known to slip away from some forms of spoken English. The root cause is that R takes effort to say: It has a relatively demanding pronunciation, requiring a stiff tongue tip. Witness the speech of young children, or of adults with impediments, who may replace R with the more easily formed W. "Pesky wabbit!" declares Elmer Fudd, perpetually frustrated enemy of Warner cartoon hero Bugs Bunny. And this writer recalls playing Three Little Pigs with a three-year-old daughter who, when threatened with destruction of her last piggy house, would reply gleefully, "No! It's stwong of bwicks!"

Studies of the Brooklyn-type accent show that R is pronounced properly before vowels but is dropped often at the ends of words—whence the cry "Beeh heeh!" from vendors who carried tall, foam-brimmed paper cups on sided trays through the stands of Yankee Stadium in the 1960s—and is especially prone to be dropped before a D, L, N, or TH. Those consonants send the tongue tip to a position rather different from the R position; thus they render the R inconvenient as a preliminary. Why say "weird" when "weeyd" is more restful to the tongue? (Not that it's a conscious personal choice, of course; rather, the group accent develops along lines of convenience.) The human wish to conserve tongue energy lies behind many changes to spoken languages through the ages, including the kinds of slurring that helped to transform late Latin into Europe's Romance tongues, around 200 to 800 A.D.

Far from New York City, you can find the dropped R (minus the Brooklyn vowels) in Boston. *Pahk yuh cah in Hahvahd Yahd*— and it'll get towed away by the police! Linguists go so far as to divide all English-language pronunciation into two accent groups:

Hail to the chief. Carved in limestone, these two primitive Semitic letters are part of the world's oldest known alphabetic writing, left in the Egyptian desert in about 1800 B.C., perhaps 200 years after the first alphabet's invention. (See pages 38–39.) The two letters occupy the far right-hand side of one inscription and would be the opening letters if the writing runs from right to left. (We're not sure it does.) The letter here at right, resembling a cartoon head in profile, is thought to be an early form of R. The figure-9 letter is identified as an early B. (See pages 67–68.) From right to left, the two would spell R-B, that is, the Semitic word reb, *"chief." Perhaps denoting a tribal leader or army captain, "chief" would seem to be the title of the man who carved the inscription; the full message (probably never to be deciphered by us) may say something like "Chief so-and-so wrote this." The ancient Semitic word* reb *connects linguistically to the Hebrew-English word "rabbi."*

rhotic and nonrhotic. (The adjective "rhotic," from *rho*, the name of the ancient Greek R letter, is just a fancy word meaning "of R" or, in this case, "using R.")

Rhotic speakers pronounce the R as written; nonrhotic ones drop R or diminish it in certain positions in words. Nonrhotic local accents occur in the American South, the mid-Atlantic states, and New England (but not the Midwest or West), also in Australia, New Zealand, South Africa, much of the Caribbean, much of England, and Wales (but not Scotland).

The divide between rhotic and nonrhotic can be social as well as geographic. Linguistic surveys of the greater New York City area confirm that nonrhotic speakers tend to come from longtime local families of traditionally lower income, as compared with rhotic speakers. In the greater London area, just the opposite: Nonrhoticism is a part of ideal British speech—"euhl" for "earl"— and signifies education and higher income.

The history of R is among the most gratifying of any letter's. R appears in the oldest known alphabetic writing: the two rock-carved Semitic inscriptions at Wadi el-Hol in central Egypt, from about 1800 B.C. The inscriptions contain perhaps three examples of a letter shape that could be a human head in profile. Modern experts, drawing on information from later stages of the alphabet, identify this as the early Semitic R letter, called *resh* (probably pronounced "raysh"). The name meant "head" in ancient Semitic tongues. The *resh* signified the "r" sound that began its name.

Other head-shape letters, presumably *resh*, show up in the rock-carved Semitic writing of western Sinai, dating perhaps from 1750 B.C. But as is usual for the early letters, the *resh*'s uses and qualities are best known to us from a later stage of the ancient Semitic alphabet, namely, the Phoenician alphabet of 1000 B.C.

The Phoenician *resh* was the 20th letter in sequence. Much like our own R, it fell after the Q letter and before the letters denoting "sh" and T. The Phoenician name still meant "head," but the Phoenician letter was a greatly simplifed shape, a kind of ꟼ.

This stylized form was still enough to suggest a person's head (and neck) in profile, thereby fulfilling the pictorial role of an early Semitic letter: The reader saw the shape and thought, "Head, *resh*, the 'r' sound." The letter shape projected leftward, in keeping with the right-to-left direction of Phoenician writing. Despite first appearance, this Phoenician shape would not supply our letter P but rather our letter resembling P: the R.

Today a letter called *resh* endures as number 20 in the Hebrew alphabet. Copied originally from the Phoenician letter, probably soon after 1000 B.C., the Hebrew *resh* still represents the "r" sound and its name is still understood to mean "head." The Hebrew letter's shape, while much changed since the Iron Age, still slightly resembles its Phoenician model.

Similarly, the Semitic word *resh* lives on, with slight alterations, in the Hebrew and Arabic languages—for example, in

The Hebrew letter resh. *Its shape still recalls aspects of the ancient Phoenician letter from which it was copied.*

the name of the autumnal Jewish New Year holy day, Rosh Hashanah, "head of the year," and in Arabic place-names like Ras al Khaimah ("headland of the tent"), one of the United Arab Emirate states.

When the ancient Greeks copied the Phoenician letters around 800 B.C., they basically kept the *resh*'s sound, shape, and number-20 place in the alphabet, while modifying the name so as to sound more Greek: *rho*. Unlike the Phoenician "head," the name *rho* meant nothing in Greek aside from the letter.

Greek pronunciation gave *rho* a small breathy element—as shown in the fact that eventually the Romans, when transliterat-

(*1*) *The Semitic letter* resh, *the "head," from the Wadi el-Hol carved inscriptions of about 1800 B.C. The* resh *took the "r" sound that began its name. Scholars believe the letter shape was copied originally from an Egyptian hieroglyph of a human head in profile (a symbol that carried an entirely different name and meaning from the Semitic letter). (*2*) A* resh *from the inscriptions at Serabit el-Khadem in central-west Sinai, from perhaps 1750 B.C. Compared with the earlier letter shape, this one is more developed as a picture, perhaps due to the carver's skill and to Serabit's receptive sandstone, versus the tougher limestone at Wadi el-Hol. (*3*) The Phoenician* resh *of about 1000 B.C. shows drastic reduction in shape yet still suggests a head in profile. Although it faces leftward for Phoenician right-to-left writing, the letter shape is on its way to becoming our R. (*4*) The early Greek R letter,* rho—*this example from a right-to-left inscription of about 725 B.C.—duplicated the Phoenician letter in shape, sound, and alphabetic place. (*5*) Modern Greek* rho, *facing rightward, looks like our letter P but takes the sound "r." This symbol is also the R letter in the Greek-derived Cyrillic alphabet of modern Russia, Serbia, Bulgaria, Ukraine, Kazakhstan, the Mongolian republic, and other nations.*

ing Greek into Latin, would render the *rho* as two Roman letters: R + H. Today this Roman RH combination, representing the ancient Greek *rho*, is found in such Greek-derived English words as "rhetoric," "rhinoceros," and "rhythm," as well as in our spelling of the Greek letter's name itself, *rho*.

Like other Greek letters, *rho* could face in either direction in early Greek writing— ꟼ or P —insofar as the writing might run in either direction. By about 500 B.C., as the Greek system settled at left to right, *rho* normally faced rightward. The neatly carved *rho* of Greek marble inscriptions of the 400s and 300s B.C. looks exactly like our letter P. Meanwhile (as the prior chapter describes) the ancient Greek letter *pi*, for the sound "p," developed a different shape.

R's diagonal leg or tail, which distinguishes the letter in appearance from our P, was introduced in ancient Rome, after the Greek alphabet had passed to the Etruscans of Italy (700 B.C.) and the Etruscan one to the Romans (600 B.C.). In extant Roman inscriptions, R's identifying tail first appears as a stub ending in midair, then as a stroke to the baseline: R.

Our lowercase r shape grew out of the semi-uncial handwriting style of the early Middle Ages. To save time, scribes began abbreviating the right-hand part of the letter. Instead of the half-loop and tail, they drew just one, slightly curled stroke from the vertical bar: r. Adopted by the influential Carolingian minuscule style of about A.D. 800, this pleasant little shape was then copied by the humanist handwriting school of Italy in the early 1400s. From there, the r was taken up by early printers in Italy, who copied humanist letter shapes in designing lowercase letters of type (around 1470).

Most of our consonants' names in English have two elements: (1) the sound of the letter itself, floated on (2) a vowel sound. For example, "dee," "jay," "que." Chapter F, pages 126–27, describes how seven of our consonant names acquired an initial vowel rather than a following one—not "dee" but "eff." The seven are F, L, M, N, R, S, and X. Their names all begin with a short-E sound except for R, the name "ar" being the only English letter name with a short-A sound. R's name may have developed that way because the A sound displays the R sound better than E does.

R's name in the spoken Latin of the Roman Empire's common folk, around A.D. 300, was probably "erray" (perhaps spelled *erre*), similar to the modern Spanish name. Descending to early French and imported to England with the Norman Conquest of 1066, the letter name in medieval French and English reached a

1   2   3   4   5

(1) The early Etruscan R—seen here from a right-to-left inscription of about 660 B.C.—simply copied the Greek rho in shape, sound, and alphabetic place. The Etruscan letter, in turn, would be copied to provide the earliest Roman R. (2) Roman R of the 200s B.C. The letter shape faces rightward (Roman writing having by then settled in that direction) and displays the beginning of R's distinctive tail. The Romans added the tail to distinguish R from their letter P. (3) Mature Roman R from the Trajan Inscription, A.D. 113. This form would become the model for our modern print capitals. (4) The inked R of the uncial handwriting style—this example from a Latin biblical text of the 600s—closely imitated the old Roman capital. (5) Our lowercase r shape emerged in the semi-uncial handwriting style, an early medieval Latin "business hand" for which scribes created certain abbreviated letter forms to save time and effort. This example comes from a manuscript of the 500s, from France.

form something like "air." R's name still sounds close to "air" in modern French and in certain regional dialects of England.

In modern emblems, R may stand for Latin *rex* or *regina*, "king" or "queen," as in the monogram ER (not the TV show but "Elizabeth Regina"). The mechanical R2D2, one of the more endearing characters from the epic *Star Wars* film series, has a name (never explained) that suggests "robot design number 2." According to Hollywood legend, the name was inspired by a film-editing term meaning "reel number 2, dialogue number 2."

Our Rx prescription symbol, familiar from druggists' sign-posting, commemorates a word from medieval Latin: the imperative verb *recipe* (pronounced "re-SIP-eh"), meaning "take." This was the official first word of a doctor's prescription written in Latin (as they generally were, until the early 20th century, in Western Europe and the Americas). The x represents what was once a fancy crossbar, inked onto the R's tail as an identifying sign at the prescription's start.

Leaving R, let's recall one of our earliest health writers, the Elizabethan English physician William Butler. In his eating guide *Dyet's Dry Dinner* (1599), Butler fashioned the proverbial advice that "It is unseasonable and unwholesome in all months that have not an *r* in their name to eat an oyster."

The shape and sound of S are put to their natural use—rather excitingly—in an illustrated alphabet in the 1844 children's book Wonderful Stories.

[UNIVERSAL S]

UNIVERSAL S

Serpent's letter. So Ben Jonson calls it in his *English Grammar* (1640), and no one has trouble guessing which letter he means. For centuries, in language, poetry, and art, S's sinuous shape and hissing sound have conjured up a certain kind of reptile.

Take for example a memorable scene in Hell, near the end of John Milton's epic poem *Paradise Lost* (1667), where the Devil gets his comeuppance from God for having ruined the Garden of Eden. Listen to the sounds as Satan and his army are metamorphosed, unwillingly, into giant snakes:

On all sides, from innumerable tongues
A dismal universal hiss, the sound
Of public scorn . . . / Now were all transform'd
Alike, to Serpents . . . / Dreadful was the din
Of hissing through the Hall, thick swarming now
With complicated monsters, head and tail . . . (Book 10)

S is the primary sibilant in English, a sibilant being a hissing or hushing sound or a symbol representing same. Other sibilants are SH-, Z, and soft C. For English spellings, S does most of the work—although in words like "nose" and "pies," it could be said to be hogging Z's job.

Among the 26 letters, S ranks about number 8 in frequency of use in printed English. And it ranks number 1 as an initial letter: More of our words start with letter S than with any other—one reason being that S encompasses all of our "sh" words, too, as English (unlike some tongues) has no separate "sh" letter.

Sibilants as a category, from language to language, tend to contain many possible shades of pronunciation. English S has about four sounds. The two main ones occur in the word "season"—the sharp, front-of-mouth "s" and the flatter "z." Say them and you'll notice that the second S engages the vocal cords while the first does not. The "z" sound often occurs when S falls between two vowels ("lose") or at a word's end after a vowel ("sales").

Otherwise, S may sometimes be sounded "sh" on its own, as in "sure" and "mansion." Or it can sound like French J, as in "fusion" and "closure." Or S may be mute: island.

Sibilants are known to travel badly: Their subtle sounds may get mispronounced or misinterpreted from one language to another. Spanish or Italian speakers, for example, often have trouble pronouncing S at the start of English words and so insert an initial vowel as a buffer: "eh-song," "eh-slice." (Fitting the humor of a bygone era, this trait was a hallmark of the Italian character played by Chico Marx in Marx Brothers films of the 1930s and '40s.)

Similarly, "sh" can be impossible to pronounce for those not used to it. English-speaking children up through age three or four generally substitute "s" for "sh," saying "sooz" for "shoes" and "sy" for "shy," until they grow into more perfect speech. The biblical book of Judges relates the harrowing tale of the shibboleth: a password involving a sibilant, used to distinguish friend from foe in civil war. Two tribes of Israel, the Ephraimites and Gileadites, became enemies and fought a battle in which the Ephraimite invaders were beaten, far from home. The victorious Gileadites seized the Jordan River ford to block the homeward route of Ephraimite survivors. When any unknown man reached the roadblock, he was ordered to say the password, *shibboleth* (meaning "ear of wheat")—the point being that a native Gileadite would know how to say the "sh," but an Ephraimite, speaking just a different dialect of Hebrew, would not. "He said Sibboleth: for he could not frame to pronounce it right. Then they took him and slew him, at the passages of Jordan." The Ephraimites lost 42,000 men in all, according to the Bible.

Shape-wise, S has been sinuous from the start. The primitive Semitic language inscriptions at Serabit el-Khadem in Sinai, from perhaps 1750 B.C., include examples of a letter shaped like a curlicue W: ∽. Modern experts believe the shape probably represented the picture of an archer's bow: a "composite bow," from two joined animal horns, such as commonly used in the ancient Near East. What exactly the letter's name and sound were, at this formative stage, remains unclear to us.

As usual in the study of the early Semitic alphabet, clearer information comes from a later stage, namely, the Phoenician alphabet of about 1000 B.C. We know the Phoenicians had four sibilant letters, named *zayin, samek, tsade,* and *shin.* Because the sound represented by a Phoenician letter was always demonstrated in the opening sound of the letter's name, the four names give an idea of the letters' different sounds. *Samek* was the basic "s." *Zayin* and *tsade* took sounds "z" and "ts," respectively. And *shin* was "sh."

By coincidence, *shin* was shaped almost exactly like our W. Modern experts see in the W shape the stylized development of the earlier letter shaped like an archer's bow. Reasonable enough: The bow shape had been simplified to a mere zigzag. However, the Phoenician name *shin* is understood by scholars to mean "tooth," not "bow." Yet the letter's W shape looked not much like a tooth (although perhaps like two upper shark teeth). For whatever murky reason, the original letter's name had changed, to "tooth."

Shin came 21st in the Phoenician alphabet. Today, in the Hebrew alphabet (copied originally from the Phoenician soon after 1000 B.C.), the 21st Hebrew letter is still called *shin,* meaning "tooth." Hebrew *shin* takes the sound "sh," and, unlike most Hebrew letters, it still resembles its Phoenician forebear in shape.

As mentioned, the plain "s" sound belonged to a different Phoenician letter, named *samek* (meaning "pillar"). Logically, *samek* should have become the ancestor of our S. But events would take a different turn, due to the Greeks inadvertently throwing a monkey wrench into the works.

The Greeks spoke a language totally unlike Phoenician, including differences in sounds. We have already seen how sibilants

The Hebrew letter shin, at left, *still looks rather like the Phoenician* shin *of 1000 B.C.,* right, *from which it derives.*

can have tough times crossing language borders. When the Greeks came along and copied the Phoenician alphabet sometime around 800 B.C., they chose one letter to be their "s" sound . . . yet they got the written symbols mixed up.

What the Greeks needed simply to do was to copy the Phoenician letter *samek*'s symbol and sound. Instead, they copied the symbol for *shin* and kept it at *shin*'s place, number 21 in the alphabet, yet they gave this new Greek letter the plain "s" sound of *samek,* and they called it "samek"—that is, they called it *sigma,* which is the Greek styling of the Phoenician name.

On one hand, it didn't matter: Letters are just agreed-on symbols, and Greek writing got an S letter as needed, so who cares? On the other hand, the "sigma" error was part of a larger foul-up in the transmission of the alphabet from Phoenician to Greek, a foul-up involving all four Phoenician sibilants, *zayin, samek, tsade,* and *shin.* (We'll skip the other details here.) The issue has fascinated some scholars, as possibly offering clues about the creation of the Greek alphabet.

The scholarly consensus is that it isn't the type of mistake a group of scribes would make over a generation's time; it's a mistake an individual person would make in an afternoon. It supports (albeit slenderly) a scholarly theory that the Greek alphabet was devised by an individual, one whose name has been lost to history, without doubt a Greek, demonstrably a genius. Situated presumably at one of the east Mediterranean seaports where Greek and Phoenician traders coexisted, probably working from a written Phoenician letter list, probably with guidance from Phoenicians, this person copied and adapted Phoenician letters as tools for Greek use—however, making minor errors in translating the Phoenician sibilants.

Quickly, Greek *sigma* changed its appearance. The Greeks for some reason preferred to tilt the W shape on its side and allow it to zigzag up into the air. The *sigma* produced several variant shapes, including one resembling an elongated Z: ⟨ or ⟩, depending on the direction of the writing. This design passed to the Etruscans (700 B.C.) and Romans (600 B.C.) of Italy. The Romans eventually rounded out the shape, making our familiar S, and bequeathed it to Western European alphabets of the early Middle Ages.

Between the 300s and 800s A.D. in European handwriting, most letters spawned newer shapes for easier penmanship. Al-

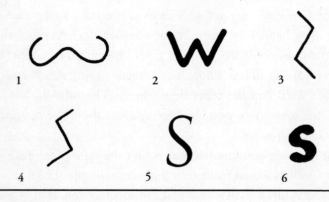

(1) The "archer's bow" letter of ancient Semitic writing, around 1750 B.C. In shape, at least, this was the earliest ancestor of our S. (2) Phoenician shin, from an inscription of about 800 B.C. Although heir to the bow letter shape, shin in name meant "tooth." It took the sound "sh" that began its name. (3) Greek sigma from a left-to-right inscription of the 600s B.C. The shape and sound had changed from the Phoenician version: The Greek letter denoted the sound "s" (not "sh"). This sigma was shaped much like our Z in facing backward, toward the previous letters in the flow of writing, not ahead like our S. (Modern Greek sigma has yet a different shape.) (4) Early Roman S, from a left-to-right inscription of about 500 B.C. The Roman letter shape faced ahead, the opposite direction from the Greek. (5) Roman S from the famous Trajan Inscription, A.D. 113. The mature Roman letter had achieved the familiar curves, with elegant finishing strokes (serifs) at both ends. Preserved in carved stone, this shape would provide the model for the uppercase S of the first roman typefaces of about 1470. (6) Minuscule s in the humanist handwriting style of Renaissance Italy, from a Latin book written at Naples in 1477. This little s, copied by printers for their lowercase type, would eventually prevail over a rival lowercase shape: the f-like "long" s.

The cover of the 1598 quarto edition of Shakespeare's Love's Labour's Lost *(as the title is normally spelled today). The lettering shows both forms of lowercase s as printed in Shakespeare's England: There is our familiar s shape but also the f-like "long" s, which was not to be used at the end of a word.*

though no one knew it at the time, some of these shapes would later supply the models for early printers' lowercase type. S developed *two* handwritten shapes: the "short" s, basically our modern lowercase letter, and the "long" s, shaped rather like an f. Long s, easy to write, was by custom used at the start or middle of a word, never at the end.

With the spread of printing in the second half of the 1400s, the long s became one of the printer's lowercase letters (along with the short s). This f-like s continued to appear in English-language print and handwriting right through the 1700s, before falling out of vogue. It still is used occasionally in German print, where certain medieval typefaces remain popular.

The S of evil. Distinguished by his twin-S collar emblem, a captured German SS officer is searched by an American military policeman (MP) in a photograph by Robert Capa for Life *magazine, somewhere in Normandy, June or July 1944, soon after D-day, during World War II. The blandly named* Schutzstaffel *(defense squadron) had been created by Hitler in 1925 as his personal bodyguard and later enlarged as a Nazi loyalist army outside the regular German army. Feared and despised by the Nazis' victims, the black-uniformed SS ran concentration camps and provided combat units; this officer may be from the 2nd SS Panzer "Das Reich" Division, which had recently massacred 642 French villagers near Limoges in reprisal for French Resistance action.*

The Schutzstaffel's zigzag S shapes resembled lightning bolts and the carved S of Germany's medieval runic alphabet, thus evoking power, atavism, and patriotism. In the 1970s, the jagged double-S would be adopted—in atrocious taste—as part of the name logo of the heavy-metal rock band Kiss.

S is one of a handful of letters—like A, O, V, and Z—that invite philosophical or spiritual interpretation. S's hissing sound need not always be bad: In Jewish mystical tradition, the Hebrew sibilant *shin* was equated by sound with the element of fire and was exalted as one of three "mother" letters. (The other two were the A and M equivalents.) With our Roman S, there is also the evocative shape: Being nearly an infinity symbol, S can imply timeless continuity. Or it could be a link in a chain or (as we've seen) a serpent, whether an evil one or the nutritive, encompassing, mother-of-waters type found in some mythologies.

On the dark side of S traditionally are its ties to sin and Satan. Also, in the past 70 years, another evil association: the Nazi *Schutzstaffel* (defense squadron) that was Hitler's private army of terror and genocide—the infamous SS.

Yet S's happier cosmic aspect has had its advocates, too, including Irish author James Joyce in his epic novel *Ulysses* (1922), a work that aims at universal significance. Based loosely on the ancient Greek epic poem the *Odyssey* (about the wanderings of the hero named Odysseus or Ulysses), *Ulysses* follows a main character and several lesser ones on perambulations though Dublin during a single day and night in June 1904. Not only does the book's title contain three S's, but the text begins and ends with an S—that is, with words containing S. The multiple S's perhaps signify: (1) the links of a chain, connecting us all but also limiting us to our mortality; (2) the image of meandering, relevant to the story; and (3) the infinity symbol and the continuing cycles of life and human history. From the novel's opening words, printed with a drop-capital S ("Stately, plump Buck Mulligan came from the stairhead . . ."), we proceed through 750-plus pages, 20 hours of story line, and countless incidents and themes, to end on the famously affirmative note of Molly Bloom's reverie, ". . . yes and his heart was going like mad and yes I said yes I will Yes."

A detail from German artist Albrecht Dürer's woodcut of the Lamentation (about 1496), which is shown on page 188. In the scene, women mourn the dead Christ, taken down from the cross. Medieval and Renaissance artists often pictured the cross in the form of a capital T, and the letter T might be associated with the crucifixion, in senses of both tragedy and triumph.

$\begin{bmatrix} \text{T} & \textsf{PARTY} \end{bmatrix}$

he sign of the cross. The mark of Cain. The final letter of the Hebrew alphabet. The image of containment or suppression. The profile of a spike or nail. Associations like these have given T a sometimes sinister or daunting air through the centuries.

In ancient times, the Greek T and Roman T each looked like our capital letter. To literate people of the Greco-Roman world, the shape might suggest the idea of crucifixion, a standard method of death penalty in that day. Early Christian mystics considered T a reminder of Christ's suffering on the cross. Pagan thinkers made a similar connection, although without necessary reference to Jesus.

The pagan Greek author Lucian, in a witty essay written around A.D. 100, titled "Consonants at Court," imagines a lawsuit between two rival letters: the Greek S letter, named *sigma,* and the T letter, *tau.* Speaking before the judges, S denounces T as an agent of dictators and repression: "They say it was T's shape that tyrants copied when first they set up the cross to crucify men. This vile device is called *stauros,* and it gets its vile name from *tau.*"

Ill-omened though it may be, T is fundamental to English language and spelling. Surprisingly, it is our second-most-often-used letter in print, after E. (The letter A finishes a close third.) A frequent sound in words from Old English, T occurs more often at the middle or end of our words than at the beginning, which explains why the "T" section of your dictionary isn't especially thick.

T's strong showing on the printed page owes more than a little to the word "the" and to the family of TH words generally (there, other, cloth). In English, TH amounts virtually to a separate letter of the alphabet, with its own sound and history, apart from T. (See "Tales of TH," pages 308–9.)

T's snare-drum sound has benefited poetry. For example, the English soldier-poet Wilfred Owen—who served two gruesome years on the front line in World War I, to be killed while helping to lead an attack one week before the Armistice—employed T to memorable onomatopoetic effect, along with other letters, both consonants and vowels, in his 1917 "Anthem for Doomed Youth." The poem reflects on the horror and insane waste of that particular war:

What passing-bells for these who die as cattle?
Only the monstrous anger of the guns.
Only the stuttering rifles' rapid rattle
Can patter out their hasty orisons.

Phonetically, T is the brother of D. In English, both letters create sound through a spurt of breath around the tongue tip set against the sockets of the upper front teeth. D engages the vocal cords while T does not. Thus, T is an unvoiced stop; D is the voiced counterpart. Yet the T can sound mighty similar to D in certain uses at the middle of a word, at least in American accents. Many a country-western song rhymes "saddle" with "cattle," and we all know what happened when the cow tried to jump over the barbed-wire fence: udder disaster.

The midword position is a vulnerable one for T generally. There, historically, the letter has been known to soften, not just to the unofficial American "d" but to other sounds or even to silence. The Cockney swallowing of the middle T's in the word "bottle"— yielding the pronunciation "bah-owe"—has been mentioned back on page 50. Other examples of softened T, in mainstream English worldwide, include "nation," "creature," and "listen."

In "listen" or "castle," the T was at one time pronounced. But the "nation" category represents the biggest use of alternative T. In hundreds of words where T precedes the letter I plus a second vowel, T has acquired the sound "sh": inertia, patience, facetious, and so on.

Most such words come from Latin; the "sh" commemorates a slurring of T in those positions in spoken Latin of the late Roman Empire. A Latin word like *natio* (meaning "a race of people"), originally pronounced "nah-tio," came to sound more like "nah-shio" in common folk's Latin, but with no change in spelling. Likewise, the word *gratia* (favor, pardon, charm) went from "grah-tia" to "grah-shia."

After Rome's fall (A.D. 500), this secondary pronunciation of T became part of Europe's emerging Romance languages, where it gradually slurred further, to the sound "s." Sometimes it effected a change in spelling and sometimes not. Modern Spanish acknowledges reality with spellings like *nación* (pronounced "nah-see-on") and *gracia* ("grah-sia"). The soft C in those words replaces the T that once stood there. In modern Italian, the old T has turned to Z: *nazione, grazia*.

Medieval French, meanwhile, apparently recognized two levels of decayed T. Where the T had slurred completely to "s," the spelling changed to C, as in medieval French *grace* (pronounced something like "grahss"). But where T had stuck at "sh," it remained spelled as T: *nation* ("nah-shee-on"). Such French spellings and pronunciations were imported to medieval England after the Norman Conquest of 1066. Today, medieval French's "nah-shee-on" has become our "nation."

The best-known story of T's pronunciation involves the British countess and society wit Margot Asquith (1864–1945), wife of Herbert Asquith, who was Britain's prime minister from 1908 to 1916 and who later became Earl of Oxford. Legend places this razor-minded, aging, titled lady at a 1930s dinner party that included blond American screen siren and bad girl Jean Harlow. (The connection isn't impossible, as the Asquiths' son was the movie director Anthony Asquith.) Jean Harlow, recognizing her, asked loudly, "Say, aren't you Margot Asquith?"—but mispronouncing the name as "Mar-got." To which her ladyship replied, "Oh, no, dear, the T is silent, as in Harlow."

The T enters history in the oldest alphabetic writing yet known: the limestone-carved inscriptions at Wadi el-Hol, from about 1800 B.C. Although the two messages in ancient Semitic language may never be satisfactorily deciphered, one of them clearly shows two examples of a primeval letter T (photograph on page 39, inscription number 2). However, the letter's properties are better known to us from a later stage of the early Semitic alphabet, namely the Phoenician alphabet of about 1000 B.C.

Phoenician T was the last letter of that alphabet, number 22. Called by the Semitic name *taw,* it took the "t" sound that began its name. The word *taw* meant "mark," probably as in an agricultural identifying sign, like a cattle brand or the dye mark that modern Near Eastern shepherds daub on their sheep. *Taw's* shape was usually cruciform, either perfectly even, like a plus sign, or favored lengthwise, like a church cross. Alternatively, in some inscriptions, *taw* looks like an X. There being no other X-shaped Phoenician letter, the variation didn't matter.

Today, *taw* survives as *tav,* the 22nd and last letter of the Hebrew alphabet. It still takes the "t" sound and its name is still understood in Hebrew to mean "mark," although its modern shape looks nothing like the Phoenician letter. According to legend, this branding, final letter, *tav,* was the "mark" mentioned in the biblical book of Genesis as being placed by God upon Cain, after Cain murdered his brother, Abel.

When the Greeks copied the Phoenician letters around 800 B.C., *taw* was ushered right into the newborn Greek alphabet as letter number 22, with the sound "t" and the Greek name *tau* (probably rhyming with "cow"). *Tau* wasn't the last letter of the Greek alphabet, for the Greeks invented new letters to follow, starting with their letter U. (Today U still follows T in our own alphabet.)

One small change the Greeks made: From the earliest extant Greek inscriptions, carved in stone or ceramic, the *tau* shows a T shape, not a cross shape. A very few early examples where the vertical stroke does pierce the crossbar seem to represent manual error, a slip of the carver's hand, not a variant letter form. Because the Greek alphabet also contained an X-shaped letter, the Greeks evidently took care to cap their T, to help keep the two letter shapes distinct. In Western tradition, T's shape would remain exclusively capped for 2,000 years, roughly 800 B.C. to A.D. 1200.

From the Greek alphabet, the simple, handy T letter was appropriated into the Etruscan alphabet (700 B.C.) and thence into the Roman (600 B.C.). The Romans called it something like *te* (pronounced "tay"). That name, eventually reaching English via medieval French, would yield our modern "tee" through a shift in English vowel pronunciations culminating in the 1500s A.D. The story parallels that of B's name and others (see pages 71-73). Modern French still calls T the "tay."

Most of our lowercase shapes—a, b, d, e, f, g, h, i, m, n, p, q, r, u, and y—were born as ink shapes in European handwriting between about A.D. 300 and 800. The impetus for creating such minuscule forms was ease and speed in penmanship. Yet a few of the simpler-shaped letters, like O and X, never produced a minuscule, as not needing one: They were already perfectly simple to write. For centuries, T remained in this category, taking the shape T in all handwriting styles.

Not until about 1200 did our familiar t shape emerge, in the Northern European pen style known as black letter. The t shape's advantage in penmanship was minor: It offered a slightly easier

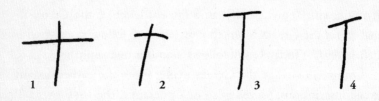

Letter T's simple shape has weathered the centuries with little change. (1) Perhaps 200 years after the alphabet's invention, this T letter was part of a message (probably never to be deciphered by us) carved by a Semitic-language speaker in desert rock in central Egypt, about 1800 B.C. (2) Phoenician taw, *the "mark," from an inscription in southeastern Cyprus, about 800 B.C. Taw took the "t" sound that begins its name. Descended through the Near Eastern alphabetic tradition, this letter shape is hardly different from its forerunner of 1,000 years before. (3) Greek* tau, *from an early Greek inscription, about 740 B.C. Although* tau *copied the Phoenician letter in sound, name, and alphabetic place, the Greeks had adjusted its shape, making it into a capped T so as to better distinguish it from an X-shaped Greek letter. (4) Early Roman T, from an inscription of about 520 B.C. The letter imitated its Etruscan and Greek forebears.*

1   2   3

(1) Roman capital T from the famous Trajan Inscription, A.D. 113. The letter's austere lines have been dignified through serifs and subtle tapering of both bars at midpoint, to produce one of the most beautiful Roman letter shapes. (2) Ink T in the Carolingian minuscule handwriting style, from an English legal document in Latin, dated 1018. Historically, the Carolingian style produced finalized forms for nearly all letter shapes that we would call lowercase: a, b, d, e, and so on. Yet the Carolingian T remained a capped figure. (3) Our lowercase shape finally emerges in the Northern European "black letter" handwriting style of about 1200. Imitated in Italian handwriting styles of about 1420, this shape would be adopted by printers in Italy around 1470 to be their lowercase t.

crossbar for the scribe, with less aiming of the pen. Of the minuscule shapes that we inherit, the t is probably the second to youngest. Only the letter L would be later in spawning a minuscule, around 1400. Prior to t, the latest born was probably the little n, coming from the Carolingian minuscule pen style around 800.

Ironically—although no one could have known so in 1200—the new, minuscule t simply re-created the cruciform shape of the earliest T letter, the Bronze Age Semitic *taw.*

Due mainly to its shape, T contributes modestly to English vocabulary: for example, golf tee, curling tee, engineer's T-square. Every plumber's truck carries a certain pipe section called a "tee" or T-fitting. The term "T-shirt," which does indeed refer to the letter shape (although it seems a stretch), dates back to the standard-issue cotton undergarment of U.S. servicemen in World War II. Our tea beverage, however, gets its name from Mandarin Chinese *ch'a.*

Something of a mystery is posed by the old expression "fits to a T," as in "Those eyeglass frames fit her to a T." First documented

Despite appearances in spelling, the sound of TH—as in "Think thin, father"—can be fairly distinct from that of T. In words like "father," where it engages the vocal cords, TH steers closer to D than to T.

The symbol TH in English actually embraces two (very similar) sounds: the voiced dental fricative, as in "then," "father," and "mother," and the *un*voiced version of same, as in "thin," "faith," and "moth." (For "fricative" defined, see page 122.) Our TH words come primarily from Old English and secondarily from ancient Greek. (The Greek words typically have been conveyed via ancient Latin and medieval French. Example: theater.)

Theoretically, our "th" sounds as a group deserve a single letter of their own. Such symbols have existed in the Greek and Old English alphabets, but not in the Roman. As described on pages 165–66, the T-H combination was an attempt—first in ancient Rome, then in medieval England—to symbolize a sound for which no Roman letter existed.

þ ð p ȝ

The extra letters of Old English. English writing of the early Middle Ages included at least four letters that were not part of the Roman alphabet. These were four Anglo-Saxon signs, which supplemented the traditional Roman letters, to capture Old English sounds not otherwise covered. The signs' names, from left, were thorn, eth, wyn, *and* yogh. Wyn *denoted the sound "w," in days before W was invented, and* yogh *meant a breathy sound hovering between "y" and "g." Further information about* wyn *and* yogh *appears on pages 335 and 354–56.*

Thorn *and* eth *both denoted English "th" sounds. Strictly,* thorn *was meant for unvoiced pronunciations ("thin," "thank") and* eth *for voiced ones ("then," "than"). Yet extant manuscript show the two symbols being used often inconsistently, with* thorn *preferred.* Thorn *had been borrowed from the old runic alphabet of Northern Europe (see pages 149–50), but* eth *was an Anglo-Saxon invention. In shape,* eth *looks like an uncial letter D with a crossbar added, and this resemblance was no doubt intended: The "d" sound was similar to eth's voiced "th." (Compare "den" and "then.")*

The use of the Anglo-Saxon letters would gradually cease after the Norman Conquest of England in A.D. 1066. The change came due to pressure from Norman-educated clergy and teachers, who sought to give written English a more "proper" Franco-Roman form. Drawing on the ancient example of the Romans' transliteration of the Greek "th" sound, Norman authorities began writing TH in place of thorn *and* eth.

Eth would disappear by about 1300, replaced by TH in English spelling. Thorn, while largely dislodged by TH, would hang on in a few uses in England right into the 19th century: See pages 356–57.

in English print in 1693, the phrase could be a play on the spelling F-I-T or a reference to mechanical drawing with a T-square. Richard Firmage, in his book *The Alphabet Abecedarium,* theorizes that the meaning lies in the printer's and calligrapher's use of letter T, which can have various crossbar widths, to fit into or fill out a line of lettering. But the *Oxford English Dictionary* finds significance in a phrase "fits to a tittle," first documented in 1607, nearly a century earlier than "fits to a T."

A tittle (from Latin *titulus,* "sign") is a dot, a tiny amount. It was also, in some medieval English traditions, the name of the final character of the alphabet as learned at school. After X, Y, Z, the child would write two more symbols to be memorized: & and ÷, the first one representing the word *et* (meaning "and" in Latin) and the second representing the word *est* ("is" in Latin). The latter symbol was called "tittle." After tittle, the child might write "amen." Reciting his ABC's aloud, the student would finish with "eks, wye, zed, et, tittle, amen."

So "fits to a tittle," meaning to the smallest *and last* detail, could have been the original expression. But when tittles fell out of schoolroom use at the end of the Middle Ages, the phrasing evolved to "to a T." To which we can say, "et, tittle, amen."

U for us all. The letter U seems mystically present in the vibrant pose of Bono Vox of the Irish rock band U2, at the start of U2's historic 1997 charity concert in Sarajevo, in Bosnia-Herzegovina. As a healing celebration after the end of Bosnia's brutal ethnic war, the rock event was Sarajevo's biggest ever, attended by 50,000 young people from across the former Yugoslavia and Central Europe. (For the meaning of U2's name, see page 319.)

MAKING SENSE OF U

Utter confusion may result from the story of letter U, unless a few quirky facts can first be ironed out. So please let's approach it as a parable, "U and Her Family."

U, our fifth vowel, has two daughters: the consonants V and W, which follow U in alphabetical order. V and W were born gradually from U, during the European Middle Ages and Renaissance. Before that, in ancient Roman times, U was alone. She had no children (the Roman alphabet going: T, U, X, Y, Z) and was compelled to do some of their current work herself. Ancient Roman U could represent either the familiar "u" sound or, when placed before a vowel, the sound "w."

Today this Roman U for "w" lives on in English, wherever U falls between Q and a vowel: quart, quest, require. (One of the few exceptions is "queue.") Also, occasionally where U falls between S and a vowel or between G and a vowel: suave, persuade, sanguine, language. Most such words originate in Latin as delivered to English by medieval French, yet a few (queen, quick) come from Old English itself, their modern spellings having followed the Franco-Latin way.

Like many mothers of grown children, U looked rather different in days before the kids came along. Back when Julius Caesar or Marcus Aurelius ruled Rome, U's shape was sharper, more svelte. In fact, U looked *exactly like* her future daughter V (without V's sound). Thus, in Roman stone-carved inscriptions, the above-mentioned emperors' names would appear as IVLIVS CAESAR and MARCVS AVRELIVS.

There have been other letters in U's life. The letter Y, specifically vowel Y, is U's half-brother: They both come from the ancient Greek U letter. But the letter with the oldest and deepest involvement with U, believe it or not, is F.

F and U? It sounds like a gag. F and U are signal letters of the worst vulgarism in English: The two letters clinch secretly, shamefully, in the muddy storage barn of every adult English speaker's mind. Yet it seems they share an honorable connection, too. Both U and F emerged from the selfsame letter of the ancient Phoenician alphabet sometime around 800 B.C., when the Greeks copied and adapted Phoenician letters. From a single Phoenician letter, the Greeks differentiated two letters for themselves, one a consonant, one a vowel, which grew eventually to be our F and U. So they are cousins, whether immoral together or not.

To this day, a family resemblance exists among the sounds of F, V, and W in English. F and V, classed together as fricatives, are pronounced very similarly. And the "f" may substitute for "w" (or "v" for "w") in the mouths of foreign speakers learning English, who find "w" difficult. Germans and certain Eastern Europeans, for example, might say "fhat" for "what," "fich" for "which."

Keeping in mind this extended family, we can start to make sense of U. The tale begins with *waw,* the sixth letter of the ancient Phoenician alphabet. As explained in the F chapter, the name *waw* meant "peg" and the letter had a peglike Y shape. It took the sound "w," demonstrated in the start of its name.

All of our vowel letters were born from the ancient Greeks. Prior chapters of this book have detailed how the Greeks created A, E, I, and O from a Phoenician alphabet of all consonants: Selecting a few Phoenician letters whose sounds were unneeded for Greek, the Greeks changed those letters' meanings to vowel sounds. For their letter U, they copied and altered Phoenician *waw.* Their choice of *waw* surely was prompted by a slight similarity between the sounds "w" and "u."

But one complication: The *waw* had already been copied once by the Greeks, to supply their letter number 6, which took a "w" sound. This Greek letter became the ancestor of our F (our sixth letter today). For letter U, the Greeks evidently copied Phoenician *waw* a second time, putting the resultant letter at the end of their alphabet, which was still in a formative stage. (Also, they doctored the shape of their "w" letter, so it wouldn't look like the U.) At that moment in history, Greek U was the last letter of the Greek alphabet, number 23, coming after Greek letter T, number 22. Later the Greeks invented four more letters, placing them after U in alphabetical order. All of which explains why, some 27 centuries later, in our own alphabet, letter U follows T, toward the end.

Greek U was called *u psilon* (pronounced "ew-psil-on"), meaning "naked U." The name basically presented the letter's sound.

(Today *upsilon* as one word is the preferred form.) Greek U was pronounced probably like German *ü*: a narrowed sound, approaching "ew" or even "ih."

In shape, *upsilon* looked like the Y figure of Phoenician *waw.* Centuries later, by another route, the Y shape would also supply our letter Y.

By 700 B.C., Greek U had been copied into the Etruscan alphabet of Italy. From there it was copied, before 600 B.C., into the Roman alphabet, for Latin speakers around the village of Rome. Probably following Etruscan usage, the Romans called the letter *u* ("oo"). Latin U evidently sounded flatter than the Greek, more like our English vowel. Latin employed a long-U sound, pronounced perhaps as in "rude," and a short-U sound, as in "put."

U could sound mournful or primordial to the Romans, particularly in verse and oratory. There was a Latin imitative verb meaning "to howl," *ululare* ("oo-loo-lah-reh"), which the poet Vergil favored and which has since supplied English "ululate." And the U's carry what is probably the single finest line by the Roman poet Horace, around 15 B.C., musing on the brevity of human happiness and achievement: *Pulvis et umbra sumus* ("pulwis et um-brah soomus"). We are but dust and shadow (Ode 4.7).

Officially, Roman U took the shape V, derived from the Y-minus-the-stem shape favored by the Etruscans. The shape V would remain letter U's principal form for 1,000 years, about 500 B.C. to A.D. 500, and a contender for 12 centuries after that.

V-shaped U's parade across imperial Roman inscriptions like that from Trajan's Column (illustrated on page 104), and they appear in various ancient Roman ink styles. An irregular tendency toward a more rounded U can be seen in surviving scraps of Latin graffiti and other informal writing as early as the first century B.C. This isn't surprising, for although the V form is far easier to carve, the U form is easier to write quickly in ink, and more so on a

M HOLCONIVM
PRISCVM·II·VIR·I·D· POMARI·VNIVERSI CVM·HFIVIOVESTA·FRO·

yielding surface like papyrus or vellum. In everyday Roman writing, shape V probably often came out looking like U.

Rounded U first appears systematically in the late Roman pen style known as uncial, which emerged around A.D. 300. Uncial being an adaption of Roman capitals to pen strokes, rounded forms were naturally preferred. The U shape became standard in certain (not all) handwriting traditions of the early Middle Ages, including the influential Carolingian minuscule style, developed around 800. For capital positions, such as headings or the beginning of a sentence, the shape V remained the favorite, although Anglo-Saxon Latin writing did develop a capital U. Several medieval styles used capital V alongside minuscule u. For penning Latin documents, such variations seemed trivial.

But not trivial outside of Latin, in the emerging languages and literatures of Western Europe. Here the contest between shapes V and U was forced to conclusion. Within medieval French, Italian, and English there existed a relatively new consonant sound, "v" (about which more will be said in the next chapter). It was a sound in search of a letter. Medieval English or French speakers understood the sound "v" as a consonantal pronunciation of letter U, and they wrote "v" with the same letter shapes as for "u." So the shapes V and U were being used *interchangeably* for sounds "v" and "u."

The inadequacy of this method—two sounds, two symbols, yet not coordinated—was felt in Middle English in the 1300s and 1400s. An attempt at order came in a tendency to write V at the start of a word and U elsewhere, regardless of sound. Such manuscript spellings include *vnder* and *vpon* along with *vain* and *vice, saue* and *euer* along with *cure* and *full*. The custom continued in England after printing's arrival (1476) for another two centuries. Among many examples, the earliest print versions of Shakespeare's plays (around 1600) show spellings like *loue* and *knaue, vndo* and *vnison* throughout.

What happened finally in print: the two sounds and two symbols squared off. Sound "v" was given to letter-form V, and "u" got U, babe. (Theoretically it could have gone the other way, with vowel "u" receiving the symbol V. The factors that recommended sign V for sound "v" will be examined in the next chapter.)

This ordering of U and V began in the mid-1500s, among Italian printers. Not until about 1700 did the custom become general to English print. Meanwhile in England and Germany, another language sound, "w," had acquired its own letter: the "double U." Thus were born W and V, the two daughters of U.

U is refreshingly uncomplicated in sound. Its main English pronunciations are two, short and long, as in "mud rules." Technically, long U is the high, back vowel and short U the low, front vowel (referring to the tongue's position in each case). Both these tongue positions occur also for certain pronunciations of O, as in the homonyms "loot" and "lute," "son" and "sun." Typically, when U and O overlap in sound, O is poaching on U's territory.

The "oo" sound of long U is distinguished as one of three vowel sounds—the other two being "ah" and "ee"—that are gen-

The Tragedie of

HAMLET

Prince of Denmarke.

Enter Barnardo, and Fransisco, two Centinels.

Bar. **VV**Hofe there?
Fran. Nay anfwere me. Stand and vnfolde your felfe.
Bar. Long liue the King,
Fran. *Barnardo.*
Bar. Hee.
Fran. You come moft carefully vpon your houre,
Bar. Tis now ftrooke twelfe, get thee to bed *Francifco,*
Fran. For this reliefe much thanks, tis bitter cold,
    And I am fick at hart.
Bar. Haue you had quiet guard?
Fran. Not a moufe ftirring.
Bar. Well, good night :
    If you doe meete *Horatio* and *Marcellus,*
    The riualls of my watch, bid them make haft.
        Enter Horatio, and Marcellus.
Fran. I thinke I heare them, ftand ho, who is there?
Hora. Friends to this ground.
Mar. And Leedgemen to the Dane,
Fran. Giue you good night.
Mar. O, farwell honeft fouldiers, who hath relieu'd you?
Fran. *Barnardo* hath my place; giue you good night. *Exit Fran.*
        B. *Mar.*

The letter U and her young family are much in evidence on the opening page of Shake-speare's Hamlet, *in the London second-quarto edition of 1604, corrected and reprinted from the inaccurate 1603 first quarto. Although the sounds "u" and "v" were both used in Shakespeare's English, they are not distinguished in shape here: Either sound can appear as the shape u or shape v in lowercase text, with v reserved for the start of words (vnfolde, vpon) and u employed elsewhere (your, liue, much, riualls). The letter W is printed usu-ally as we would recognize it, except in the drop capital of the first line—where its bro-ken shape probably stems from the printer having no newfangled W letters in so large a font, hence two V's were used. The VV reminds us of W's name, the "double U" (or, in French, "double V").*

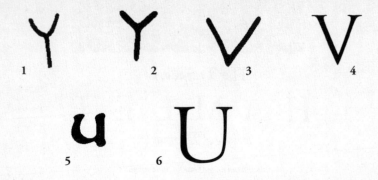

erally considered the earliest sounds of infant speech, emerging sometimes by the second month of life. Baby talk at subsequent stages involves the child floating easily pronounced consonants, like "g" or "m," in front of these vowels.

With its evocative shape and name, U has made contribution to English vocabulary. A U-turn is faster and more hazardous than a K-turn, and engineers or scientists might use a U-frame, U-tube, or U-section. U meaning "you" is a favorite in rebuses like the old print ad "Reeboks let U B U" or the message on the letter board outside the church: "Ch_ _ch: What's missing?"

The stellar Irish rock band U2 chose its punning name partly in reference to an Irish federal unemployment-insurance form called a U-2, evocative of the world the boys came from, circa 1978. (The band UB40 is similarly named, from *British* unemployment paperwork.) A very different U-2 is the high-flying U.S. Air Force spy jet, named for the deliberately vague category "utility." This once-secret aircraft embarrassingly became a household word in 1960 after the Soviet Union shot one down, capturing its pilot; a more recent U-2 design has provided reconnaissance over Saddam Hussein's Iraq. The dreaded German U-boats of two world wars were submarines, named simply from German *Unterseeboot,* "undersea boat."

U shares with letters C and O the oddly pleasing effect of a neatly curved shape. U suggests a horseshoe or magnet: strong, potent, made of iron. The nuance has been exploited in advertising and other print—not least in official emblems of, and other reference to, the United States. After the disastrous terrorist attacks of September 11, 2001, among the most poignant and encouraging responses was a simple slogan, appearing in bus shelters, shop windows, and elsewhere, featuring a confident capital U: "United We Stand."

History's famous V. British prime minister Winston Churchill gives the "V for Victory" hand sign to a London crowd in June 1943, during World War II. Conceived by Churchill in summer 1941 to help boost British morale after Britain's darkest war year, the V sign proved hugely popular in armies and homelands of the Commonwealth and, eventually, the United States, a symbol of defiance against Nazi Germany and Imperial Japan. Churchill had initiated the sign as a knuckles-outward gesture but had reversed it to thumb-outward after learning that the other one already had the vulgar meaning of "Up yours." Without a doubt, that continued nuance helped the V sign's popularity.

THE BIRTH OF V-NESS

Victory at sea. Venus in furs. Venture capital. Verizon and Viacom. The letter V can add zest and drama to words it inhabits. Its compelling shape and zippy sound imply purpose, immersion, advancement. V could be a searchlight, a spear point, a drill bit, a praying gesture, a ship's cutwater, or geese winging in a formation 80 million years old.

Some of these associations appear in Thomas Pynchon's novel *V,* published in 1961, about two characters' time-chase from the 1950s to the 1910s in quest of a mysterious lady known as V. Throughout, the shadowy V. supplies a distant goalpost of enlightenment, until she is imperfectly revealed to symbolize both the 20th century (French: *vingtième siècle*) and human sexuality: letter V as the goddess Venus or a pair of legs.

V and J share the distinction of being the youngest letters in English: Both were fully accepted into our alphabet only in the mid-19th century. Prior to that, although V and J were appearing systematically in print by year 1700, they were considered by some people to be consonantal variants of U and I, respectively— that is, variants of the vowels they now follow in letter order.

V was born from U (so was W), while J was born from I. The histories of V and J run parallel. Both letters emerged as latter-day responses to vast European language changes that began before the Roman Empire collapsed (A.D. 500) and accelerated after. From the decay of spoken Latin came medieval Romance tongues like French and Spanish, containing new sounds not necessarily represented in the old Roman alphabet. Such sounds eventually demanded their own letters.

But back in A.D. 100 or so, the Romans were doing just fine with 23 letters. That was all they needed for the writing of Latin words, plus a bunch of cultural-type words borrowed from Greek. The three letters absent were J, W, and V.

Here the reader may pause: No ancient Roman V? Wasn't Venus a Roman goddess? Wasn't there an Italian volcano called Vesuvius, a Roman emperor named Vespasian? Didn't Julius Caesar send home a postbattle message, *"Veni, vidi, vici"* (I came, I saw, I conquered)? So how no Roman V?

The answer is that the Roman letter in those examples was never V. It was U, only written as V and pronounced as "w."

According to modern analysis, spoken ancient Latin had no sound "v." The closest was sound "f," written as F. But Latin did have "w" sounds, often beginning a syllable. Caesar's boast would have been spoken as "*Way*-nee, *wee*-dee, *wee*-kee." Venus's name was really pronounced "Way-nus." A new country house was a *villa nova*, "willa no-wa." In a line of verse by the Roman poet Horace, quoted in the preceding chapter (page 314)—*Pulvis et umbra sumus* (We are but dust and shadow)—the Latin word for "dust" was pronounced "pul-wis," sounding a bit like ashes on the wind.

To represent their "w" sound, the Romans used the letter U as a consonant. That was U's second job. Its main job was as a vowel. It was a vowel when placed before a consonant letter or at a word's end, in Latin words like *murus* (wall) and *manu* (by hand). But before a vowel letter, Roman U was recognized as consonant "w." The word *quercus* (oak tree), pronounced "kwair-cus," demonstrates both uses: U first as a consonant, then as a vowel.

The letter at the front of Latin words Venus and *villa* was the consonantal U. In *Venus,* the first and fourth letters look different only due to modern printing convention. Ancient Romans would have written Venvs or, in informal style, Uenus. The shapes V and U were considered in those days to be the same letter, the letter U—a point explained in the preceding chapter. The spelling Uenus would show us modern readers that U was being used twice, in different ways, as in the word *quercus.* Compare our word "yearly," which begins with a Y consonant and ends with a Y vowel, yet offers no confusion. The context tells us which Y it is.

Latin consonantal U had logic behind it. The logic came from the vowel U, which tends naturally to create the sound "w" in front of another vowel. You hear this phenomenon in English words like "nuance," "fluent," "suing." Most two-sound vowel combinations generate either a "w" (example: co-op) or a "y" (Fiona). The U being strong on "w," it must have seemed a natural choice to the Roman adapters of the alphabet, circa 600 B.C., to symbolize their sound "w." The situation mirrors that of Roman letter I, which also had a second job, as a consonant representing sound "y."

Consonantal U is still at work in modern Romance languages, in words like Spanish *agua* (water), pronounced "ah-gwa," and

French *huit* (eight), "hweet." It occupies one whole corner of English vocabulary, in uses after letter Q. Q hardly ever appears in English without being followed by two vowels, the first of which is U, almost always sounded as "w"—quart, question, inquire. English consonantal U occurs also after G or S, in a handful of words from Latin, French, or Spanish, like "anguish," "iguana," "suite," and "suede" (from *Suède,* the French word for Sweden, whereby the English "Swed-" corresponds to the French "Sued-").

Notice that these uses involve U near the middle of a syllable, sheltering in the lee of Q, S, or G. That's the typical position where U for "w" has survived since ancient Rome. Yet in a different position, at the *front* of a syllable, it has been weathered and changed by time. In countless Latin words like *victoria* ("victory"), *caverna* ("cavern"), or *pulvis* ("dust"), consonantal U subsequently slurred from sound "w" to sound "v."

Let's follow the sound through a millennium or so. By A.D. 300, spoken Latin of the Roman Empire had begun shifting to new pronunciations, particularly of certain consonants—a development mentioned throughout this book. First, Roman "w" in many words slipped toward sound "b," allowing a more relaxed position of the lips, yet with no change in traditional Latin spellings. A new country house, still written as *villa nova* or *uilla noua,* was pronounced "billa no-ba," not "willa no-wa" anymore.

Modern Spanish, a language generally close to ancient Latin, retains this early evolutionary stage. In most regional accents of Spain and Latin America, letter V is routinely pronounced the same as B. Spanish *villa* (meaning "town") is pronounced "billa"; *victoria* is "bictoria"; *caverna,* "caberna."

Outside of old Spain—as the Roman Empire crumbled and spoken Latin broke into regional dialects that grew into medieval Romance tongues—the consonantal U slurred further, from "b" to "v." The fledgling languages French and Italian reached this second stage by about A.D. 900. A medieval Parisian would say *ville* or *caverne* with a sound we would call a V. (Compare with this the medieval French slurring of letter B itself: page 73.)

Next stop: England. According to modern scholarship, the Old English of 1000 already had its own "v" sound, courtesy of prior development in the Germanic language family. The Old English sound survives today as the V in "love," "drive" (as in herding), "even," and other words dating back to the Anglo-Saxons. The Old English alphabet—with no legacy of Latin consonantal U—denoted the sound "v" with the letter F. Archaic "love," pronounced "luv-uh," was written *lufu*. That was F's second job, for it also represented the sound "f."

Sounds "f" and "v" are as close as two consonants can be. Classed together as dento-labial fricatives, they both involve air being pushed through the barrier of your front teeth against your lower lip. The main difference is that "v" engages the vocal cords while "f" does not. To write the letter F for both sounds was adequate for Old English. Yet that usage would soon be hosed away in history.

The Norman Conquest of 1066 brought French vocabulary and spelling rules to England. By 1300 medieval English had been enlarged with thousands of Norman French words, many incorporating the sound "v"—for instance, *caverne, victorie,* and *village.* The written symbol for French "v" being V or U, this system was imposed on native English words, also, eventually producing modern spellings like "love" and "drive." If you could ask an educated Londoner of 1400 to name the first letter of "victorie" or the third letter of "love," she would say it was U, used as a consonant.

The letter-U chapter here has sketched the somewhat tedious issue of shape V versus shape U in medieval writing. Both shapes occurred interchangeably to mean the letter U, including consonantal U. A written U could signify sound "u" or "v"—and ditto a written V could signify either. Shape V was the prevalent capital form; shape U often appeared in minuscule styles.

A step toward order had come by 1400, with the practice of writing V at the start of a word and U at other positions, regardless of sound. The custom was observed in Italy, France, and England for writing those countries' languages. Late medieval English manuscripts show spellings like *vpon* and *vse*, *vile* and *victorie*, *loue* and *euer*, and *rule* and *huge*, a practice maintained after printing's arrival in England (1476) and reflected in such print documents as the original King James Bible (1611) and the Shakespeare First Folio collection (1623).

Two symbols, two sounds. By about 1650, a need was felt to bring sounds "v" and "u" into line, obviously by giving each to one symbol, U or V. But which to which? Conceivably, the sound "v" could have gone to the shape U. Here the path had been cleared by certain printers in Italy and France, who in the latter 1500s had begun to print "v" as V exclusively. The choice had been prompted by the prior stage of usage, where shape V had normally appeared at the start of a word, regardless of sound. By nature of the Italian and French tongues, the V shape in that position had captured the sound "v" far more often than "u," and so the association arose. By 1700 it was standard in English, too.

The new letter's sound helped supply its name. English "vee" comes from the letter's French name, *vé*. Theoretically, the letter could have been called "voo," meaning "the v-sound U," yet this nowhere happened.

Like its fellow latecomer J, the V had to wait about another 150 years before being finally accepted as a letter of our alphabet. Until around 1840, some scholars (not all) treated V as a variant of U and J as a variant of I, thereby recognizing only 24 letters. A 26-letter alphabet, with J and V, appeared in London schoolmaster Thomas Dyche's *Guide to the English Tongue* of 1707 (yet notice the interesting letter order in his chart, page 328). But Samuel Johnson's landmark 1755 English dictionary held the line at 24 letters, thus delaying J and V's official arrival by at least 75 years.

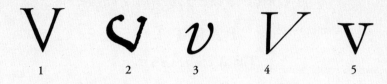

1	2	3	4	5

(1) The ancient Roman U of stone-carved inscriptions has supplied the shape for our modern print V. (2) From a Latin manuscript of Italy of the early 1100s A.D., this inked letter, beginning the word Veni *(imperative: "Come"), anticipates not only our modern use of shape V for the consonant sound "v" but also the slant of our modern italic typeface. (3) Lowercase italic print v, designed in France around 1615 by Jean Jannon. (4) The uppercase italic V from Jannon's same series has no such rounded look but more resembles his roman V, shown here (5) in lowercase. Designs like Jannon's would inspire subsequent serif typefaces, and today most follow this biform treatment of italic V.*

Although Johnson uses V and J in spellings throughout, he excludes them from the letter list. His dictionary headings run "H, I, K" and "T, U, W." The "U" heading presents all words starting with U or V in one alphabetical sequence. Johnson's first U entry is "V" meaning the Roman numeral for 5, followed immediately by "Vacancy" and "Vacant," then eventually by "Vagrancy," "Valley," and "Vat." After the Va-'s finish, we come to "Ubiquity" and "Udder," then eventually "Veal" and "Ugly." Significantly, Johnson prefaces an editorial note regretting that "the old custom" prevents him from treating U and V separately as they deserve.

J and V were still being excluded from the British alphabet as late as 1836, in Charles Richardson's *New Dictionary of the English Language.* Yet a milestone had been reached in Noah Webster's *American Dictionary of the English Language* (1828), which presents a 26-letter alphabet, including J and V.

V contributes modestly to our vocabulary. The V-8 car engine, available since the 1915 Cadillac, was named for its two rows of four cylinders, each row standing at an angle, forming a V in profile. The V-chip is a TV-reception scrambler, named originally for

A Guide to the English Tongue.

PART I.

The ALPHABET.

English Letters.	Roman Letters.	Italian Letters.	The Names of the Letters.
a b	A B	a b	A B	ay bee
c	C	c	C	see
d	D	d	D	dee
e	E	e	E	e
f	F	f	F	eff
g h	G H	g h	G H	jee aytſh
i	I	i	I	i
j	J	j	J	jay
k	K	k	K	cay
l	L	l	L	ell
m	M	m	M	em
n	N	n	N	en
o	O	o	O	o
p	P	p	P	pee
q	Q	q	Q	cu
r ſ	R S	r ſ	R S	ar eſs
t	T	t	T	tee
v	V	v	V	vee
u	U	u	U	yu
w	W	w	W	double yu
x	X	x	X	eks
y	Y	y	Y	wi
z	Z	z	Z	zed

Not as a printer's error, letter V precedes U in the alphabet of Thomas Dyche's A Guide to the English Tongue, *published in London in 1707. Among the earliest scholars to treat V and J as sovereign letters, Dyche wrote at a time when their place in alphabetical sequence was unclear, beyond the fact that V stood in relationship to U and J to I. The logic in putting V first is that, if you treat V and U as equivalent and start listing all V-words and U-words together, the V-words kick in first alphabetically: Words like "vacate" and "vat" attach the V to an A, while U must wait for B in order to form an English word, "ubiquitous." So V beats U to the punch. Dyche's letter I precedes J because I itself is an English word, the pronoun "I," which comes before the A attachments of "jabber," "Jack," etc. Eventually, a wish for consistency would push both newcomers, J and V, to the rear of their respective mother vowels.*

A retired Sir Winston (with his wife, Clementine) jubilantly exchanges V signs with well-wishers sometime in the early 1960s, not long before his death in 1965. After the war, the V remained Churchill's personal signature in politics and other public appearances. For the last two decades of his life, he routinely met demands by news photographers and supporters to "give us a V."

"viewer" when first issued in the mid-1990s yet now more often thought of as meaning "violence."

But the most famous V of all has been Winston Churchill's "V for Victory" hand sign, symbol of British defiance and resolve during World War II. Churchill launched the V sign in a now-famous speech in Parliament in July 1941, just when events had begun to suggest that Hitler might not win after all. (Ironically, Hitler later launched his own V's against England: the V-1 and V-2 flying bombs, named from German *Vergeltungswaffe*, "retaliation weapon.")

Churchill's V was powerful propaganda—yet perhaps not so powerful as claimed by mystical British scholar Alfred Kallir, who theorized that the whole Allied war effort was being boosted by cosmic energy, channeled down through the letter's shape, imitative of a praying person's hands. It was, as Kallir touchingly asserted in a postwar booklet, *The Victory of V.*

This W has legs. Republican presidential candidate George Walker Bush makes his three-fingered W sign to supporters in Tampa, Florida, in November 2000, days before the election. Referring to the middle initial that distinguishes Bush from his father, President George Herbert Walker Bush—and modeled on Winston Churchill's "V for Victory" (see page 320)—the W sign perhaps helped "Dubya" to his narrow victory over Democrat Al Gore.

USEFUL W

Widest of all our letters in standard typefaces, W is more than just an M turned upside-down. While M may stand securely on two vertical legs, W's arms typically angle outward, commemorating W's early days as two linked V forms.

W symbolizes a sound that reaches back to the ancient Germanic roots of English. Technically, it is the voiced bilabial semivowel—one of two consonants (the other being Y) that sound through your open throat in much the same way as a vowel does. The term "voiced bilabial," as we all know by now, just means that W uses your vocal cords and both lips.

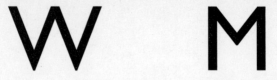

W M

Fairly dwarfing the M in width, W surely has its own shape in the celebrated 1927 sans-serif typeface called Gill Sans, designed by Englishman Eric Gill. Not all designs so strongly distinguish the two letters.

With no subtle tongue positioning, "w" is one of the easier letter sounds for English speakers to say. Babies can say it ("wa-wa"), and many children and some adults may substitute it for the more complex "r" sound, as in "Wudolph the wed-nosed weindeeh."

W has a most interesting history. The 23rd letter of our alphabet, it was chronologically the 24th to join our English alphabet, somewhat ahead of rear-runners J and V. The W was invented during the first millennium A.D. to answer a specific need of language. It exemplifies how letters can be created to accommodate speech.

As mentioned elsewhere, the ancient Roman alphabet had only 23 letters: no W, V, or J. Those three came into general use during the Middle Ages or Renaissance, abetted after the mid-1400s by the printing press. V and W were born as variants of U and now follow their mother in alphabetical order. Today U is commemorated in the name of W, the "double U."

During ancient Roman times, U did the job of our W. Prior chapters have detailed how Roman writing used U to show both the vowel sound "u" and the consonant sound "w." The Latin word *equus* (horse) demonstrates the "w" sound in its first U, while the second U takes the familiar "u." This U with two hats was feasible because the Latin "w" sound occurred only before a vowel; thus, a U written before a vowel would almost always be consonantal.

But then spoken Latin gradually lost much of its "w" sound as pronunciations slurred, over centuries. According to modern analysis, by A.D. 300 Latin "w" had disappeared from the heads of syllables, replaced by the sound "b." Following the Roman Empire's fall in about 500, the "b" slurred to "v" in early medieval French and Italian (tongues derived from Latin). Eventually these changes would prompt the invention of the letter V.

The Latin "w" sound survived mainly in uses in midsyllable, such as after the letter Q. Here it continued to be shown by the letter U, as in our words "quantum" or "frequent."

So: Sound "w" disappeared from much of late Latin, and letter U came to symbolize what remained of it. Neat, simple, and yet . . .

Life and language being sometimes complicated, the Latin sound "w" occasionally did hang on at the front of a syllable, where by the rules it should have turned to "b" instead. This happened in a few deeply ingrained uses, like place-names. Modern epigraphists (scholars who study old writing) find relevant evidence in place-name spellings in extant inscriptions and manuscripts. For example, the eastern-Italian mountain region that the Romans called Seuo ("Seh-wo") apparently retained its "w" sound during the empire's final centuries, never slurring to "Seh-bo" as logically it might have. As early as A.D. 150, the name's spelling begins to change in extant inscriptions, from Seuo to Seuuo—a doubling of the U. This seems to be ancient writers' way of showing an abiding "w" sound.

Such evidence suggests that a doubled U was an informal device used by Latin writing of the later Roman Empire to represent the old "w" sound that survived (although rarely) at the head of a syllable in spoken Latin. This double U was destined, more than 1,000 years on, to become standardized as W.

Meanwhile, outside of Latin and early medieval Romance tongues, the sound "w" thrived in the Germanic language family of Northern Europe. The Anglo-Saxons who invaded England from northern Germany (latter 400s A.D.) said "w" all the time: Think of "Wotan," "wassail," "weapons," "witches," "woods," and "swine," and you've covered most of their hobbies. On the continent, German sounds of "w" show up, represented by Latin-style double U's, in the earliest known book in German, a rhyming translation of the Gospels written at Weissburg, in Alsace, in around 865. (During a later era, in northern German, at least, the "w" sound would shift generally to "v.")

Germanic "w" was native also to the Vikings who sailed from Denmark and Norway to plunder and capture parts of northern France, northern England, and elsewhere, starting around 800. By 1000, in Viking-occupied Normandy in France, the infusion of Scandinavian vocabulary had created Norman French words that used "w" while Parisian French did not. Particularly, Norman "w" might occur as an opening sound in place of mainstream French "g."

For example, the medieval Norman French word for a document granting authority or security was *warant* (ancestor of our "warrant"). This was a variant of the French word *guarant* (as in "guarantee"). Similarly, a Norman French border castle might have a *wardein* named *William,* earning a *wage* and ready for *warre,* whereas on the royal French side the same thing would be *guarden Guillaume* with his *gage,* ready for *guerre.*

Thus possessed of this un-French sound "w," the medieval Normans needed a way to show it in writing. Their solution: the double U of late Latin and of German writings.

The English meantime had their own way of doing things (no surprise). The citizens of Anglo-Saxon England used a Roman alphabet that omitted J, Q, V, and the irregular double U. Yet in order to accommodate Old English language sounds, the Anglo-Saxons had supplemented their alphabet with four non-Roman letters, two of them invented in England and two borrowed from northern European tradition. (See "Tales of TH," pages 308–9.) One such letter, called *wyn* or *wen,* looked like a second P but denoted the sound "w."

Medieval England was destined to be a fertile breeding ground of the letter W. In 1066 the most famous William of Normandy, Duke William the Conqueror, landed an army in southeastern England, defeated an English army, and grabbed the English throne. The Norman occupation changed everything, including, gradually, the speaking and writing of English. Among other developments, English *wyn* eventually disappeared, pushed out by Norman double U.

Like its sibling V, but to a less extreme degree, the double U spent a few centuries being viewed as a variant of letter U rather than a letter on its own. Its cause was helped by printing's arrival in England (1476): The double-U shape was necessarily included with other metal letter blocks for printing English, and so its status as a separate letter became secure.

During the 1500s, W started to be admitted to the letter list, as taught to English children at school. It was inserted into the order next to its mother, U, either before or after. Richard Mulcaster puts W directly after U in his landmark English grammar book, *The First Part of the Elementarie* (1582), yet the "double-u," spelled out, comes *before* U in a 1597 written recitation of the alphabet set to music by English composer Thomas Morley. These are two of W's earliest appearances in the English alphabet list.

The shape of English W emerged during the centuries 1100 to 1500. The rounded double-U shape of late Roman script was the common handwritten form in days before printing. (Today it is preserved in our lowercase script w.) But with the advent of print, type designers in England eventually produced a double-V shape, in reference to the V-shaped U of ancient Roman stone inscriptions. Some early typefaces showed the two constituent V's as slightly separated: VV. More often, they touched or overlapped: W.

In Germany, a print W had been used since the 1470s, with a shape based on traditional German handwriting: **𝖂**. Today W represents mainly the German sound "v," due to changes in German since the Middle Ages. Many modern German uses of W for "v" correspond to English W for "w" in related words, for example: *Wasser* ("vahsser"), "water"; *wunderbar* ("vuhnderbar"), "wonderful"; *Wilhelm* ("Vilhelm"), "William."

The W fared less well in southern Europe. The sound "w" having largely departed from late Latin, the Romance languages of 1600 were in no desperate need of a new letter in this category. The legacy of ancient consonantal U sufficed to cover surviving "w" sounds, as in Italian Guido or Spanish *iguana*. To this day, W is not properly a letter of the Italian or Spanish alphabets, although it is employed to render foreign words already in print.

French, likewise, was very reluctant over W. French got along fine with consonantal U to show "w," as in the word *suave* (which English shares). To show an initial "w," French employed the combination OU-, as in *oui,* meaning "yes," or *ouest,* pronounced "west," meaning "west." Not until the late 19th century was W accepted into the French alphabet, the last to arrive. Previously the alphabet of Victor Hugo and other French authors had 25 letters, no W.

In keeping with this tardy recognition, the French name for the letter describes the print shape—*double vé* (double vee)— whereas the English name describes the earlier, handwritten shape. It is the only instance of an English letter name inspiring a French one, rather than vice versa. Today French W remains rarely used, except for foreign-derived names and English-borrowed words, in which it tends to be pronounced "v," as in *wagon-lit* (railroad sleeper car).

Certain English words like "answer" and "two" hold a silent W that was at one time pronounced—a fact hinted at in the related words "swear" and "twain." In an anxious line from Shakespeare's 1607 tragedy *Antony and Cleopatra*, "Our Italy shines o'er with civil swords," the word "swords" would have been spoken much like "wars," which is the context's meaning.

The letter combination WH-, occurring mostly in words of native English origin (white whale), usually commemorates the medieval English spelling HW-, which was pronounced just as "hw." By 1300 the two letters were being transposed in English writing, partly to look more Norman and genteel. Today the H has fallen silent in almost all such words. Yet a very few, for complex reasons, gradually saw their W fall silent: whom, whole. The situation would be trivial except that it prompted a memorable comment from Samuel Johnson in his 1755 dictionary: "In *whore* only, and sometimes in *wholesome, wh* is sounded like a simple *h*."

(*1*) Classical ancient Roman U, A.D. 113. Shaped for carving into stone, the letter could be read as either "u" or "w," in context. (*2*) The double U, here in Carolingian minuscules of the 800s, denoted the sound "w" in the writing of late Latin, early medieval German, and Norman French. (*3*) Combining both elements of the past is the broken W from the opening page of the Hamlet *second-quarto edition of 1604 (shown in full on page 317). By that date, English W was more usually printed as a single, continuous shape.* (*4*) The letter's historical background is acknowledged in the Times New Roman font, created in 1932 for the London Times *newspaper and now one of the world's most widespread typefaces.*

X PERSONS UNDER 17 NOT ADMITTED

Forbidding X. Notations like this one began appearing on movie posters and other advertising in 1968, after the Motion Picture Association of America introduced audience-related ratings. The X stood for "extreme," which was the category including pornography—but not only. One X-rated film, Midnight Cowboy *(1969), about a young Texan's misadventures in New York City, went on to win three Oscars, including Best Picture. The "X" category has since been renamed as the less-notorious-seeming "NC-17" (meaning "no children, 17 or under, admitted").*

LIVING WITH YOUR X

Xenophobia means "fear of foreigners," and no word better displays the alien and forbidding spirit that once belonged to X. True, the letter has mellowed in the last 12 years or so. But in olden days—before there were *X-Files,* X Games, or the Xbox—the X was an outsider, slightly sinister, sparingly used.

Thirty years ago X stood mainly for a movie off-limits to kids or for the "poison" warning on a product label. If X marked the spot on a treasure map, you could bet it was someplace remote and dangerous. Remote if fabulous was Xanadu, capital of Kubla Khan in Samuel Coleridge's poem of 1798. The X-Men of 1960s Marvel comic books were mutant superheroes:

good guys but, well, mutants. Even the gas called xenon (abbreviated as Xe on the elemental chart) was never exactly the substance next door. Indeed, the name "xenon" means "foreign thing" in Greek, carrying the same word root as in "xenophobia."

Some of X's mystery comes from its low rate of use: In printed English it ranks second or third to last, above Z and (in some surveys) Q or J. As an initial letter, X ranks dead last: It's the one that appears least at the start of English words.

Yet more important to X's mystique is its traditional job denoting an unknown or unrevealed mathematical quantity: "If $3X = X + 3$, what is X?" (Answer: 1.5.)

This use of X was introduced in 1637 by none less than French philosopher-mathematician-scientist René Descartes in his treatise *La Géométrie*. Descartes assigned letters X, Y, and Z to symbolize any three unknowns in a geometric equation, but he favored X (see "Why Isn't Z the Unknown?," page 344). The association stuck: Down later centuries of math and science, X came to be used almost as a question mark.

In 1895, when German physicist Wilhelm Konrad Röntgen discovered a strange new radiation, he called it the X-ray because he didn't know what it contained. A similar scientific fog enshrouds such 1950s and '60s sci-fi movie duds as *The X from Outer Space, Strange World of Planet X,* and *X—The Unknown.*

In fiction and even journalism well into the 20th century, the letter X might be published in place of someone's name, to preserve anonymity and guard against libel lawsuits, a custom reflected in the title of a silly 1938 Laurence Olivier and Merle Oberon movie, *The Divorce of Lady X.* Similarly, in 1952, American Black Liberation advocate Malcolm Little, to commemorate his forgotten African lineage, changed his name to Malcolm X. And who above age 40 could forget the disesteemed "Brand X," the name used in certain 1960s TV commercials to cloak the identity of the competitor's product being shown as inferior to Lestoil floor cleaner or Brillo scouring pads?

If X had any place in genuine product names of those days, it was for something dangerous or racy—perhaps literally so. The U.S. X-1 aircraft (X for "experimental") was the first to break the sound barrier, in October 1947, with a young Chuck Yeager piloting. The next year a British motor company launched the first Jaguar sports car, the XK 120, in which X stood for "experimental engine," K for "11th in development," and 120 for the top speed in miles per hour.

In 1968 the Motion Picture Association of America introduced lettered ratings to alert moviegoers to levels of sex, profanity, and violence in new releases. At the adult-content end of the spectrum, R stood for "restricted" and X for "extreme"—the category including pornography. Practically overnight, X took on a new association in the American mind: dirty, explicit sex.

Thus, by the end of the 1960s, X could mean either "mystery," "danger," or "sex"—a memorable combination. X was the Unknown, the Sinister, the Extreme. Subsequent decades have seen the letter's public relations improve dramatically. But first, some background.

X comes to us from the ancient Roman alphabet. Originally it was the last of 21 Roman letters, but by about A.D. 100 it had been joined by two added rear-runners: Y and Z. Roman X represented the "ks" sound in Latin words like *rex* (king) or *exit* (he goes out); its name was formed by prefixing a vowel to the sound: *eks* or *ex*.

The Romans had acquired the letter, and probably its name, too, in copying the Etruscan alphabet, around 600 B.C. Previously the Etruscan letters had been copied from the Greek: Etruscan X had come from the letter *ksi* of the West Greek alphabet, used by Greek settlers at the Bay of Naples. West Greek *ksi* carried the

1   2   3   4

X's simple, distinctive shape has changed little over the millennia. (1) Letter ksi of the West Greek alphabet, about 700 B.C. Coming toward the end of the alphabet and carrying sound "ks," this Greek letter was copied into the Etruscans' alphabet to become their letter eks, or X. (2) The elegant X of Roman carved inscriptions, around A.D. 113, had one bar slightly widened. The letter symbolized a "ks" sound that occurred at the middle or end of Latin words. (3) An inked X in the uncial handwriting style, 600s. Although designed for the pen, the shape made reference to the Roman capital. (4) An X in the 1925 typeface called Broadway reflects prior traditions, more so than you might expect.

sound "ks," fell near the end of the alphabet, and took the shape X. Scholars theorize that the Etruscans changed the name to *eks* to better demonstrate the letter's sound in their language, because while Greek *ksi* might often begin a Greek word or syllable, the Etruscan "ks" sound came never at the beginning of a syllable but only at the end, with a vowel preceding. Much the same rule has held for Latin and for English (see below).

Passing to the Roman alphabets of medieval European languages after Rome's fall (A.D. 500), X became an English letter. Its "ks" sound occurred at the middle or end of Old English words, not at the beginning. Today the Anglo-Saxon sound is retained in old words like "Saxon," "ox," and "mix," while words delivered through Norman French may have a softer X (luxury, anxious) or not (tax, execute). At the start of a word, X takes yet a softer sound: "z," as in "xylophone."

Most modern English words starting with X derive from ancient Greek: xylophone (wooden voice), xanthine (yellow), xiphoid (sword-shaped). The name Xena—warrior princess of comic books and TV—means "foreign lady." The name Xerox takes off from Greek *xeros* (dry), as in xerography, a dry copying method perfected in the late 1950s to improve on mimeographing.

In such X-words, our X represents what in the original Greek was that letter *ksi,* sounded as "ks." Greek *xeros* was actually pronounced "ksehr-os." The Athenian author-soldier-gentleman Xenophon would have called himself "Ksehnophon." His name meant "foreign voice," and too foreign indeed for the start of an English word was that Greek "ks," which has softened systematically to "z" in English borrowings. But only where it falls as the first letter. In other placements, in countless Greek-derived English words, letter X still carries its authentic Greek sound: exodus, lexicon, oxygen.

Since the early 1990s, X has come roaring into the mainstream, to the extent that it is one of the defining letters of the new millennium. Like Q, e, and i, the X has been drafted for

The "other" Greek X. In the Christian symbol known as the Cross of Constantine (whose meaning is explained on page 266), the X shape belongs to a Greek letter called khi, *taking the sound "kh." Our X, meanwhile, comes from the Greek letter* ksi, *with the sound "ks." Confusingly, this symbol X was shared, with two different meanings, between two versions of the early Greek alphabet: the East and West Greek. Our alphabet descends from the West Greek version, while the East Greek eventually became official for ancient and modern Greece. See the chart on page 61.*

According to legend, a 17th-century printer's problem helped X to land its major job symbolizing something unknown. For the many equations in his now-famous 1637 mathematical work *La Géométrie,* René Descartes chose letters A, B, and C to represent any three constants and X, Y, and Z to represent any three unknown quantities. He intended that Z be the first unknown (corresponding to A), with Y second and X third.

But the story goes that the printer, while typesetting the manuscript, found himself repeatedly running short of letter blocks for Y and Z, due in part to Descartes' many equations calling for these letters. However, the printer still had plenty of X's, a letter that in French-language print is used far less than Y or Z.

So the printer wrote to Descartes, asking whether it made any difference which of the three, Z, Y, or X, appeared in equations of one or two unknowns—and might X be the preferred letter for printing purposes? The great man replied that this was acceptable. And that is why the *Géométrie* tends to favor X as the letter of an unknown quantity, especially in the second half of the treatise.

marketing and advertising; it now signifies something like "computer magic and control" or "cutting edge." Witness such software company names as X-Collaboration, Xpoint Technologies, and Xvision Eclipse, not to mention X-Ceptor bioresearch and Germany's X-Filme production company *(Run, Lola, Run).* Microsoft's Xbox video game console actually carries an X across its top: a plastic repoussé shape that seems to hold it all in there. In its look and name, the Xbox promises fun and control, across the board, for the whole family.

Brand names like these—which in part exploit X's rarity in normal English—would have looked really odd 30 or 35 years ago. In 1972, when the X-rated film *Deep Throat* was out, a prod-

French philosopher-mathematician-scientist René Descartes (1596–1650) in an engraving based on a famous portrait by Dutch painter Frans Hals. Best remembered for his philosophical statement "I think, therefore I am" (meaning, perhaps: "To doubt is to approach reality"), Descartes changed his contemporaries' way of seeing the world and anticipated an era of science and reason. In his most important mathematical work, La Géométrie (1637), he pioneered the use of algebra for solving geometric problems. Here the words around the picture frame include his titles: "knight, lord of Perron" (a family estate near Poitiers). Presumably it is just coincidence that the armorial badge at bottom center shows an X shape.

uct name like "X Box" would have seemed laughably obscene. Today corporate choice of trademark X belongs to a new climate, in which the letter has been rehabilitated.

How so? One groundbreaking change in this direction was the 1991 fiction best-seller *Generation X: Tales for an Accelerated Culture* by Douglas Coupland. Published during a recession, the book addressed the diminished expectations of American post–Baby Boomers, born between about 1965 and 1975; its title played on the Brand X of 1960s TV. Soon the media were referring to 20-somethings of the early '90s as "X-ers." (By the late '90s we had "Y-ers," too.)

Computer jargon had changed, too, by the early '90s. The development of the X Window System for graphics display (1986) was followed by the popular QuarkXPress software program (1987) and the arrival of mature desktop publishing. Soon capital X began to imply "page-layout software" in brand names. Today we have Xpert Tools, Punch XT, Xdream, and HexWeb XT, all software "Xtensions" of basic Quark programs. In addition, there's the whole Window "X Server" software category: SecureX, X-ThinPro, WinaXe, and so on.

Then came *The X-Files.* Debuting in 1993 and titled for the traditional X of mystery, this Fox TV hit series—about two good-looking FBI agents pursuing evidence of an alien-planet conspiracy to take over the world—helped to normalize X and give it associations of thrills and pleasure for millions of the show's fans. By the time the series folded in 2002, X had reached legitimacy. It wasn't just for sex and danger anymore.

The custom of writing X's for kisses in signing off a letter dates from the Middle Ages, when much of Europe's population remained illiterate. On legal documents, in lieu of a signature, a person might write an X or the sign of the cross. The signatory would then kiss the X, to promise to stick to the agreement. Over later centuries, the written X came to mean not the signature but the kiss.

 *A Roman capital Y symbolizes our moral choice in our conduct of life, in an ink drawing from Geofroy Tory's 1529 treatise on the letters,* Champ Fleury. *The broad and easy road of vice delivers violence, punishment (scourging rods, a penal yoke), and Hell, while virtue's narrow road brings honor and office: a laurel wreath, a scepter, a crown. Associated with a legend about the young Hercules, in which the future hero had to choose his life's direction, the fork of a road was a popular symbol in Renaissance writing and art.*

THE WHEREFORE OF Y

You were born with your legs apart. They'll send you to the grave in a Y-shaped coffin." This farcical rebuke goes to the imperious hypocrite Mrs. Prentice from her equally reprehensible husband in English playwright Joe Orton's subversive 1969 comedy, *What the Butler Saw.*

The letter Y's forked shape has inspired thinkers throughout history—although usually in terms less sensational than Joe Orton's. The 16th-century French type designer and scholar Geofroy Tory found in Y the symbolized choice between vice and virtue (see facing illustration). The French author Victor Hugo, in his 1839 *Travel Notebooks,* rhapsodized thus: "Have you ever noticed that the letter Y is a picturesque letter open to countless different interpretations? A tree is in the shape of a Y; the fork of two roads forms a Y; two rivers flow together in a Y; the head of a donkey or that of an ox is in the shape of a Y; the stem of a glass is Y-shaped; a lily on its stalk is a Y; a man who prays to the heavens raises his arms in the shape of a Y."

Y is the only letter commonly used as both vowel and consonant in English. As a vowel, it overlaps with letter I, often pronounced like short or long I (myth, fly), although sometimes like long E (messy) and occasionally as a schwa (myrtle, satyr). In "say" and "boy," vowel Y forms a single sound with the preceding vowel, similar to the double-vowel combinations in "paid," "void," and many other words.

As a consonant, Y in English has one sound: the "y" of youth and yearning. Technically known as the palatal semivowel or voiced palatal spirant, it is pronounced with the tongue poised below the palate and with the vocal cords engaged. The title "semivowel," shared in English phonetics only by W, means that the letter's pronunciation approaches a vowel sound in the way it uses throat and vocal cords.

The symbol Y has never had a monopoly on representing the spoken sound "y." Native to Indo-European languages including Old English, the sound has been to a lot of places where written Y hasn't gone. For example, modern German and Czech write "y" as the letter J: German "year" is *Jahr,* pronounced "yahr." Ancient Latin had a common "y" sound, which it wrote as a consonantal I (see Chapter J, pages 186–87).

Even English at one time had no consonant Y. For the first 600 years of English writing, from the 600s A.D. onward, the sound "y" was shown with a symbol called a *yogh,* one of four Old English letters not from the Roman alphabet. Only after 1200 did letter Y start to take over in representing the sound "y."

Thus Y can be thought of as two different letters, vowel and consonant. They look identical but have distinct personalities, and the vowel is the elder by more than 2,000 years.

Let's tackle vowel Y first. As mentioned several times already in these pages, the ancient Greeks had a vowel letter called *upsilon,* which took a narrowed "u" sound and looked just like our Y shape. Like other letters of the early Greek alphabet, *upsilon* was copied into the Etruscan alphabet (700 B.C.) and thence into the Roman alphabet (600 B.C.) as the letter U. Thus *upsilon* is the grandmother of our U.

But unlike most letters, *upsilon* gave birth a second time into the family of Latin and English. Around A.D. 100, some 700 years after the Roman alphabet had been created, the Romans added two more letters, which are our Y and Z. The two were copied directly from the Athenian Greek alphabet of the day. Z was the Greek consonant *zeta*; Y was the vowel *upsilon* (again). The Romans imported them expressly for help in transliterating Greek words into Latin, a need created by the influx of Greek technical and cultural vocabulary into Roman science and society during the prior centuries. The Romans called their Y letter *upsilon,* and with it they were better able to write such useful Greek terms as *symphonia, symmetria,* and *stylus.*

The point of creating a Roman Y was that Greek *upsilon* sounded different from Roman U and thus properly needed its own Greek symbol for Latin spellings. To Roman ears, Greek *upsilon* probably sounded halfway between "u" and "i." Therefore, Roman Y probably sounded rather like "i," too.

Evidence suggests that by the late Roman Empire (A.D. 300), Roman Y was being pronounced the same as Roman I. The situation is commemorated imperfectly in the modern French and Spanish names for Y: *i grec* and *i griega,* "Greek I."

Whereas ancient Roman Y was confined to words borrowed

from Greek, Y in the early Middle Ages, A.D. 500 to 1000, began to spread to other words in written Latin, French, English. Scribes would often substitute Y for I as a way to break up a row of pen strokes that otherwise would be difficult to read. For instance, the Latin word for "impassable," written as *inuium* in medieval script, would be a bunch of short strokes; by spelling it *ynuyum*, the writer made it more legible.

Medieval Y was often dotted, suggesting a form of I. Likewise Y's peculiar English name "wye"—dating from the Middle Ages and never adequately explained—seems to relate to letter I.

Partly for legibility but partly through appeal of its handsome shape, Y enjoyed a heyday in English spelling between about 1250 and 1600. Extant writings show Y instead of I all over the place, even in uses like "hys" that would not have been hard to read with an I.

The spread of printing in Britain in the 1500s removed the legibility issue and had a standardizing effect that gradually returned many word spellings to I. Today the old Y versus I rivalry can still be glimpsed in such alternative spellings as flyer/flier, cyper/cipher, and tyre/tire.

Yet the medieval Y fad did leave one large legacy: Y's plum job representing any final "i" sound in English. Today we use a "-y" suffix that encompasses four diverse categories: (1) adjectival forms of Old English words (stony, mighty, my); (2) nouns from Greek, Latin, or Old French that originally had endings like -ia, -ium, or -ie (empathy, remedy, tally); (3) other anglicizations (Henry, from French Henri); and (4) certain diminutives (Jimmy, kitty, dummy).

Elsewhere Y still does the work the Romans hired it for—transliterating Greek *upsilon* in countless Greek loan words like "system," "phylum," "hypodermic." A word like "sympathy" shows two different layers of Y use: After the ancient Greco-

". . . But too late, for the Frenchmen beynge gredye of spoyle and seyinge some advantage, entered and slew all wythyne, saving the capitayne, hys wyfe, and hys two daughters . . ." (text beginning at middle of photograph). The Y's show as thickly as the sword blades in this letter of 1552, from young English nobleman Barnaby Fitzpatrick to England's King Edward VI, recounting Fitzpatrick's experiences on military campaign with King Henri II of France. In English handwriting of the era, vowel Y offered a legible and handsome alternative to I.

Latin *upsilon* of *sympatheia,* there comes the handy anglicizing –y suffix of medieval English.

Today Y is treated purely as a vowel in many languages of northern and eastern Europe, such as German, Swedish, Polish, and Czech. While these tongues include a frequent sound "y," they write it, as mentioned already, with the letter J. (As to the sound "j," they either omit it in speech or they show it with a variant letter G.) In German, Y appears mainly in Greek-derived words like *Psychologie* and *symbolisch,* where it represents the original Greek *upsilon.* In fact, Y's name in German is *üpsilon.*

Now, as to Y the consonant. This aspect of Y—one of the most characteristic English spelling traits, in which the English uses the letter differently from many other European tongues—goes back to medieval French. Emerging from late Latin at the start of the Middle Ages, French inherited the Roman alphabet of 23 letters, including a vowel Y (as in medieval French *symphonie*) and an I that could be either a vowel or a consonant (as in *iustice,* pronounced "joos-tee-seh"). But French writing began to use Y more often than Latin had, substituting it for I as a vowel or a consonant. Gradually Y came to denote the French consonantal sound "y," particularly at the start of a syllable, in medieval spellings like *yeulx* (eyes) and *ioyeulx* (joyous). Spanish, too, developed this use of Y, although Italian did not.

Like all French spelling rules of the day, the Y consonant was forcibly imported to England with the Norman Conquest of A.D. 1066. Here Y found fertile soil. For whereas the consonantal sound "y" was a minor part of spoken French, it occurred far more frequently in the northern European tongue of Old English. The Y had suddenly gotten a big promotion, much like its sibling W, for the same reasons.

Let's have a quick look at England before the Normans came. Mention has been made, at the start of the chapter, of the Old English letter *yogh,* which was a squiggle shape resembling a modern lowercase script Z. The Anglo-Saxons wrote *yogh* for their prevalent sound "y"—a sound found today in such grand old words as "Yule," "yoke," and "yeoman." Theoretically, Old English could have chosen to represent the sound with a Roman consonantal I, but the I was evidently seen as inadequate, due to its indistinct shape and its existing job as a vowel. So an Englishwoman of A.D. 1000 would have written the word "Yule" as something like **3**eol, that first symbol being the *yogh,* denoting "y." (In other uses, *yogh* might represent a sound closer to our "g.")

But *yogh* was targeted for redundancy after the Norman Conquest brought a new, French-speaking ruling class to England. Norman French used Y, not *yogh*. Under pressure from Norman clergy who sought to bring English writing into line with Norman, the Y for "y" became standard gradually for English, as well. By the late 1400s, the useful *yogh* was history, at least in England.

However, it survived farther afield, in writing in Scotland. With the arrival of Scottish printing in 1508, *yogh* even got into print. It was not given its own metal letter block but was assigned to the Roman letter closest to its shape: the Z. Thus, in Scottish print until the 1700s, a letter Z might mean either "z" or "y" (or sometimes "g") in sound; the word "year," pronounced normally, might appear printed as *zer.*

The Scottish Z variant became extinct, yet a remnant can be found today. The Scottish surnames MacKenzie and Menzies, among others, carry a Z that at one time represented a Gaelic

---

3   þ

The yogh *and* thorn, *representing the sounds "y" and "th," respectively, were two Anglo-Saxon letters that supplemented the Roman alphabet for Old English writing. (There were four in all: See page 308.) Amid the emergence of modern English, both* yogh *and* thorn *would be replaced, sometimes by the print letter Y.*

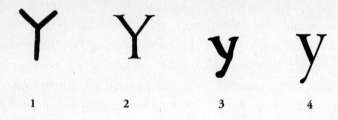

1 2 3 4

(1) The ancient Greek vowel upsilon *became the ancestor of our U and, centuries later, of our Y. Today Y loyally keeps* upsilon's *shape. (2) Roman inscriptional Y of about* A.D. *100. Copied from* upsilon, *the Roman letter was called* upsilon *and took a vowel sound between U and I. (3) An inked uncial Y of the 600s retains aspects of the Roman capital, while reducing the number of pen strokes to two. The shape of the uncial Y anticipates the modern lowercase shape. (4) Lowercase y in Baskerville Old Face, a modern version of Englishman John Baskerville's design of about 1768.*

sound of "g"—a fact not understood in England and eventually forgotten in Scotland.

Not so different from the fate of *yogh* was that of another Old English letter, *thorn,* denoting the plentiful English sound "th." *Thorn,* too, came under pressure in Norman England to get lost, and by the 1400s it was giving way to the letter combination TH in many spellings. Yet *thorn* would hold on for centuries more— the longest-lived of Old English letters—as a convenient abbreviation in words like "the," "them," "there," and "that," especially in informal writing.

Handwritten *thorn* had by the 1400s grown to resemble the Roman letter Y. With the advent of English printing (1476), *thorn* remained popular enough to be represented in print. The job of impersonating *thorn* on a typeset page was given to the Roman letter that *thorn* most resembled: Y. Therefore, the word "the,"

A curling tail distinguishes the shape of thorn, *as opposed to Y, on a carved gravestone now in Devon, from the mid-1700s, of adult twins who died young. As a convenient abbreviation and space-saver in words like "the" (lines 2, 6, 7, 9) and "this" (line 8), thorn remained in use for epitaphs and other signposting through the 1700s in England and for personal handwriting into the 1800s.*

printed with a *thorn*, would look like *ye*, or *Ye* in a headline. The word "that" would look like *yat*. Such words would be pronounced exactly as we pronounce them—"the," "that"—but with slightly different symbolization.

The Y *thorn* remained in English print and signposting through the 1700s and in personal handwriting into the 1800s. Today it is recalled, although not usually understood, in such quaint archaisms as the signpost "Ye Olde English Pub."

Three medieval ink styles of the letter Z, as penned by American type designer Frederic W. Goudy.

EXZOTIC Z

Zeroing in on the end of the alphabet, let's pause to salute one indispensable letter: U (yes, you). Your time and companionship, on this voyage of discovery, are much appreciated. For me, this book has been a chance to share a personal fascination and to promote respect for those miraculous little shapes that show language; along the way, I've learned much about things I never understood before. Here's hoping that readers, likewise, have gained something in enjoyment and knowledge. Now at journey's end, I thank U.

The last letter of our Roman alphabet is Z, a consonant that can seem racy and elusive or just plain disadvantaged. The potential indignity of being the alphabet's caboose is compounded by one real weakness: Z is, on average, the least-used letter in printed English. Of the 26 letters, Z finishes last in *this* race, too, behind Q and X. For every 1,000 appearances by E (our most-used letter), Q appears about 50 times, X 44, and Z a measly 22.

No wonder Z has been called superfluous, mere excess baggage. In Shakespeare's *King Lear* (A.D. 1605), the irascible Earl of Kent insults the fatuous courtier Oswald, calling him by the British name for Z: "Thou whoreson zed, thou unnecessary letter!"

Still, don't cry for Z, Venezuela. For not only has Z benefited from the romance of being rare and elusive, but also, in the past decade, Z has exploded in print: The Z's now shower down on us in company names like Z-Com (communications) and Capital Z (investments), signpostings like Kidz Korner, and movie titles like *eXistenZ*.

First, the old spelling issue. For centuries, letter S has been robbing Z of jobs. Phonetically Z and S are cousins. Both are sibilants, the category of hissing and hushing, and they take similar tongue positions. But where Z vibrates the tongue's blade section, S vibrates the tip, and Z engages the vocal cords, which S does not.

Soothing and intriguing, the "z" sound suggests sleep, bees, or high-flying prop planes. It is distinct from "s." Yet in countless English words like "rose," "raise," and "ties," sound "z" has been awarded to letter S. Of our words spelled with Z, a fair percentage seem to have been given the letter only because an S spelling would have duplicated an existing word: thus, "doze" instead of "dose" and "prize" instead of "prise" (but back to S for "surprise"). As English grammarian Richard Mulcaster observed in 1582, "Z is a consonant much heard amongst us, and seldom seen."

Why the bar against Z? One reason: Amid the fluid spellings of the Middle Ages (500 to 1500), scribes preferred S for its ease and legibility; Z was harder to handwrite clearly, as still today.

The problem could have been fixed amid the spread of printing (late 1400s), but in England a deeper prejudice remained: Z just looked too foreign. Being rarely used in Latin or Old English, Z was associated in English minds with French and ancient Greek, and it became reserved mainly for borrowed words: Amazon and zodiac (from Greek), azimuth and zenith (from Arabic).

Z never had such popularity problems as a youngster. Back in 1000 B.C., the seventh letter of the Phoenician alphabet was *zayin,* which took a "z" sound, as demonstrated in the opening sound of its name. The name probably meant "ax." The letter looked like our capital I, which might suggest a pole-ax if someone could just erase that bottom crossbar.

Copied into the Greek alphabet around 800 B.C., the letter was renamed *zeta*—evidently in confused reference to a different Phoenician sibilant letter, called *tsade.* (See pages 16–17, 61–62.) The *zeta*—the name meant nothing in Greek aside from the letter—began its life as an I shape but morphed gradually to the familiar Z shape. It represented the common Greek sound "zd."

However, neither "zd" nor "z" was a sound used in the Latin language of the Romans of Italy. After the alphabet was copied from the Greeks to the Etruscans and from the Etruscans to the Romans (by 600 B.C.), *zeta* dropped out of Roman use. The Roman alphabet of 250 B.C. had 21 letters, ending in X, with no *zeta.*

Then, around A.D. 100, a change: To help transliterate the Greek loan words that were flooding into Roman scientific and cultural vocabulary at that time, the Romans selected two Greek letters and added them to the end of their own alphabet: *upsilon* and *zeta,* or Y and Z. The two newcomers were never written for Latin but only for foreign-borrowed words, mainly Greek. As Greek *zeta* had by now shifted to the sound "z," that was the new Roman letter's sound, too. The Romans called Z by its Greek name, *zeta.*

Here Z languished—the underused tail end of Roman letters—until the early Middle Ages, when the emergence of Romance languages invited the use of Z for the sounds "ts" or "tz," common in Old French and Italian. Z spread modestly through medieval French-language spelling circles, both in France and in Norman England; in both countries, Z's sound slurred eventually to our "z." Z's rival for this sound was the letter S—a rivalry still seen in such alternative spellings as British "analyse" and American "analyze." By 1600, S was the clear winner and Z was rare in printed English.

For centuries after, Z retained an aura of foreignness or mystery: Zanzibar, Zoroastrianism, Nebuchadnezzar. If creative media minds chose a Z-word, it usually was for that effect. On 1920s and '30s movie screens and on 1950s TV, the hero Zorro's name seemed almost as exotic as his Z-slash calling card. The Houston rock group ZZ Top (formed in 1970, still going strong) were innovators, and the beloved "Z" consumer sports car line from Datsun (now Nissan), launched in 1970 and recently reintroduced, was meant to seem as racy as its letter. Meanwhile, director Costa-Gavras's 1969 political film, Z—named factually from a left-wing symbol of defiance in contemporary, authoritarian Greece—spoke of government conspiracy and the end of freedom. Z was a place you didn't casually go.

But that was then. Today Z is visible everywhere, borne on a recent tide of advertising and marketing that exploits certain letters as visual hoods, often in oddball phonetic spellings. Favorites are X, Q, K, and Z—normally rare letters, with strong sounds. Z, once so alien or extreme seeming, now signifies "hip" or "techno fun" or "ultimate service" in countless brand names.

The names form two categories. Where Z provides a flamboyant misspelling, as in the movie title *Antz* (1998) or Fox TV's Girlz Channel and Boyz Channel, the product is generally aimed at

The letter Z, slashed with a sword point into fabric, is the signature of the fictional hero Zorro, as immortalized in popular novels, movies, and a 1950s Walt Disney TV series. Introduced in a 1919 novel by American writer Johnston McCulley, Zorro ("fox" in Spanish) is a mysterious, cloaked, masked figure who operates against injustice and a corrupt Spanish governor in the Spanish Californian settlement of Los Angeles in around 1820. A dazzling swordsman, Zorro might spare a defeated adversary's life, instead slicing his "Z" into the man's clothing or nearby furnishings. Only a trusted few know that Zorro is the alter-ego of a seemingly frivolous local gentleman. Zorro reached the silver screen in the 1920 Douglas Fairbanks silent film The Mark of Zorro, *but the classic treatment was perhaps the 12-part 1937 movie-house serial,* Zorro Rides Again.*

teens or preteens. Kids recognize the Z spelling as a signal to them, inviting their trust. To this category also belong Racerz snack chips, the coyly named *Dragon Ball Z* animated TV series, and such abundant signposting as Whizz-Kidz (website) and "Kidz' Dentist."

Where Z stands alone, the appeal is meant as more adult: Z-Tel (telecommunications), Z-World (computer hardware), Z-Corp (printers), Z-Tech (electronics), Z-Team (video production), Z-man (audio), Z Systems (ditto), Z Spot (tattoo parlor), Z magazine, Rachel Z (jazz pianist), and so on. So *much* so on, in fact, that Z now seems in danger of becoming a cliché.

Much of Z's momentum may derive from the 1991 hit film *Boyz N the Hood,* set in the Los Angeles ghetto of Watts. The ti-

1   2   3   4

(1) Phoenician zayin, *the "ax," about 1000 B.C. One of four Phoenician sibilant letters,* zayin *came seventh in the alphabet and took the sound "z." (2) Greek* zeta *of the 700s B.C. It duplicated* zayin's *shape and alphabetic place, and took a similar sound. (3) Greek* zeta *had morphed to a shape more familiar to us by about 400 B.C. (4) Roman Z, the 23rd and last ancient Roman letter, about A.D. 120. The Romans had copied Greek* zeta *into their alphabet for help in transliterating Greek loan words and had put the new letter at the end of the letter row, where it remains for us today.*

tle popularized the kind of misspellings long used as a password of American Black hip-hop culture. Like backward baseball caps and baggy pants, the emblem was then copied into the North American teen mainstream. Yet the hip-hop tradition lives on in such rapper names as Ghetto Twiinz, Youngbloodz, and Jay-Z.

No aspect of Z is more intriguing than the puzzle of its name: "zed" in Britain, Canada, and other Commonwealth nations, "zee" in the United States. The American version follows the normal system for naming a consonant in English: Take the letter's sound and add a long vowel, typically E, as in our names for B, T, or V. But the British version is more in line with the letter's ancient and medieval names.

As mentioned, the Romans called it *zeta* (pronounced "zayta"). The name passed to Romance languages of the early Middle Ages, and in modern Italian it is still *zeta,* in Spanish *zeta* or *zeda.* The Old French name evolved to *zède,* with a shortened form, *zé*. These are the grandfathers of the two modern English-language names.

Most of our letter names come from medieval French, brought to England with the Norman Conquest of A.D. 1066. It was not a neat process: Medieval and Renaissance English had a surprising number of variant letter names, based on local dialect and social class in an age before mass communication. Z's official name in England was "zed," yet variants—zad, zard, izzard, izard, uzzard, and ezod, as well as zee—crop up in extant British writings into the 19th century.

The izzard, ezod types seem to represent a separate puzzle. Samuel Johnson, in his 1755 English dictionary, explains them as decayed forms of an earlier name for Z: "S hard" (pronounced "ess hard"). Other scholars theorize they come from the French words *et zède* ("and Z"), which is how a medieval Norman English schoolboy might have ended his alphabet recitation.

But as to zee versus zed. Apparently both names came to America with locally drawn groups who emigrated from England to build the earliest settlements in Virginia and Massachusetts, in the 1600s. Both names endured in the young United States. As late as 1882, a certain journalistic item noted that the name of Z "in New England is always *zee;* in the South it is *zed.*" Meanwhile an influential New Englander had been advocating "zee." Lexicographer Noah Webster, from Connecticut, sought generally to disassociate American English from British. In his 1828 *American Dictionary of the English Language,* destined to set the standard for American usage, Webster says absolutely of the letter's name, "It is pronounced *zee.*"

To the 19th-century French novelist-poet-playwright Victor Hugo goes the privilege of the last word. The author of *The Hunchback of Notre-Dame* (1831) and *Les Misérables* (1862) was an ardent admirer of the 25 letters—no French W in those days—as being images of language, civilization, and principles even more profound. In his memoir *Travel Notebooks* (1839), he interprets the alphabet mystically, musing on the significance of each letter. Beginning with comments on Y (quoted here already on pages 349–50), he proceeds through all the letters, not always in faithful order. With apologies to the omitted W, here is Victor Hugo:

> *Human society, the world, and the whole of mankind is to be found in the alphabet. Freemasonry, astronomy, philosophy, all the sciences find their true, albeit imperceptible, beginnings there; and so it must be. The alphabet is a wellspring.*
>
> *A is the roof, the gable with its crossbar, the arch; or it is the greeting of two friends who embrace and shake hands; D is the back; B is D upon D, the back on the back, the hump; C is the crescent, the moon; E is the foundations, the pillar, the console, and the architrave, the whole of architecture in a single letter; F is the gallows, the gibbet, furca; G is the French horn; H is the façade of a building with its two towers; I is a war machine launching its projectile; J is the plowshare and the horn of plenty; K is the angle of reflection equal to the angle of incidence, one of the keys to geometry; L is the leg and the foot; M is a mountain or a camp where the tents are pitched in pairs; N is a gate closed by a diagonal bar; O is the sun; P is the porter standing with a burden on his back; Q is the rump and the tail; R represents rest, the porter leaning on his stick; S is the snake; T the hammer; U is the urn, V the vase (hence the two are often confused); I*

have already discussed Y; X is crossed swords, combat—Who will be the victor? We do not know—so the mystics adopted X as the sign of destiny, and algebraists chose it to represent the unknown; Z is lightning, it is God.

The letter aleph *in the Semitic word* el, *"god." From the oldest known alphabet writing, at Wadi el-Hol in central Egypt, about 1800* B.C.

BIBLIOGRAPHY

Backhouse, Janet. *The Lindisfarne Gospels.* Ithaca, N.Y.: Cornell University Press, 1981.

Barber, Alleen. "X Appeal," *Fortune,* September 28, 1998, p. 64.

Barber, Katherine, ed. *The Canadian Oxford Dictionary.* New York: Oxford University Press, 1998.

Beament, Justin, and Esther Dudley. *In Blessed Memory: Incised Headstones of North & West Devon and North Cornwall, 1650–1850.* Exeter: Exeter School of Arts & Design, University of Plymouth, 2000.

Bishop, T. A. M. *English Caroline Minuscule.* New York: Oxford University Press, 1971.

Blumenthal, Joseph. *Art of the Printed Book: 1455–1955.* New York: Pierpont Morgan Library, 1973.

Bonfante, Larissa. *Etruscan.* London: British Museum Publications, 1990.

———. *The Etruscan Language: An Introduction.* New York: New York University Press, 1983.

Bowman, Alan K. *Life and Letters on the Roman Frontier: Vindolanda and Its People.* New York: Routledge, 1994.

Campbell, George L. *Handbook of Scripts and Alphabets.* New York: Routledge, 1997.

Catich, Edward M. *The Trajan Inscription in Rome,* 2nd ed. Davenport, Ia.: Catfish Press (St. Ambrose College), 1961.

Chappell, Warren, and Robert Bringhurst. *A Short History of the Printed Word,* 2nd ed., rev. Point Roberts, Wash.: Hartley & Marks, 1999.

Claiborne, Robert. *Our Marvelous Native Tongue: The Life and Times of the English Language.* New York: Times Books, 1983.

Cook, B. F. *Greek Inscriptions.* London: British Museum Publications, 1987.

Crystal, David. *The Cambridge Encyclopedia of the English Language.* New York: Cambridge University Press, 1995.

———. *The Cambridge Encyclopedia of Language,* 2nd ed. New York: Cambridge University Press, 1997.

Current, Richard N. *The Typewriter and the Men Who Made It,* 2nd ed. Arcadia, Calif.: Post-Era Books, 1988.

Daniels, Peter T., and William Bright, eds. *The World's Writing Systems.* New York: Oxford University Press, 1996.

Diamond, Jared. *Guns, Germs, and Steel: The Fates of Human Societies.* New York: W. W. Norton, 1997. Chapter 12: "Blueprints and Borrowed Letters: The Evolution of Writing."

Diringer, David. *The Alphabet: A Key to the History of Mankind,* 3rd ed. London: Hutchinson & Co., 1968.

———. *Writing.* New York: Frederick A. Praeger, 1962.

Drogin, Marc. *Medieval Calligraphy: Its History and Technique.* Montclair, N.J.: Allanheld & Schram, 1980.

Drucker, Johanna. *The Alphabetic Labyrinth: The Letters in History and Imagination.* New York: Thames & Hudson, 1995.

Dyche, Thomas. *A Guide to the English Tongue,* facsimile ed. Menston, Yorkshire: The Scolar Press, 1967. First published: London, 1707.

Elliott, Stuart. "The Last Letter of the Alphabet," *New York Times,* October 26, 1999.

Encyclopedia Americana. Brief articles on letters of the alphabet. Danbury, Conn.: Grolier Inc., 1998.

Fairbank, Alfred, and Berthold Wolpe. *Renaissance Handwriting.* London: Faber and Faber, 1960.

Firmage, Richard A. *The Alphabet Abecedarium: Some Notes on Letters.* Boston: David R. Godine, Publisher, 1993.

Fischer, Steven Roger. *A History of Writing.* London: Reaktion Books, 2001.

Gardiner, Sir Alan. *Egyptian Grammar: Being an Introduction to the Study of Hieroglyphics,* 3rd ed., rev. Oxford: Griffith Institute, Ashmolean Museum, 1988.

Goldberg, Jonathan. *Writing Matter: From the Hands of the English Renaissance.* Stanford, Calif.: Stanford University Press, 1990.

Gordon, Arthur E. *Illustrated Introduction to Latin Epigraphy.* Berkeley: University of California Press, 1983.

Gray, Nicolete. *A History of Lettering: Creative Experiment and Letter Identity.* Oxford: Phaidon Press, 1986.

Hamilton, Gordon J. *Development of the Early Alphabet,* Ph.D. diss. Harvard University, 1985.

Harden, Donald. *The Phoenicians,* rev. ed. New York: Thames & Hudson, 1963.

Harling, Robert. *The Letter Forms and Type Designs of Eric Gill.* Boston: David R. Godine, Publisher, 1976.

Hart, John. "The Opening of the Unreasonable Writing of Our Inglish Toung." Written in 1551. Reprinted in *John Hart's Works on English Orthography and Pronunciation,* Volume 1, ed. Bror Danielsson. Stockholm: Almquist & Wiksell, 1955.

―――. *An Orthographie.* op. cit. First published London: 1569. Reprinted in *John Hart's Works on English Orthography and Pronunciation,* Volume 1, ed. Bror Danielsson. Stockholm: Almquist & Wiksell, 1955.

Havelock, Eric Alfred. *Origins of Western Literacy.* Toronto: Ontario Institute for Studies in Education, 1976.

Healey, John F. *The Early Alphabet.* Berkeley: University of California Press, 1990.

Hoffman, Edward. *The Hebrew Alphabet: A Mystical Journey.* San Francisco: Chronicle Books, 1998.

The Holy Bible. King James Version.

Hornblower, Simon, and Anthony Spawforth, eds. *The Oxford Classical Dictionary.* New York: Oxford University Press, 1996.

Isserlin, B. S. J. "The Earliest Alphabetic Writing," in *The Cambridge An-*

cient History, Volume 3, Part 1: The Prehistory of the Balkans; and the Middle East and the Aegean World, Tenth to Eighth Centuries B.C., 2nd ed., ed. John Boardman, I. E. S. Edwards, et al. New York: Cambridge University Press, 1982.

Jackson, Donald. The Story of Writing. New York: Taplinger Publishing Company, 1981.

Jean, Georges. Writing: The Story of Alphabets and Scripts, trans. Jenny Oates. New York: Harry N. Abrams, 1992.

Jeffery, L. H. "Greek Alphabetic Writing" in The Cambridge Ancient History, Volume 3, Part 1: The Prehistory of the Balkans; and the Middle East and the Aegean World, Tenth to Eighth Centuries B.C., 2nd ed., ed. John Boardman, I. E. S. Edwards, et al. New York: Cambridge University Press, 1982.

————. The Local Scripts of Archaic Greece: A Study of the Origin of the Greek Alphabet and Its Development from the Eighth to the Fifth Centuries B.C., 2nd ed., rev. by A. W. Johnston. New York: Oxford University Press, 1990.

Johnson, Samuel. A Dictionary of the English Language, 2nd ed., rev. by H. J. Todd. London: Longman, Rees, et al., 1827.

Johnston, Edward. Writing and Illuminating, and Lettering. London: Sir Isaac Pitman & Sons, 1932 (1906 edition).

Jonson, Ben. The English Grammar. London: Lanston Monotype Corporation, 1928. First published London: 1640.

Katzner, Kenneth. The Languages of the World, 3rd ed. New York: Routledge, 1995.

Knight, Stan. Historical Scripts: From Classical Times to the Renaissance, 2nd ed., rev. New Castle, Del.: Oak Knoll Press, 1998.

Maittaire, Michael. The English Grammar: Or, an Essay on the Art of Grammar, Applied to and Exemplified in the English Tongue, facsimile ed. Menston, Yorkshire: The Scolar Press, 1967. First published: London, 1712.

Man, John. Alpha Beta: How Our Alphabet Changed the Western World. London: Headline Book Publishing, 2000.

Mares, G. C. The History of the Typewriter, Successor to the Pen. Arcadia, Calif.: Post-Era Books, 1985. First published: London, 1909.

Markoe, Glenn E. *Phoenicians.* Berkeley: University of California Press, 2000.

Martin, Henri-Jean. *The History and Power of Writing,* trans. Lydia G. Cochrane. Chicago: University of Chicago Press, 1994.

Massin. *Letter and Image,* trans. Caroline Hillier and Vivienne Menkes. London: Studio Vista, 1970.

McArthur, Tom, ed. *The Oxford Companion to the English Language.* New York: Oxford University Press, 1992.

McCarter, P. Kyle, Jr. *The Antiquity of the Greek Alphabet and the Early Phoenician Scripts.* Missoula, Mont.: Scholars Press, 1975.

Meggs, Philip B. *A History of Graphic Design,* 3rd ed. New York: John Wiley & Sons, 1998.

Mencken, H. L. *The American Language: An Inquiry into the Development of English in the United States,* 4th ed. New York: Alfred A. Knopf, 1955. Chapters: "The Two Streams of English" and "American Spelling."

———. *The American Language: Supplement I.* New York: Alfred A. Knopf, 1952. Chapter: "The Two Streams of English."

———. *The American Language: Supplement II.* New York: Alfred A. Knopf, 1956. Chapter: "American Spelling."

Mish, Frederick C., ed. *Merriam-Webster's Collegiate Dictionary,* 10th ed. Springfield, Mass.: Merriam-Webster, Inc., 2001.

Monaghan, E. Jennifer. *A Common Heritage: Noah Webster's Blue-Back Speller.* Hamden, Conn.: Archon Books, 1983.

Moscati, Sabatino. *The World of the Phoenicians,* trans. Alastair Hamilton. London: Weidenfeld and Nicolson, 1968.

Mulcaster, Richard. *The First Part of the Elementarie which entreateth chefelie of the right writing of our English tung,* facsimile ed. Menston, Yorkshire: The Scolar Press, 1970. First published: London, 1582.

Murray, James A. H., Henry Bradley, et al., eds. *The Oxford English Dictionary.* New York: Oxford University Press, 1933.

Naveh, Joseph. *Origins of the Alphabet.* London: Cassell & Company, 1975.

Nesbitt, Alexander. *Lettering: The History and Technique of Lettering as Design.* New York: Prentice-Hall, 1950.

The New Encyclopaedia Britannica, 15th ed. Chicago: Encyclopedia Britannica, Inc., 2002.

Ouaknin, Marc–Alain. *Mysteries of the Alphabet: The Origins of Writing,* trans. Josephine Bacon. New York: Abbeville Press Publishers, 1999.

Pei, Mario. *Invitation to Linguistics: A Basic Introduction to the Science of Language.* London: George Allen & Unwin Ltd., 1965.

———. *The Story of Language,* 2nd ed. London: George Allen & Unwin Ltd., 1966.

———. *The Story of Latin and the Romance Languages.* New York: Harper & Row, 1976.

Penney, J. H. W. "The Languages of Italy," in *The Cambridge Ancient History, Volume 4: Persia, Greece and the Western Mediterranean c. 525 to 479 B.C.,* 2nd ed., ed. John Boardman, N. G. L. Hammond, et al. New York: Cambridge University Press, 1988.

Potter, Simeon. "English Language" entry in "Languages of the World" article in *The New Encylcopaedia Britannica,* Volume 22, 15th ed. Chicago: Encyclopaedia Britannica, Inc., 2002.

Powell, Barry B. *Homer and the Origin of the Greek Alphabet.* New York: Cambridge University Press, 1991.

Robinson, Andrew. *The Story of Writing.* New York: Thames & Hudson, 1995.

Sacks, David. *Encyclopedia of the Ancient Greek World.* New York: Facts On File, 1995.

Sandys, Sir John Edwin. *Latin Epigraphy: An Introduction to the Study of Latin Inscriptions,* 2nd ed., rev. by S. G. Campbell. Groningen, Holland: Bouma's Boekhuis N.V., 1969.

Sass, Benjamin. *The Genesis of the Alphabet and Its Development in the Second Millennium B.C.* Wiesbaden, Germany: Otto Harrassowitz, 1988.

Scragg, D. G. *A History of English Spelling.* New York: Barnes & Noble Books, 1974.

Senner, Wayne M., ed. *The Origins of Writing.* Lincoln, Neb.: University of Nebraska Press, 1989.

Sihler, Andrew L. *New Comparative Grammar of Greek and Latin.* New York: Oxford University Press, 1995.

Simpson, J. A., and E. S. C. Weiner, eds. *The Oxford English Dictionary,* 2nd ed. New York: Oxford University Press, 1989.

Steinberg, S. H. *Five Hundred Years of Printing,* 3rd ed., rev. by John Trevitt. New Castle, Del.: Oak Knoll Press, 1996.

Tory, Geofroy. *Champ Fleury* (Field of Flowers), trans. and annotated by George B. Ives, 1927. New York: Dover Publications, 1967. Originally published in French in Paris, 1529.

Tuer, Andrew W. *History of the Horn-book.* Amsterdam: S. Emmering, 1971.

Ullman, B. L. *The Origin and Development of Humanistic Script.* Rome: Edizioni di Storia e Letteratura, 1960.

V & M Typographical, Inc. *The Type Specimen Book.* New York: Van Nostrand Reinhold Company, 1974.

Wilford, John Noble. "Finds in Egypt Date Alphabet in Earlier Era," *New York Times,* November 14, 1999.

Woodard, Roger D. *Greek Writing from Knossos to Homer: A Linguistic Interpretation of the Origin of the Greek Alphabet and the Continuity of Ancient Greek Literacy.* New York: Oxford University Press, 1997.

INTERVIEWS

Darnell, John Coleman. Assistant professor, Department of Egyptology, Yale University. Telephone interview, November 2001.

Dobbs-Allsopp, F. W. Associate professor of Old Testament, Princeton Theological Seminary. Telephone interview and e-mail correspondence, January 2002.

Hamilton, Gordon J. Professor, Old Testament Language and Literature, Huron University College. E-mail correspondence, July 2002.

ILLUSTRATION CREDITS
AND ACKNOWLEDGMENTS

Pages 3 and 279: cartoon images of "dog," "doctor"' "knot," "deer," "waist," and "nose" by kind permission of AM Productions, Ottawa, Ontario.

Page 6: Attic red-figure cup fragment by Akestorides Painter from The J. Paul Getty Museum, Malibu, CA. Photograph © The J. Paul Getty Museum.

Page 11: Map reprinted from A. Bernard Knapp, *The History and Culture of Ancient Western Asia and Egypt,* 1st ed., Chicago: Dorsey Press, 1988. © 1988. Reprinted with permission of Wadsworth, a division of Thomson Learning. *www.thomsonrights.com.* Fax 800-730-2215.

Page 14: Painting © by Björn Landström. Reprinted from Björn Landström, *The Ship,* Garden City, NY: Doubleday & Company, 1961. By permission of Olof Landström.

Page 22: Courtesy Israel Antiquities Authority.

Page 27: From Sir Alan Gardiner, *Egyptian Grammar,* 3rd ed. Oxford: Griffith Institute, Ashmolean Museum, 1957. Reprinted by permission of the Griffith Institute, Oxford.

Page 38: Photograph by Bruce Zuckerman and Marilyn Lundberg, West Semitic Research. Drawing by Marilyn Lundberg, West Semitic Research.

Page 39: Photographs by Bruce Zuckerman and Marilyn Lundberg, West Semitic Research.

Page 42: Reproduced with permission of Punch Ltd.

Page 44: From the U.S. Department of Agriculture website: *www.ams. usda.gov.*

Pages 46, 214, 215, 268, and 348: Reprinted from Geofroy Tory, *Champ Fleury* (English translation), New York: Dover Publications, 1967.

Page 56: Lyrics from "The Sadder But Wiser Girl," from Meredith Willson's *The Music Man,* by Meredith Willson. © 1957 (renewed) FRANK MUSIC CORP. and MEREDITH WILLSON MUSIC. All rights reserved.

Page 57: Map reprinted from A. T. Reyes, *Archaic Cyprus: A Study of the Textual and Archaeological Evidence,* New York: Oxford University Press, 1994. Reprinted by permission of Oxford University Press.

Page 63: © American School of Classical Studies at Athens: Agora Excavations.

Pages 64, 65: By permission of the British Library. Manuscript G.12216.

Page 69: Photograph © The British Museum. GR 1870.3-20.88.

Page 74: The Metropolitan Museum of Art, Fletcher Fund, 1924. All rights reserved, The Metropolitan Museum of Art.

Page 75: Map reprinted from Graeme Barker and Tom Rasmussen, *The Etruscans,* Oxford: Blackwell Publishers, 1998.

Page 82: © The Coca-Cola Company, Atlanta, Georgia. Used by permission.

Pages 93, 172, 246, 278, and 290: Reprinted from Massin, *Letter and Image* (English translation), London: Studio Vista, 1970.

Page 103: Map reprinted from Michael Grant, *The Antonines: The Roman Empire in Transition,* New York: Routledge, 1994.

Page 104: Trajan Inscription photograph by kind permission of Mobium Creative Group, a subsidiary of R.R. Donnelley & Sons Company, Chicago, IL.

Page 105: Alinari/Art Resource, NY.

Page 110: Reuters/Richard Carson.

Page 115: Photograph by Bruce Zuckerman and Marilyn Lundberg, West Semitic Research.

Page 121: © F Company Design, Minneapolis, MN. By permission.

Pages 131, 185 and 358: Reprinted from Frederic W. Goudy, *The Alphabet and Elements of Lettering,* Berkeley: University Press, 1942.

Page 141: Kunsthistorisches Museum, Vienna.

Page 142: The Bodleian Library, University of Oxford, Manuscript Auct. T.2.26, f.82 r.

Page 154: The Bayeux Tapestry, 11th century. By special permission of the City of Bayeux.

Pages 156, 157: By permission of the British Library. Manuscript Add. 10546, f.26 det.

Page 179: By permission of the British Library. Yates Thompson Manuscript 6, f.127 r.

Page 180: St. Bride Printing Library, London, England. Photo by Geremy Butler Photography.

Pages 188 and 301: © The British Museum. Dodgson Burl. Mag. 1922, p. 18.

Pages 194–195: Reprinted from a Yale University Press facsimile edition of the Henry Hoth copy of the Shakespeare First Folio at the Elizabethan Club, Yale University. By kind permission of the Elizabethan Club.

Page 199: By kind permission of the Master, Fellows, and Scholars of Pembroke College in the University of Oxford.

Page 201: Reprinted from Edward M. Gottschall, *Typographic Communications Today,* New York: International Typeface Coroporation, 1989. By kind permission of Agfa Monotype, Wilmington, MA.

Page 213: From Charles Olson, *The Collected Poems of Charles Olson,* edited by George Butterick. Berkeley: University of California Press, 1987. © 1987 Estate of Charles Olson.

Page 226: The Metropolitan Museum of Art, bequest of Charles Allan Munn, 1924. All rights reserved, The Metropolitan Museum of Art.

Page 238: Courtesy of Newman's Own.

Pages 255, 266, and 343: Reprinted from *A Book of Alphabets with Plain, Ornamental, Ancient, and Medieval Styles,* Ottawa, Ontario: Algrove Publishing Limited, 2000. By kind permission.

Pages 258, 259: By permission of the British Library. Manuscript Cott. Nero Div. f.5 v.

Page 282: Photograph by Bruce Zuckerman and Marilyn Lundberg, West Semitic Research.

Page 297: By permission of the British Library. Heber copy C. 34.1.14.

Page 298: © Robert Capa/Magnum Photos.

Page 302: By Wilfred Owen, from THE COLLECTED POEMS OF WILFRED OWEN, copyright © 1963 by Chatto & Windus, Ltd. Reprinted by permission of New Directions Publishing Corp.

Page 310: Reuters/Damir Sagolj.

Page 315: Reprinted from Sir John Edwin Sandys, *Latin Epigraphy: An Introduction to the Study of Latin Inscriptions,* 2nd ed., Groningen, Holland: Bouma's Boekhuis N.V., 1969. By permission of Ares Publishers, Golden, CO.

Page 317: This item is reproduced by permission of the Huntington Library, San Marino, California. RB 69305.

Pages 320 and 329: © Bettmann/CORBIS/MAGMA.

Page 328: Reprinted from Thomas Dyche, *A Guide to the English Tongue* (facsimile edition), Menston, Yorkshire: The Scolar Press, 1967.

Page 330: AP/Wide World Photos.

Page 345: Reprinted from Elizabeth S. Haldane, *Descartes, His Life and Times,* London: J. Murray, 1905.

Pages 349–50, 366–67: Victor Hugo excerpt reprinted from Georges Jean, *Writing: The Story of Alphabets and Scripts,* New York: Harry N. Abrams, Inc., 1992. English translation by Jenny Oates, © 1992 by Harry N. Abrams, Inc.

Page 353: By permission of the British Library. Manuscript Cott. Cali. E.III f.273.

Page 357: Gravestone on the east wall of St. Swithuns Church, Shobrooke, Devon, from Justin Beament and Esther Dudley, *In Blessed Memory: Incised Headstones of North & West Devon and North Cornwall, 1650–1850,* Exeter: Exeter School of Arts & Design, University of Plymouth, 2000. Photograph courtesy of Justin Beament.

Page 363: "Z" ™ is used with the express permission of Zorro Productions, Inc., Berkeley, CA. © 2003. All rights reserved.

Page 367: Photograph by Bruce Zuckerman and Marilyn Lundberg, West Semitic Research.

INDEX

ABOUT THE AUTHOR

David Sacks grew up in Summit, New Jersey, and studied Greek and Latin at Swarthmore College and Oxford University. He has written on cultural topics for many magazines and newspapers, including the *New York Times Book Review,* the *Wall Street Journal,* and the *Ottawa Citizen.* The author of one prior nonfiction book, *Encyclopedia of the Ancient Greek World,* he lives with his wife and two daughters in Ottawa, Ontario.